BICYCLING THE BACKROADS AROUND PUGET SOUND

By Erin and Bill Wood

Fourth Edition 1995

Maps by Helen Sherman and Bill Woods

Cartoons by Dale Martin

The Mountaineers, Seattle

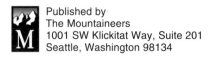
Published by
The Mountaineers
1001 SW Klickitat Way, Suite 201
Seattle, Washington 98134

9 8 7 6 5
5 4 3 2 1

Published simultaneously in Canada by Douglas & McIntyre, Ltd., 1615 Venables Street, Vancouver, B.C. V5L 2H1

Published simultaneously in Great Britain by Cordee, 3a DeMontfort Street, Leicester, England, LE1 7HD

Manufactured in the United States of America

Edited by Dana Fos
Maps by Helen Sherman and Bill Woods
Cover design by The Mountaineers Books
Cartoons by Dale Martin

Cover photograph by Kirkendall/Spring of bicycler with sculpture "Slip Stream" by David Govedare, Kent Arts Commission, KCAP 1986.2.

Library of Congress Cataloging-in-Publication Data

Woods, Erin.
    Bicycling the backroads around Puget Sound / by Erin and Bill Woods. — 4th ed.
        p.   cm.
    Includes index.
    ISBN 0-89886-451-8
    1. Bicycle touring—Washington (State)—Puget Sound Region— Guidebooks.   2. Puget Sound Region (Wash.)—Guidebooks. I. Woods, Bill, 1925–   . II. Mountaineers (Society)   III. Title.
GV1045.5.W22P838   1995
796.6'09797—dc20   95–33203
                                                                      CIP

CONTENTS

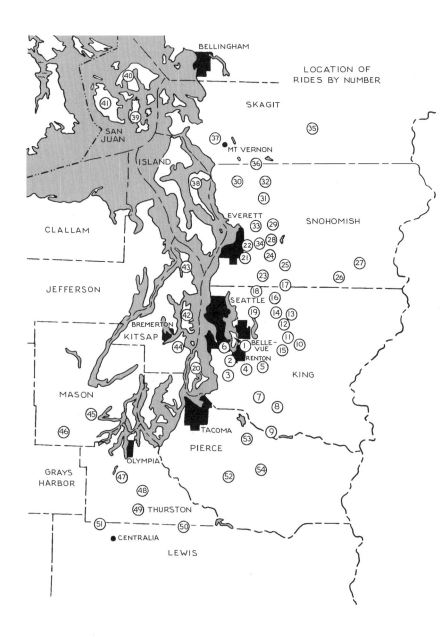

LOCATION OF
RIDES BY NUMBER

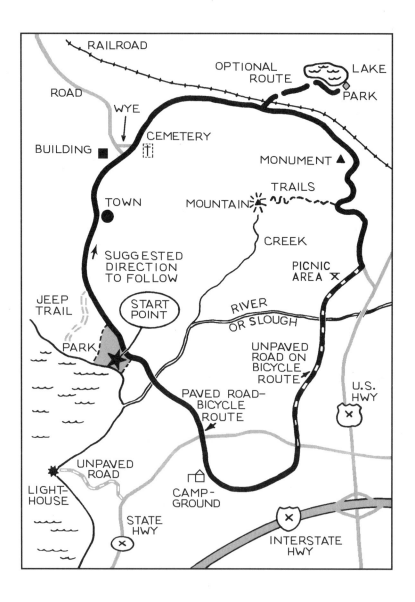

RAILROAD

OPTIONAL ROUTE

LAKE

ROAD

PARK

WYE

CEMETERY

BUILDING

MONUMENT

TOWN

TRAILS

MOUNTAIN

CREEK

SUGGESTED DIRECTION TO FOLLOW

PICNIC AREA

JEEP TRAIL

START POINT

RIVER OR SLOUGH

PARK

UNPAVED ROAD ON BICYCLE ROUTE

U.S. HWY

PAVED ROAD-BICYCLE ROUTE

LIGHT-HOUSE

UNPAVED ROAD

CAMP-GROUND

STATE HWY

INTERSTATE HWY

INTRODUCTION

BICYCLING IS FUN

Bicycling is fun and it is invigorating! It can be indulged in by almost everyone, young and old. A good machine, the desire to get out and do something, and a place to ride are all that are required. For most people, the first two are easy to come by; the third often is harder to find. Some cities have bicycle paths of limited scope and streets posted as bicycle routes. Occasionally on special days, a few streets are blocked off for exclusive use of bicyclists.

Soon, however, the bicyclist tires of circling small lakes or parks and of dodging roller skaters and joggers on trails or cars on city streets. We find young people, map in hand, setting off in desperation down main highways toward distant goals. If they try backroads, often not on their map, they may encounter dead ends or find themselves cut off by freeways and forced back onto main thoroughfares. Main highway travel, even where not specifically prohibited by law, is dangerous and disturbing to both the cyclist and motorist. A cyclist cannot relax and enjoy riding when teetering along the edge of the pavement as cars and trucks whiz by inches away, spouting noxious exhaust fumes.

An alternative is to organize or join a bicycle club, which can pool its members' knowledge of backroads to come up with a few good rides. These rides soon need documentation because assignment to different leaders and education of new members require preparation of maps and tour descriptions. The responsibility for maintaining a tour book eventually falls upon a few dedicated members, with perhaps one or two people occasionally generating a new ride.

With the recent rise in popularity of bicycling, the need for comprehensive books of tours has become increasingly apparent, not only for the burgeoning bicycle clubs, but also for people who lack either the opportunity or the desire to tour with a club. As energetic ride scouts, the authors of this guide have been increasingly called upon to provide information about tours in Puget Sound country. Accordingly, we have collected the material in this and two additional books to summarize the more popular club rides, and we have added many new tours suitable for club or family touring. We have personally bicycled each of these tours and have periodically updated them to ensure the authenticity of the descriptions.

We have found that in most cases maps alone are not adequate. Information on terrain, hills, traffic, road conditions, and food concessions is of vital interest to the bicyclist in determining which ride to take and what supplies to pack. Because most bicyclists enjoy the flora, fauna, and scenic views, we have included a general description of the rides. Mile-by-mile directions are included to help prevent that lost feeling often generated by intricate turns and poorly marked roads.

The tours in this book encompass more than 2000 miles of roads in ten counties of western Washington, but they cannot be considered exhaustive coverage of the area. Two additional *Bicycling the Backroads* books cover northwestern Washington—up into British Columbia—and southwestern Washington—down into Oregon. Although a stringent effort has been made to ensure completeness and accuracy of maps and description, a few errors may still remain. Also, conditions do change, since roads are continually being rebuilt, renamed, closed, or rerouted. Some of these changes have been projected in the write-ups. Others will certainly occur. Maps have been provided with enough detail on alternate routes to handle many such problems, but it would be wise to have a complete local map for emergency consultation. County maps are recommended for this purpose.

SAFETY IN BICYCLING

The primary purpose of this book is to introduce bicycle tour routes on little-used public roads where the cyclist can enjoy a day or weekend with minimum traffic hazard. Metropolitan riding, except as necessary to link up with rural routes, is left to others to document. In all areas, the bicycle tourist must be continually conscious of hazards such as automobiles, weather, road conditions, dogs, and other cyclists.

Bicyclists should allow for the fluctuations in auto activity that occur on almost any route depending on the hour, day, or season. For example, the beginning and end of church services, school hours, or working shifts may cause roads to become suddenly very busy. Special events or hunting and fishing activities may bring many cars to even the most remote backroads.

SEASONS FOR TOURING—CLOTHING

Most bicyclists consider summer, when rain is less likely to occur, the only season for touring. Warm weather requires little if any extra clothing in the pack; parks and their restrooms, rural stores, and food concessions are open. In summer, however, many more vehicles are on the road, especially the wide pickup-campers and house trailers. Parks are jammed to the limit, making it difficult for the overnight cycle tourist to find a camping spot. Insect hordes and roadside nettles abound, and stops are less enjoyable.

What then are the possibilities for other seasons? As long as heavy rain is avoided, any season can be enjoyable for bicycling. Springtime brings the flowering trees, shrubs, and other flora. Fall comes alive with colors of maple, willow, dogwood, tamarack, and ash trees. In winter, deciduous trees have lost their foliage, allowing views of the countryside that are unavailable in summer. Along Puget Sound, flocks of ducks, grebes, and other waterfowl congregate, waiting for warm weather to return to their northern nesting grounds.

During the cooler seasons, the question of keeping warm must be considered carefully. Here the cyclist may benefit by taking a page from the book of the mountaineer. Several layers of clothing, especially on the upper torso, may be adjusted or peeled to adjust the heat exchange. Hat and gloves have a very noticeable effect as well. An outer, lightweight shell keeps the wind from penetrating the inner, insulating layers. Insulated boots keep the feet comfortable. With adequate upper clothing, shorts can be quite comfortable in air temperatures down to freezing. If this seems incongruous, remember that a touring bicyclist is exercising vigorously.

By the same token, once stopped, if only for a few minutes, the cyclist must immediately put on clothing to conserve heat. Lightweight wind pants or warm-ups and all extra clothing in the pack should be put on immediately. With this precaution, extended stops are enjoyed without discomfort.

Rain in the Puget Sound country is an almost omnipresent hazard. Light, warm summer rains are little problem. The skin is waterproof and light clothing dries rapidly. In other seasons, however, a cold rain can penetrate clothing, making the rider miserable. If a waterproof outer covering is worn, evaporated perspiration condenses on the inside, leaving the exerciser almost as wet as without the waterproofing. Water-repellent outer clothing, such as a Gore-Tex parka or anorak that will breathe and allow the inside water vapor to escape, avoids condensation and can generally be counted upon for a few hours of comfortable riding in a gentle rain. Eventually, however, rain will penetrate. Then, if the insulating undergarments are polypropylene, the loss of insulating value will not be great and the ride can be completed in reasonable comfort. Cotton and many of the synthetic fabrics do not retain their insulating value when wet and are not recommended.

The hiker's lightweight poncho is of little value on a bicycle because it balloons and flaps in the breeze. A somewhat similar garment, the rain cape or cycle cape, can be advantageous in the rain.

For the lower legs and feet, solutions vary widely, from almost no protection (sneakers and bare legs) to total encasement in polypropylene, wet-suit fabric, and Gore-Tex. Pick the level of comfort, encumbrance, and cost desired, and proceed accordingly.

Riding the Highway

HELMETS

The price of accident-free touring is vigilance and adherence to rules of the road. Even with careful attention, however, sooner or later almost anyone who does a lot of riding will have an accident of some sort. To lessen the consequences, certain bicycling accessories are recommended. The foremost is a safety helmet. The traditional leather-strap bicycle racing helmet provides the most ventilation, but also the least protection. Even with its shortcomings, however, it is far better than nothing when one's noggin hits the pavement. The best and most expensive helmets available are those designed and manufactured specifically for bicycling. They are hot in summer and a nuisance to wear, and some whistle in the wind, but one look at a helmet with a crushed liner or distended strap supports after it has been removed from an undamaged head is enough to make one a true believer. Other accident victims without helmets have not been so fortunate.

EYE PROTECTION

In summer, sunglasses are recommended to improve vision and protect against damage from ultraviolet radiation. In early fall, insect swarms present a real hazard to the eyes, and sunglasses or goggles are desirable. In winter or early spring, the cold wind makes eyes stream with tears unless a windbreak is provided. The use of eye shields of some form virtually all year round is advised.

SCENERY

While gaining familiarity with bicycle touring, a bicyclist discovers a major advantage over the automobile driver. A bicycle travels at the best speed for appreciation of the scenery and allows use of the full hemisphere of vision. The bicyclist is able to stop at virtually any point without blocking traffic or endangering himself or others. The roadside flora and fauna become more apparent. Unfortunately, so do the discarded cans, bottles, and other trash in the ditches, which may be the principal reason why bicyclists are concerned with conservation, ecology, and recycling of resources.

BODY CONDITIONING

So much for the fun of cycling. What else does it do for you? Bicycling is invigorating, a physical activity suitable for the young, old, weak, or strong. Like swimming and running, bicycling is one of the physical activities most recommended by the medical profession for keeping the cardiovascular system in top condition. A bicycle's gears can be regulated to match the rider's ability and desires to the amount of energy expended and the rate of travel. The cyclist's physical condition can be improved gradually and without distress or extreme fatigue. It is easy to see why so many people turn to the bicycle for recreation, local transportation, and commuting. The sudden explosion of the bicycle population on campuses has turned virtually every rack, pillar, and tree into a parking anchor. Were it not for the lack of safe areas to ride near places of employment, this sort of thing could be happening everywhere.

RULES OF THE ROAD

Before wheeling out onto the road, trail, or sidewalk, the cyclist should know the rules of the road. The state of Washington has laws pertaining specifically to bicyclists listed in the Revised Code of Washington (RCW). The applicable portions of this code are quoted in Appendix A. Most cities incorporate these laws unaltered into their ordinances by reference to applicable sections of the RCW.

The principal points of the state law are these: Bicyclists must ride on the right side of the road with automobile traffic; they should have properly equipped machines and should ride them in a responsible manner; cyclists are allowed to ride singly or two abreast but are required to pull over and let traffic pass when several cars have stacked up behind them; cyclists should obey other applicable motor vehicle regulations.

GOOD MANNERS

Good manners in any recreational activity are necessary to permit continued enjoyment by all who participate. The first point of courtesy for the backroads-touring bicyclist is where and how to park the car. As a courtesy to others, park the car in the least obtrusive spot available. This is especially true when a large group or touring club moves into an area, jams it full of cars, and then cycles off. A little courtesy here, plus inquiry on how to cause the least inconvenience to others, can avoid ill will toward bicyclists. When starting on an overnight tour, consult the local law-enforcement agency for parking suggestions.

Good manners are also important in riding habits. Riding two breast is fine where traffic is light and road visibility is good, but when cars pile up behind, riding single file or pulling over to let them go by should be an automatic reaction. In any case, weaving and clowning have no place on the highway.

When stopping to eat along the way, take care in the disposition of food wrappers. If a trash can is not handy, pack the trash with you for later disposal. Never add to the roadside litter. In most areas, automobile service stations and parks are located at frequent enough intervals to take care of personal sanitation problems, but in an emergency situation, be sure to bury all wastes well away from any watercourse or trail.

TOURING EQUIPMENT

When a bicycle is purchased, what equipment should be mounted or carried on it? The following items have been found useful, if not essential, for one-day or overnight touring.

1. Lights and reflectors. During the hours of darkness (from one-half hour after sunset to one-half hour before sunrise), a headlamp and rear reflector are the mandatory minimum by state law. For reliability in occasional use, a generator-headlamp assembly has been found most satisfactory, especially with the new halogen lamps. The generator lamp, however, stops when the bicycle stops, leaving the bicyclist invisible and vulnerable to automotive hazard. For after-dark riding, therefore, the authors strongly recommend additional visibility aids. One of these is augmentation of the rear reflector with pedal and/or wheel reflectors. The second most important is a battery-operated light, either steady or flashing. These lights are available at most bicycle stores.

Long-life alkaline batteries, although high in initial cost, are the most reliable and economical in the long run. A two-cell standard flashlight using the same size batteries may be advisable for reading maps and road signs. Carry an extra set of batteries. Of course, if being caught by darkness approaches zero probability, as in midsummer, leave the lights at home. In December or January, however, lights are an indispensable security.

2. Bell or horn. These are required by law only in certain cities where the approaching bicyclist must warn pedestrians. For rural-road touring, such devices are not essential nor required.

3. Cyclometer or speedometer. A mileage meter is advantageous, especially when following the trip descriptions in this book. Many makes and styles are available, but the electronic devices appear to have best reliability.

4. Tire pump and repair kit. These are a must for a trip of any length. Bicycle pumps are lightweight and may be clipped to the frame. Some bicycles come with pumps and brazed-on supports as standard equipment. Besides patches and cement, a canvas boot should be carried for emergency repair of a minor blowout. For longer, multi-day tours, a spare tire and tube are advisable.

5. Tools and spare parts. Tools are a must for the ever-necessary adjustments and emergency maintenance that occur on rides. Brakes, saddles, and cables are the greatest offenders, followed by fenders, chains, and spokes. On long trips, spare brake blocks, spokes, cables, and chain links often come in handy.

6. First-aid kit. People are as likely as bicycles to require emergency maintenance. Accidents do occur, mostly with only abrasions, but a good first-aid kit should be carried for the occasional serious injury.

7. Dog repellent. This is a must in most semi-rural areas. Something about a bicycle can turn a placid dog into a roaring menace. Pepper derivative spray cans with the trade name *Halt* or *Dog Shield* are available at most bicycle shops.

8. Luggage carrier. For short summer trips, a small tourist bag mounted on the handlebar or the rear of the saddle will carry a few tools, first-aid kit, and lunch. For winter trips and for long summer tours, more luggage space

is required. Various choices are available, including front and rear touring bags, luggage racks, and panniers.

9. Miscellaneous. Under this category, we list such items as water bottles, toilet paper, and, of course, emergency food. The last deserves elaboration. Bicycling, involving continued, high-level exertion, sometimes produces the sensation of "running out of gas." The cyclist may be on level ground shifting to lower and lower gears and seemingly not able to get anywhere. This can result from using up all available blood sugar and not getting food to the muscles. A candy bar or other sugar-containing food will get nutrients into the blood almost immediately and allow the cyclist to continue. Adequate meals containing high proportions of fat and carbohydrate for supper and breakfast are advised, but it is still wise to carry a certain amount of high-calorie food for emergencies.

BICYCLE CARE

A good bicycle requires periodic maintenance as does any highly refined machine. The first requisite is to keep it clean. As an automobile needs cleaning and polishing, so does a bicycle. Automotive cleaning and waxing materials work well and are recommended. One cleaning method not recommended, except in exceptionally muddy conditions, is the garden hose approach. This will put unwanted water into the bearings of the headset, wheels, crank, and freewheel and hasten their deterioration.

Areas most frequently in need of attention are the chain, chainwheels, and gear-changing mechanisms. Unless properly lubricated, the chain will absorb appreciable leg power and cause annoying jumps due to stiff links. Common petroleum-based automotive lubricants work well, but because of the exposed nature of the assembly, these pick up grit and grime. Oxidation proceeds rapidly, turning the clean oil into a black, gritty substance that is

Bicycle Sunday

difficult to get off the skin and clothing. Paradoxically, it will wash out readily in a rainstorm, leaving the chain without adequate lubrication. Furthermore, its lubricating properties on alloy chainwheels have been severely questioned. Alternatives such as wax lubricants need to be applied more often but are less messy in use.

The derailleur gear changer, being intimately coupled with the chain, suffers from the same problems. Grit and grime build up rapidly, requiring frequent cleaning and lubrication. Both the derailleur and geared-hub gear changers require occasional adjustments. Directions for adjustments on gear changers are too lengthy to be included here, but may be found in any of a number of books on bicycle maintenance. In the event of cable breakage, the bicyclist is often left in high gear, which is inconvenient in hilly country. If a replacement cable is not available, the high-gear limit stop may be adjusted to lock the transmission in mid-range. This creates the equivalent of a single-speed bicycle and is an optimum compromise for continuing to the nearest town.

Brakes are as important for descending hills as the transmission is for going up them. Brakes should be checked periodically for wear and adjustment. If worn excessively, the blocks should be replaced. If clearances are excessive, a simple adjustment should correct this. All fasteners (bolts, nuts, etc.) should be checked periodically for loosening. Few situations are more dangerous than having a brake fall off halfway down a long, steep hill.

Brake and derailleur cables stretch, wear, and eventually break. Unless properly lubricated in their housings, they will stick, causing brake drag or poor gear-changer operation. Anytime a frayed cable is observed, it should be replaced at the earliest opportunity, as its lifetime is severely limited thereafter. A broken cable in the middle of a ride is not only annoying, but also dangerous.

Bicycle wheels, as part of the rim-brake system, must be kept round and true for proper brake operation. Severe shocks from bumps, spills, rocks, or chuckholes will produce distortions in the wheels that sometimes must be trued by adjustment of spoke nipples. A spoke may break occasionally, producing wheel distortion, and should be replaced at the earliest opportunity.

Whether on wheel hubs, headset, or bottom bracket, bearings should be disassembled, cleaned, and relubricated at least every two years, unless they are the sealed type. Most bearings will keep running for several years without attention but, without lubrication, will eventually deteriorate to the point of having to be replaced.

All this points to the fact that a serious bicyclist must be willing either to find and support a good bicycle mechanic or to become one. As good mechanics may be difficult to find on a tour 100 miles or so from a major metropolis, the latter alternative is preferable. If becoming a mechanic is too formidable or undesirable, have the bicycle overhauled every six months and pick cycling companions carefully.

Before every ride, the bicyclist should verify that tires are properly inflated and free of embedded stones, glass, or metal objects. Few things will ruin a tire more quickly than riding it underinflated. Tire pressure ratings may be found printed on most tires, and recommendations should be available at any bicycle shop.

BICYCLE CARRIERS

With the bicycle equipped, the next problem is to get to the start of the tour. At this point, the cyclist usually looks to the motor vehicle. Unless a pickup truck is available, however, fitting in a fully assembled bicycle may be difficult or impossible. Even with a truck, jamming in more than two bicycles is likely to cause damage. The solution is to take a tip from ski buffs and mount a bicycle rack on the car. Bicycle shops offer roof- or trunk-lid-mounted racks for one to four bicycles. Bumper- or frame-mounted racks are available as well. If only one bicycle is to be transported, it may fit into the back of a sedan, or perhaps even into the trunk, with one or both wheels dismounted; quick-release hubs are handy for this operation.

BICYCLE TOURING

For the novice, joining a bicycle club is one of the best ways to learn the skills and the art of having fun on bicycle trips. Such clubs may offer short courses to develop bicycling proficiency. Even if they don't, observation of experienced riders will help. Few veteran bicycle tourists are reluctant to offer advice when asked or even when not asked. The advice is almost always beneficial for improving techniques or making riding easier.

If a bicycle club is unavailable or undesirable, buy a book or two on bicycling and perhaps a bicycling anthology. With these as guides, try out bicycling techniques on short rides. As confidence and proficiency increase, try longer and more difficult rides. In a short time, tours of less than 30 to 40 miles will no longer seem satisfying. At this point, tour routes may be combined or longer variations added. Eventually the excitement of planning new and untried routes takes over and new tours are born.

Happy cycling!

ERIN and BILL WOODS

SAFETY CONSIDERATIONS

Safety is an important concern in all outdoor activities. No guidebook can alert you to every hazard or anticipate the limitations of every reader, so the descriptions in this book are not representations that a particular trip is safe for your party. When you take a trip, you assume responsibility for your own safety. Some of the trips described in this book may require you to do no more than look both ways before crossing the street; on others, more attention to safety may be required due to terrain, traffic, weather, the capabilities of your party, or other factors. Keeping informed on current conditions and exercising common sense are the keys to a safe, enjoyable outing. On all trips, be sure to wear a helmet and urge your companions to do so as well.

Additionally, many of the lands in this book may be subject to development and/or change of ownership. Conditions may have changed since this book was written, making your use of some of these routes unwise. Always check for current conditions, respect posted private property signs, and avoid confrontations with property owners and managers.

KING COUNTY

1   MERCER ISLAND

STARTING POINT: Luther Burbank King County Park. Take exit 7 (Island Crest Way) from westbound I-90 and turn sharp right on S.E. 26th Street, then left to park on 84th Avenue S.E. as 26th Street ends. From eastbound I-90, take exit 7A (77 Avenue). Turn left on 77 Avenue, right on N. Mercer Way, then left on S.E. 26th Street as Island Crest Way goes right.

DISTANCE: 15 miles.
TERRAIN: Flat to moderate.
TOTAL CUMULATIVE ELEVATION GAIN: 500 feet.
RECOMMENDED TIME OF YEAR: Any season.
RECOMMENDED STARTING TIME: Any hour.
ALLOW: 2 hours.
POINTS OF INTEREST
Luther Burbank Park
Groveland Park
Clarke Beach Park

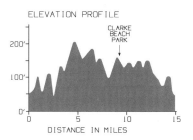

Although Mercer Island can no longer be called rural and its roads are no longer really backroads, the Mercer Way ride is still enjoyable and can be taken almost any time of the day and any day of the year. No matter what season this ride is taken, a sunny day will find dozens of cyclists enjoying the curving, woodsy roads around the island.

Luther Burbank Park, the recommended starting point, has plenty of parking space. Riding this loop in a counterclockwise direction permits convenient stops at several vantage points along the way. At Slater Park, views are toward the I-90 floating bridges and the Mt. Baker district of Seattle. Harry and Loretta Slater, strong advocates of sensible bicycle trails and legislation, bought the property and built their home on it many years before bridges connected Mercer Island to Seattle. The couple passed away in 1985 and the property was willed to the City of Mercer Island, to be developed as a park. It is now a beautifully landscaped picnic area and viewpoint. Seattle's Seward Park appears directly across the lake from Mercer Island's Groveland Park. A steep hill leads down to this park, which is popular for swimming and picnicking. Clarke Beach Park, at the south end of the island, offers hard-surfaced paths down through the trees past grassy glades with picnic tables to an expansive beach and swimming area. Mt. Rainier, the Boeing Renton plant, and the city of Renton fill the horizon on the southern end of the lake. East Mercer Way curves in and out of the densely wooded gullies that form the east side of the island.

The views again open up on the approach to I-90. Of the many buildings that once composed Seattle's former Luther Burbank school for boys, only the administration building remains. This fine brick building is the focal point

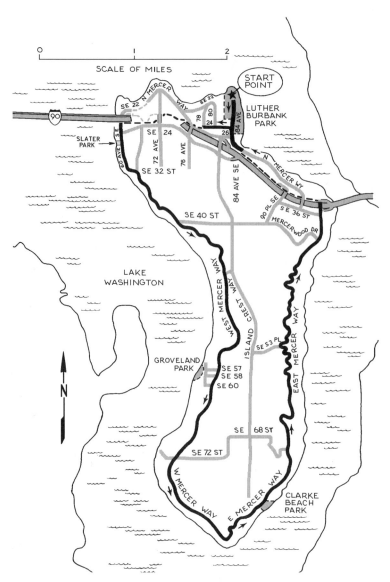

of the park, overlooking the soccer fields and shoreline. The park contains many acres of land to explore; a well-maintained trail leads to the beach at the northern tip of the island. Canada geese and other migratory waterfowl find a haven along the uninhabited lake shore. An open-air amphitheater provides an attractive backdrop for thespians. A uniquely designed play area for the young set buzzes with activity, while players of all ages fill the nearby tennis courts. Extensive docking facilities provide access to the park for the boating fraternity.

MILEAGE LOG

0.0   Leave Luther Burbank Park and head south on **84th Avenue S.E.**

0.2   Turn right on **S.E. 24th Street**.

0.5   Go past planting barricade as 24th Street ends and continue on bikeway along North Mercer Way.

0.8   Cross 76th Avenue S.E. and turn right on parallel bikeway, which soon bends left from road.

1.0   Bear left on bikeway across I-90 lid through park area underneath 72 Avenue S.E. overpass. Continue on bikeway.

1.4   Cross 70th Avenue S.E. and bear left as right fork of bikeway crosses the lid again.

1.6   Turn left on **60th Avenue S.E.** as bikeway ends. Slater Park on the right at mile 1.7. The road soon bends left and is renamed **S.E. 32nd Street**.

2.7   Turn right on **West Mercer Way** at T junction. Road to Groveland Park turns right and down steep hill at mile 5.7. Road is renamed **East Mercer Way** at mile 8.0. Clarke Beach Park is on the right at mile 8.8.

12.9   Cross I-90 on overpass and turn left on grade-separated bikeway. Cross North Mercer Way at mile 13.2.

14.0   Exit bikeway onto **North Mercer Way** and continue as roadway bends right and is renamed **84th Avenue S.E.**

14.4   End of loop ride at Luther Burbank Park.

Our Superhighways

2 DUWAMISH RIVER

STARTING POINT: Fort Dent Park (King County park system). Take exit 154 (I-405) from I-5, then exit 1 from I-405. Turn left on Interurban Avenue, pass Grady Way and the Green River and turn right on Fort Dent Way into the park.

DISTANCE: 10 miles.
TERRAIN: Flat with one major hill.
TOTAL CUMULATIVE ELEVATION GAIN: 200 feet.
RECOMMENDED TIME OF YEAR: Any season.
RECOMMENDED STARTING TIME: Not critical.
ALLOW: 2 hours.
POINTS OF INTEREST
Fort Dent Park
River valley scenery

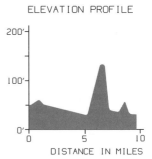

Although this tour is named Duwamish River, the waterways encountered relate to four river names. The first crossing is of the Green River. Up until the turn of the century, this was the White River, into which the Green River flowed at Auburn. In November 1906, the White overflowed its banks and formed a new channel, following Stuck Creek to join the Puyallup. The Green River then had the old channel all to itself and flowed north, joining the Black River at Tukwila to form the Duwamish. The Black River, once a prominent waterway draining Lake Washington, essentially disappeared in 1916 when the Chittenden Locks were opened and the lake was lowered several feet. Now all that remains of the Black River is a short channel between a flood-control pumping station and the junction with the Green River.

This short tour along the Duwamish River begins by following a trail, constructed in 1995, in cooperation among the political entities of King County, Metro, and Tukwila, along the Green and Duwamish rivers. The tour wanders through the little community of Allentown, tucked among freeways, railroad tracks, and the Duwamish River, where a pleasant, slow-paced atmosphere exists as children, with no fear of being run down by fast-moving cars, play and ride bicycles and horses. Lawn bowling matches are held by the older set, while anglers line the banks of the tidal Duwamish River. A muskrat swims upstream and dives beneath the waves of a passing motor boat. Little boys on the footbridge play "captain" as their homemade boats ply the river on the end of a long string. Young men work on their cars. Flower and vegetable gardens receive loving care.

The steep climb out of Allentown and over I-5 is followed by a pleasant descent down Beacon Coal Mine Road; there has not been a coal mine here for a long time. The Black River flood-control pumping station appears on the left as the road crosses the Black River channel and continues up the valley to Grady Way. From there, a broad sidewalk leads over a bridge back almost to the entrance of Fort Dent Park.

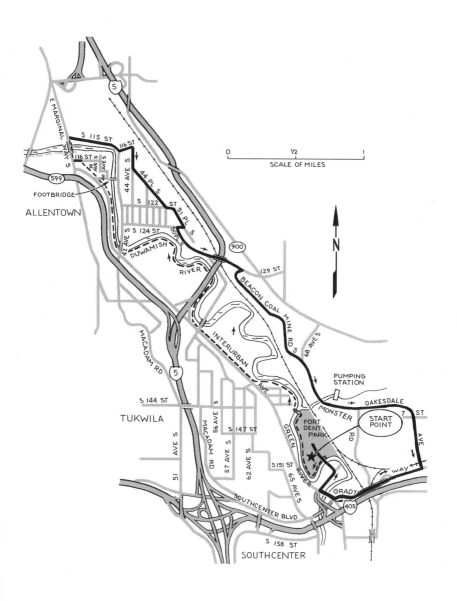

MILEAGE LOG

0.0 Fort Dent Park by restrooms. Leave the parking area, heading east toward the entrance bridge. Just before the road crosses the bridge, go up a curb cut on the left side of the roadway and turn left on the trail that loops right and under the bridge. Follow the trail along the Green River.

0.7 Turn left with trail, cross the Green River, and continue right with the trail along the Green and Duwamish rivers.

1.4 Turn right with trail along Interurban Avenue S.

2.2 Cross 56th Avenue S. and turn right with trail along I-5 entrance road. Go under the I-5 Duwamish River bridge at mile 2.7.

3.7 Turn right with trail as it approaches Interurban Avenue again, and go under 42nd Avenue S. bridge. S. 119th Street goes right to footbridge across Duwamish River at mile 4.4.

4.7 Turn left on **S. 116th Street**, then right on sidewalk along **E. Marginal Way** as it crosses the Duwamish River.

5.0 Turn right on **S. 115 Street** and ride along the river.

5.4 Turn left on **S. 116 Street**, which turns right and changes name to **44 Avenue S.**

5.7 Turn left on **44 Place S.**

6.0 Turn left on **S. 122 Street**, which bears right and is renamed **51 Place S.**

6.3 Turn right on **S. 124 Street**, then left on **50 Place S.** Continue uphill and cross I-5 on an overpass.

6.9 Turn right on **Beacon Coal Mine Road S.**

7.9 Turn right on **Monster Road** as 68 Avenue S. goes left. Cross railroad tracks and the Black River at mile 8.1.

8.4 Continue on **Oakesdale Avenue S.W.** as Monster Road turns right. Cross S.W. 7 Street at mile 8.8.

9.0 Turn right on sidewalk along **Grady Way**. Cross bridge over Monster Road and railroad tracks.

9.8 Continue along **Interurban Avenue S.** as sidewalk ends. Cross the Green River.

9.9 Turn right on **Fort Dent Way** and follow roadway left across the Green River into Fort Dent Park.

10.3 End of tour by restrooms.

3 LOWER GREEN RIVER

STARTING POINT: City of Kent's Russell Road Park. Take exit 149 from I-5 and follow State Route 516 down the hill toward Kent. Turn left on Meeker Street at traffic light at bottom of hill, cross bridge over Green River, go past first traffic light, and take next left on Russell Road.

DISTANCE: 14 to 18 miles.
TERRAIN: Flat.
TOTAL CUMULATIVE ELEVATION GAIN: 100 feet.
RECOMMENDED TIME OF YEAR: Any season.
RECOMMENDED STARTING TIME: Avoid peak traffic hours, otherwise anytime.
ALLOW: 2 hours.
POINTS OF INTEREST
Bicycle sculptures at Van Doren's
    Landing

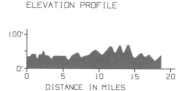

This is a pleasant ride along the flat Green River Valley through portions of Kent and Tukwila. It includes trails on dikes along the Green River and roads designated as recreational corridors by the city of Kent. Although industrial plants and shopping centers have taken over much of the Green River Valley, there are still a few truck farmers raising raspberries, strawberries, and corn. Landscape gardeners devote many acres to the growing of shrubs and trees for their clientele. Even a few dairy and beef cattle graze in the fields, and llamas decorate hillside pastures near Southcenter. Russell Road Park, beside the Green River, includes several acres of green, grassy fields for sports activities as well as trees and tables for picnickers. A cleverly designed golf course covers acres of open space. Van Doren's Landing features sculptures of touring cyclists, and smaller rest stop parks welcome the bicyclist along the way. Heavy traffic is avoided as the route traverses the dike along the Christensen Trail. On clear days, Mt. Rainier dominates the horizon to the southeast.

A major highway revision at the north end of Southcenter has cut off reasonable bicycle access to Fort Dent, and until a new trail is built, this tour does not continue to Fort Dent Park.

MILEAGE LOG

0.0 City of Kent's Russell Road Park. Starting from the center of the parking lot, head north on **Russell Road**.

0.2 Go past chain link fence and turn sharp left on **River Trail**.

1.1 Go past footbridge entrance and continue through bollards on trail beneath Meeker Street bridge.

1.9 Turn right across pedestrian bridge suspended under State Route 516 over Green River and turn right on **Frager Road**.

2.6 Bear right on blacktop path under Meeker Street. Rejoin Frager Road on the other side and continue along the Green River. City of Kent

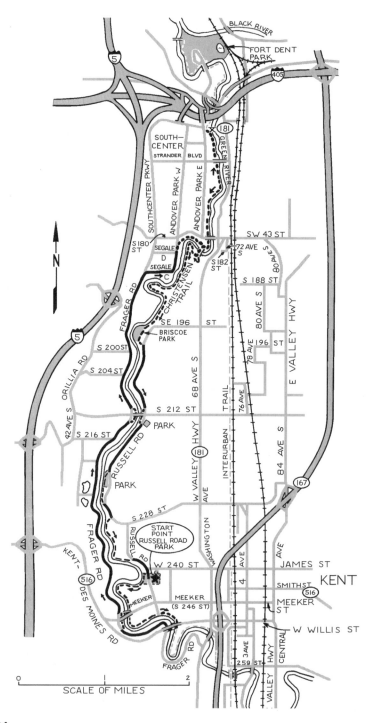

BLACK RIVER

FORT DENT PARK

5

405

181

SOUTH-CENTER

STRANDER BLVD

GREEN RIVER

SOUTHCENTER PKWY

ANDOVER PARK W

ANDOVER PARK E

SW 43 ST

S 180 ST

72 AVE S

SEGALE

D

S 182 ST

80 AVE S

SEGALE

C

S 188 ST

CHRISTENSEN TRAIL

80 AVE S

FRAGER RD

SE 196 ST

196 ST

5

BRISCOE PARK

78 AVE S

N

S 200 ST

E VALLEY HWY

S 204 ST

80 AVE S

ORILLIA RD

68 AVE S

TRAIL

76 AVE S

92 AVE S

S 212 ST

84 AVE S

RUSSELL RD

PARK

S 216 ST

INTERURBAN

181

PARK

W VALLEY HWY

167

S 228 ST

RUSSELL RD

WASHINGTON AVE

START POINT RUSSELL ROAD PARK

FRAGER RD

JAMES ST

W 240 ST

KENT

KENT- DES MOINES RD

SMITH ST

516

MEEKER

MEEKER (S 246 ST)

MEEKER ST

W WILLIS ST

FRAGER RD

VALLEY HWY

CENTRAL AVE

4 AVE

3 AVE

259 ST

0   1   2

SCALE OF MILES

Cottonwood Grove rest area at mile 3.4; picnic tables, bike rack, and trash can, but no water.

5.5 Bear right on trail under S. 212 Street bridge; rejoin Frager Road on other side.

7.4 Pass Segale Construction Company offices and asphalt plant and turn right past *No Through Traffic* sign on **Segale Park Drive C**. Road bends left at mile 7.7 and becomes **Andover Park West**.

8.0 Pass Segale Park Drive D, cross railroad spur, and turn right along tracks behind office building.

8.1 Turn right across railroad spur and up onto paved trail.

8.3 Continue on **Christensen Trail** as footbridge goes right across Green River. *Note: Turning right here shortens route by 4.1 miles.* Go under S. 180 Street bridge at mile 8.7 and Strander Boulevard bridge at mile 10.0.

10.4 Trail ends at sidewalk along Christensen Road. Picnic tables nearby on lower trail. Until new trail is completed to Fort Dent Park, this is the northerly end of this tour. Turn back along trail.

12.4 Turn left on footbridge across Green River and turn right on other side. Briscoe Park on right at mile 13.4.

14.5 Continue on **Russell Road** as trail ends. Road skirts the Boeing Space Center as it winds along the Green River. Bear right on trail under S. 212 Street bridge at mile 15.4. City of Kent's Anderson Park picnic and rest stop at mile 15.5.

15.9 Turn right on **River Trail** through Van Doren's Landing Park; picnic tables, toilets, bicycle sculptures, monument. Rejoin **Russell Road** at mile 16.2.

16.8 Go past gravel drive and turn right on **River Trail** for another 0.9-mile scenic detour, rejoining **Russell Road** at mile 17.7. Keep right through bollards as S. 240 Street goes left at mile 17.9.

18.1 Return to Russell Road Park; end of tour.

"New Member"

4 RENTON–FAIRWOOD

STARTING POINT: Cedar River Park in Renton. From I-405, take exit 4 (State Route 169, Enumclaw). Head east 0.1 mile and turn right into park. Proceed left clockwise in park to parking area near Carco Theater and Renton Community Center.

DISTANCE: 19 miles.
TERRAIN: Half hilly, half flat.
TOTAL CUMULATIVE ELEVATION GAIN: 1000 feet.
RECOMMENDED TIME OF YEAR: Any season.
RECOMMENDED STARTING TIME: Anytime.
ALLOW: 3 hours.
POINTS OF INTEREST
Lake Youngs Pipeline
Cedar River Trail

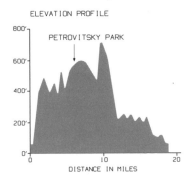

This 19-mile tour travels the hills southeast of Renton. Starting from Renton's Cedar River Park, the route briefly skirts downtown Renton before going uphill over I-405 into quiet suburban areas. The first hill, following the Seattle Water Department's Lake Youngs Reservoir pipeline right of way, is impressive, but once it is conquered the rest of the ride is comparatively easy. A gate across the roadway, blocking automobiles, makes this leg of the tour pleasantly traffic-free. Multiple sets of power lines hum overhead, electrifying the atmosphere.

Continuing to follow the general direction of the multiple water pipelines from the Lake Youngs Reservoir to downtown Renton, the route meanders along residential streets, eventually passing through the upscale Fairwood residential area and golf course. Here a choice may be made between an extra two miles to find food services in the Fairwood shopping center or a sack lunch from the pannier enjoyed at recently upgraded Petrovitsky (King County) Park.

After lunch, two miles of riding along the generously wide shoulder of Petrovitsky Road is followed by another climb over a hill with a long, exhilarating, nine-percent downgrade on the other side. At the bottom of the hill a traffic light eases a crossing of busy Maple Valley Highway to quiet, undulating Jones Road. The bridge over the Cedar River at the start of Jones Road is a great place to watch for migrating salmon in season. Following the Cedar River, Jones Road ends abruptly at the busy Maple Valley Road, but do not despair. The newly constructed Cedar River Trail, following the old Chicago, Milwaukee, St. Paul, and Pacific Railroad grade, is being improved as a grade-separated bikeway. Incomplete as this book goes to press, the trail is blocked at a crossing of the Cedar River, but an escape route to a sidewalk along the highway leads safely back to the starting point at Renton's Cedar River Park.

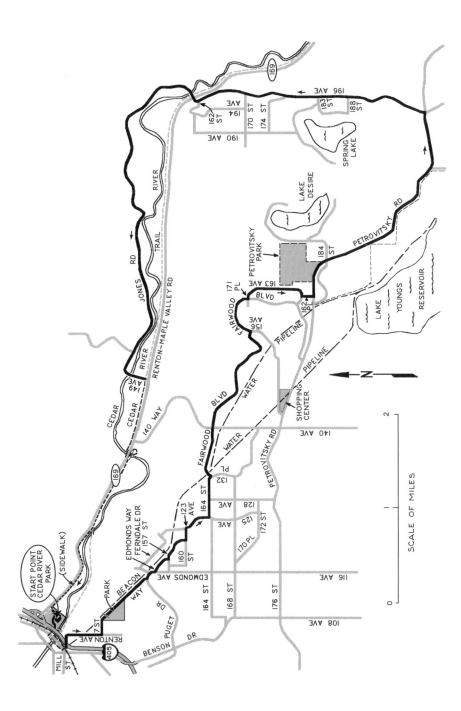

MILEAGE LOG

0.0 Starting from Renton Community Center front door (restrooms inside), follow roadway counterclockwise around the center and under I-405 and railroad trestle.

0.2 Cross **Houser Way** with pedestrian signal and turn left on sidewalk. Cross Cedar River on pedestrian bridge.

0.4 Turn left with pedestrian signal across Houser Way as Mill Street goes right. Continue uphill on steep ramp over I-405 and continue uphill on **Renton Avenue S.** Views of Renton from hill.

1.0 Turn left at stop sign on **S. 7th Street**.

1.2 Turn right at stop sign on **Beacon Way S.** by Philip Arnold Park. Go around vehicle-blocking gate and pedal uphill to top of grade at mile 1.4. Continue under ten sets of power lines.

1.9 Turn left on **Puget Drive S.E.**, right on **Edmonds Avenue S.E.**, and left on **Edmonds Way S.E.** in quick succession. The road bends right and becomes **118 Avenue S.E.**

2.3 Turn left on **S.E. 157 Street**, which bends right and is renamed **126 Avenue S.E.**

2.6 Turn left on **S.E. 160 Street**.

2.7 Turn right at yield sign on **123 Avenue S.E.**, which meanders and is renamed **126 Avenue S.E.**

3.1 Turn left on **S.E. 164 Street**.

3.5 Turn left at stop sign on **132 Place S.E.** as 164 Street ends. The road bends right shortly and is renamed **S.E. Fairwood Boulevard**. Cross 140 Avenue S.E. at traffic light at mile 4.1.

5.4 Turn left with Fairwood Boulevard at stop sign as 156 Avenue S.E. goes right. *Note: For food services, turn right on 156 Avenue one mile.* Road is evetually renamed **161 Avenue S.E.**

6.0 Turn left at stop sign on **S.E. 171 Place**. Road bends right and is renamed **163 Avenue S.E.**

6.6 Turn left on **162 Place S.E.**

6.7   Turn left on **S.E. Petrovitsky Road** as 162 Place ends. Continue on six-foot shoulder.

6.9   Petrovitsky King County Park on left with restrooms, ball fields, picnic tables; recommended brown-bag lunch stop. An inviting trail paralleling Petrovitsky Road dead-ends after 0.2 miles. Continue on shoulder of Petrovitsky Road over top of hill and down other side.

9.4   Turn left on **196 Avenue S.E.** at crossroads at base of hill and start uphill again on two-foot shoulder. Top of hill at mile 10.2; begin 9% downgrade at mile 10.9.

11.9   Cross Maple Valley Road at stop light, cross Cedar River and continue on **S.E. Jones Road**. Road is renamed **149 Avenue S.E.** after second river crossing.

16.0   Turn right on **Cedar River Trail** just before 149 Avenue ends on Renton-Maple Valley Road at traffic light. Turn left with trail at mile 16.8 under bridge and follow cloverleaf around and across trail bridge over Cedar River. Cross 131st Avenue S.E. with pedestrian signal at mile 17.1 and continue with trail as it climbs a landscaped berm along the highway.

17.6   Take right-hand side trail down off the berm and continue on sidewalk. *Note: When trail is completed as planned, it may be taken all the way back to the starting point.* Pass Maplewood Roadside Park at mile 17.8 and Cedar River Greenway Interpretive Park at mile 18.4.

18.8   Turn left on paved walkway into Cedar River Park. Turn left on roadway as walkway ends. Return to starting point at mile 19.0.

5 RENTON–MAPLE VALLEY

STARTING POINT: Cedar River Park in Renton. From I-405, take exit 4 (State Route 169, Enumclaw). Head east 0.1 mile and turn right into park. Proceed left clockwise in park to parking area near Carco Theater and Renton Community Center.

DISTANCE: 32 miles.
TERRAIN: Flat to moderate.
**TOTAL CUMULATIVE ELEVA-
TION GAIN:** 800 feet.
RECOMMENDED TIME OF YEAR:
Third Sunday of any month.
**RECOMMENDED STARTING
TIME:** 7 to 11 A.M.
ALLOW: 4 hours.
POINT OF INTEREST
Cedar River salmon run (in season)

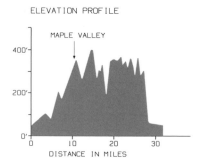

ELEVATION PROFILE

On the third Sunday of every month, the Maple Valley Grange offers its popular family-style breakfast. Featuring ham and eggs and stacks of hot-cakes at a reasonable price, the meal has been a favorite of bicyclists for many years. This is the basis for the above-recommended starting place and time for this ride. At other times, a grassy slope along the Cedar River behind the grange hall serves as an opportune picnic site.

Aside from the food, this tour has many scenic attractions. The planned Cedar River Trail, under construction at the time of this writing, promises a scenic, relaxing trip on the old Milwaukee Railroad grade by the Cedar River. Several parks along the way invite cyclists to stop. The mileage log reflects the state of trail construction as this book went to press, and further improvements may allow cyclists to avoid some of the diversions outlined below.

Maxwell Road, a seemingly forgotten strip of asphalt, climbs a gentle grade from a back door of the Maple Valley business community. Along Cedar Grove Road, the terrain changes to forest and small lakes. May Valley Road offers the rural atmosphere of horse and cattle ranching. In early spring, the prunus trees put on a show of frothy pink blossoms. The Devil's Elbow grade, abandoned as an automotive roadway, now serves as a scenic, almost secretive trail for cyclists. Low-traffic streets are followed through Renton back to the starting point.

MILEAGE LOG

0.0 Head east, then north from the parking lot toward the park entrance.
0.1 Turn right through curb cut onto sidewalk in park, then right again on sidewalk along **State Route 169 (Maple Valley Highway)**. Cedar River Greenway Interpretive Park appears at mile 1.0.
1.2 Turn right onto **Cedar River Trail** berm by Maplewood Roadside Park. Follow trail as it crosses the Cedar River on old highway bridge at mile 2.1 and turns under the bridge along the river.

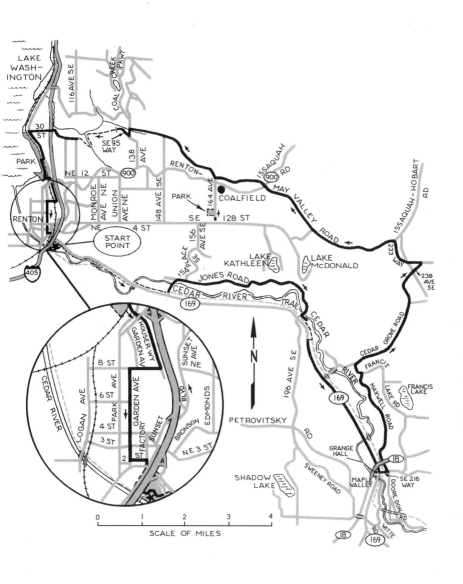

3.0 Turn left on **149 Avenue S.E.** as trail surface degenerates. Cross the Cedar River on an old steel truss bridge at mile 3.1 and continue on **S.E. Jones Road**.

7.0 Cross the Cedar River and turn left and downhill on **Cedar Mountain Place S.E.** At bottom of grade, turn sharp right on access trail, then left on **Cedar River Trail**.

7.6 Turn right on driveway as trail surface degenerates, then left on **Renton-Maple Valley Highway (State Route 169)**. A trail access point appears on the left at mile 11.0, just east of the State Route 18 high overpass.

11.2 Pass grocery and stop at Maple Valley Grange for Sunday brunch. For picnic lunches, a park is planned just across the Cedar River. After the meal, cross the highway by the grange hall and continue on **S.E. 216th Way**.

11.4 Turn left on **Maxwell Road S.E.**

12.0 Turn right with Maxwell Road on **S.E. 208 Street**, which reverts to just Maxwell Road again after 0.1 mile.

13.9 Turn left on **S.E. Lake Francis Road** as Maxwell Road ends.

14.1 Turn right on **Cedar Grove Road S.E.** as Lake Francis Road ends.

17.1 Cross Issaquah-Hobart Road and continue on **238 Avenue S.E.**

17.3 Turn left on **Tiger Mountain Road** as 238 Avenue ends.

17.5 Cross Issaquah-Hobart Road and continue downhill on **233 Way S.E.**

18.0 Turn left on **S.E. May Valley Road** as 233 Way ends. Cross Issaquah Creek and begin moderate climb. Cross State Route 900 at mile 21.8.

23.0 Turn right on **164 Avenue S.E.** as May Valley Road appears to end. Road name reverts to **S.E. May Valley Road** at mile 23.1.

25.3 Turn left on **Coal Creek Parkway S.E.** as May Valley Road ends. Cross May Creek and turn right at the next opportunity on **S.E. 95 Way**. Continue past *Road Closed* sign at mile 26.4, through gap in concrete barrier and down the Devil's Elbow, a steep, rough, curving roadway. Cross Honeydew Creek at mile 26.7 and begin moderate climb.

27.0 Go around steel A-frame gate and continue past a small wye on **N.E. 27th Street**, which changes name as it descends hill to **Kennewick Avenue N.E.** and **N.E. 30th Street**. Cross I-405 on an overpass at mile 27.8. Striking views of the Olympic Mountains, Lake Washington, and South Seattle on a clear day.

28.3 Turn left on **Lake Washington Boulevard N.** as N.E. 30th Street ends.

29.1 Turn right into entrance to Coulon Park, then left on park roadway.

29.6 Leave the south entrance to the park, cross Lake Washington Boulevard, go around gate, and turn left across railroad tracks on **Houser Way**.

30.1 Turn right at stop sign on **N. 8th Street** and cross railroad tracks.

30.4 Pass Garden Avenue as it goes right, then turn left on **Garden Avenue N.** Cross N. 4th Street (right-turn-only for automobiles) at mile 30.9.

31.1 Turn left on **N. 2nd Street**.

31.2 Turn right on **Factory Avenue N.E.** at stop sign as 2nd Street ends.

31.3 Cross Bronson Way N. with pedestrian signal and get up on sidewalk by *Do Not Enter* sign along **Houser Way**, which is One Way the opposite direction.

31.5 Turn left across Houser Way with pedestrian signal to entrance to Cedar River Park. Go under railroad trestle and I-405 and bear left, then right around Community Center to parking lot. End of tour at mile 31.7.

6 SOUTH LAKE WASHINGTON

STARTING POINT: South parking lot of Gene Coulon Park in Renton. Take exit 5 (Park Avenue, State Route 900) west from I-405, turn right at traffic light at bottom of hill on Lake Washington Boulevard N., and follow signs to the park.

DISTANCE: 26 miles.
TERRAIN: Flat to moderate.
TOTAL CUMULATIVE ELEVA-TION GAIN: 900 feet.
RECOMMENDED TIME OF YEAR: Any season.
RECOMMENDED STARTING TIME: 10 A.M.
ALLOW: 4 hours.
POINTS OF INTEREST
I-90 and Lake Washington bikeways

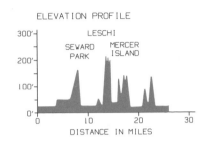

Bicycle touring around the perimeter of southern Lake Washington has long been a popular sport, but only recently has the trail system across Mercer Island and Mercer Slough and along I-405 reduced the exposure to hills and traffic to the extent that it is a pleasurable ride even for the inexperienced cyclist. Add to this the marked bicycle routes past lakeside parks and duck-watching vantage points along Seattle's Lake Washington waterfront, and this becomes a delightful, relaxing day's outing. Take a picnic lunch to enjoy in one of the many parks, or patronize one of the several food services along the way.

MILEAGE LOG

0.0 From the south parking lot of Gene Coulon Park, head out the south entrance, cross Lake Washington Boulevard N., and continue past A-frame gate and across railroad tracks on **Houser Way N.**

0.7 Turn right at stop sign on **N. 8th Street** as Houser Way is marked Dead End.

1.0 Turn left at traffic light on **Garden Avenue N.**

1.2 Turn right on **N. 6th Street**. Cross Logan Avenue at mile 1.6.

1.8 Continue straight on paved trail as roadway bends right, then turn left immediately on trail along Cedar River.

1.9 Turn right across concrete bridge, then turn left on roadway along river.

2.3 Bear right on **Airport Perimeter Road** as a stop sign appears ahead.

3.6 Turn left at stop sign, go up a short ramp, and turn right along shoulder of **Rainier Avenue S.**

6.2 Bear right at traffic light on **Seward Park Avenue S.** with Lake Washington Loop bike route sign. Start a long, gradual climb through residential neighborhood.

8.0 Turn right with Seward Park Avenue and Lake Washington Loop bike route sign as Wilson Avenue continues on.

8.5 Turn right toward Seward Park on **S. Juneau Street**, then left at bottom of hill toward UW on **Lake Washington Boulevard S.** by

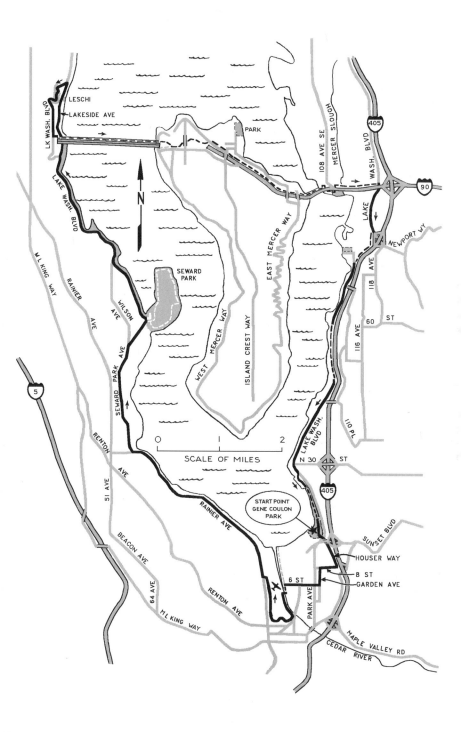

entrance to Seward Park; restrooms, trails, and fish hatchery. A sidewalk bikeway and several side loops along Lake Washington Boulevard provide closer views of the lake. Pass Sayres Park at mile 10.5.

11.6 Continue on **Lakeside Avenue S.** uphill as Lake Washington Boulevard turns left. Go under I-90 at mile 12.0. Leschi Park, marina, grocery, restaurant, and delicatessen at mile 12.8.

12.9 Turn sharp left on **Lake Washington Boulevard S.** and go uphill under E. Yesler Way viaduct and through Frink Park. Views across Lake Washington at mile 13.9.

14.0 Turn left on **S. Irwin Street** toward I-90 Trail with Lake Washington Loop bike route. Descend short, steep hill, turn right through bollards as roadway bends left, then turn left on **I-90 Trail** and cross Lake Washington to Mercer Island.

15.7 Continue uphill on I-90 lid trail on Mercer Island as a side trail goes left down to a roadway.

16.0 Cross roadway, turn left, then right through bollards, and continue uphill on bikeway. A side trail just past tennis courts goes left to picnic tables among ventilation stacks. Cross the I-90 lid past ball fields and continue downhill on the north-side trail.

16.6 Turn left across 76th Avenue S.E. and continue on bikeway along **North Mercer Way**. *Note: 76th Avenue crosses I-90 to Mercer Island business district and food services.*

17.0 Bear right across Island Crest Way with pedestrian light and continue on bikeway as it crosses Shorewood Drive, N. Mercer Way, E. Mercer Way, and the East Channel Bridge.

18.9 Turn left on **S.E. 34 Street** as bikeway ends in Bellevue. Take next left on **108th Avenue S.E.** at stop sign, go under I-90 and follow roadway left.

19.2 Bear left through bollards on bikeway and go under I-90.

19.6 Turn right across Mercer Slough bikeway bridge and floating trail.

19.9 Turn right on frontage bikeway as Mercer Slough trail ends. Continue on **Lake Washington Boulevard S.E.** as bikeway ends at mile 20.1.

20.8 Go under railroad trestle and turn right through bollards on **Lake Washington Bike Trail**. Continue on alternating stretches of boulevard and trail at miles 21.3 and 22.5.

23.3 Turn left on **Lake Washington Boulevard N.** as Lake Washington Bike Trail ends.

23.7 Turn right with Lake Washington Boulevard as N. 44th Street goes left across I-405 overpass.

24.6 Turn right on **Mtn View Avenue N.** and bear left across badly angled railroad tracks. Go through gate at end of road into Gene Coulon Park and continue on paved trail. Take left-hand, uphill trail fork at mile 25.1.

25.4 Bear left on roadway at traffic circle.

26.0 Turn right into south parking lot; end of tour.

7   UPPER GREEN RIVER

STARTING POINT: Flaming Geyser State Park. Take exit 4A, Renton-Maple Valley Road S.E. (State Route 169) from I-405 in Renton. Continue past Black Diamond 2.5 miles, turn right toward Flaming Geyser State Park on S.E. Green Valley Road for 2.7 miles, then left on S.E. Flaming Geyser Road across the Green River to the park. Parking area available near main restrooms.

DISTANCE: 19 to 34 miles.
TERRAIN: Flat to strenuous.
TOTAL CUMULATIVE ELEVATION GAIN: 1480 feet.
RECOMMENDED TIME OF YEAR: Any season.
RECOMMENDED STARTING TIME: 9 to 10 A.M.
ALLOW: 5 hours.
POINTS OF INTEREST
Flaming Geyser State Park
Black Diamond Bakery
Green River Gorge

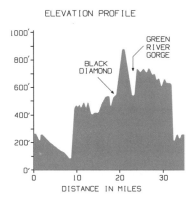

Although we call this the Upper Green River tour, only the first nine miles follow the river valley. Much of the ride is on the plateau on either side of the river. Flaming Geyser State Park, the starting point for this tour, has restrooms, picnic shelters, and tables. Managed by the State Parks and Recreation Commission, Flaming Geyser will become the western end of the larger Green River Gorge Conservation Area extending to Palmer. Trails will connect the several sections—some developed, others primitive.

As the route leaves the valley floor near the outskirts of Auburn, it climbs a steep hill to the plateau where suburban farmers keep horses, sheep, goats, chickens, and ducks. Along the Auburn-Black Diamond Road, the tour tunnels through second-growth forest.

The bakery and adjoining cafe in Black Diamond are considered by many to be the high point of the ride. Although closed on Monday and Tuesday, it is open on Saturday and Sunday to the delight of weekend skiers and bicyclists. Be sure to get there early, as it is often sold out and closed by 2 P.M. The Dinner House in Morganville features a Sunday brunch from 11 A.M. to 2 P.M. A drive-in cafe in Black Diamond offers the usual fast food.

Out of Black Diamond, the route climbs a hill, then begins a long descent to the bridge over the Green River Gorge. Views into the gorge 200 feet below the bridge are worth a stop, but be sure to keep bicycles out of the way of the automobile traffic. Maidenhair ferns cling to the moist sides as small waterfalls plunge over the cliffs. The Gorge Resort maintains trails into the gorge; picnicking and camping. Leaving the lush area of the gorge, the tour leads uphill on a good low-gear grade of five to eight percent past several springs that gush out of the hillside and disappear under the road.

Several miles of second-growth forest provide relaxing, low-traffic touring.

After passing marshy Bass and Beaver lakes, the road meanders a bit and eventually edges up to the canyon brink. A few brief glimpses of the valley below are afforded before the exhilarating swoosh down the hill and across the Kummer Bridge. In fall the vine maple provides a colorful display.

As the cyclist returns to Flaming Geyser State Park during a winter tour, steelheaders, making their yearly pilgrimage in search of the elusive seagoing trout, line the banks of the Green River.

MILEAGE LOG

0.0   Parking lot by restrooms in Flaming Geyser State Park. Go out park entrance road and cross the Green River.

1.1   Turn left on **S.E. Green Valley Road** and continue as it winds down the valley. Cross the Green River at mile 7.7. *Note: The tour may be shortened 15.4 miles by turning right on 218 Avenue S.E. at mile 1.6 and turning right on Auburn-Black Diamond Road at the top of the hill. See map.*

9.3   Turn right on **S.E. Auburn-Black Diamond Road** and cross the Green River.

9.4   Turn right on **S.E. Lake Holm Road** and start up steep hill.

11.6 Turn right on **S.E. Lake Moneysmith Road**.

14.0 Continue on **S.E. Lake Holm Road** as it joins from the left.

14.7 Turn right on **S.E. Auburn-Black Diamond Road** as Lake Holm Road ends. At mile 16.6, 218 Avenue S.E. goes right to Flaming Geyser Park.

18.6 Enter Black Diamond, ride past Dinner House and barber shop, and bear right on thoroughfare, eventually named **Railroad Avenue**.

19.2 Turn left on **Baker Street** by the Black Diamond Museum and Old Confectionery Art Gallery. Black Diamond Bakery is one block farther on Railroad Avenue.

19.4 Turn right on **3 Avenue (State Route 169)** and then immediately turn left toward Green River Gorge, passing a diner, on **Lawson Street**, which is renamed **S.E. Green River Gorge Road** as it leaves Black Diamond. Bridge over Green River Gorge at mile 22.5. Continue on **Enumclaw-Franklin Road S.E.** up out of gorge as S.E. Green River Gorge Road goes left to Cumberland.

27.8 Turn right on **S.E. 385 Street**, cross State Route 169, and continue on **S.E. 383 Street**. As it bends around Bass Lake and Beaver Lake, the road is renamed **S.E. 383 Way**, **S.E. 380 Street**, **252 Avenue S.E.**, and **S.E. 384 Street**. A one-mile interlude of straight roadway is followed by a right bend as **236 Avenue S.E.** and a left bend as **S.E. 368 Street**, which changes to **S.E. 368 Way** and begins the plunge down to the valley.

32.3 Turn right at stop sign on **212 Way S.E.** and continue downhill.

32.8 Cross the Green River on the Kummer Bridge and turn right on **S.E. Green Valley Road** as 218 Avenue S.E. goes on.

33.4 Turn right on **S.E. Flaming Geyser Road** toward Flaming Geyser State Park and cross the Green River. End of tour at mile 34.5.

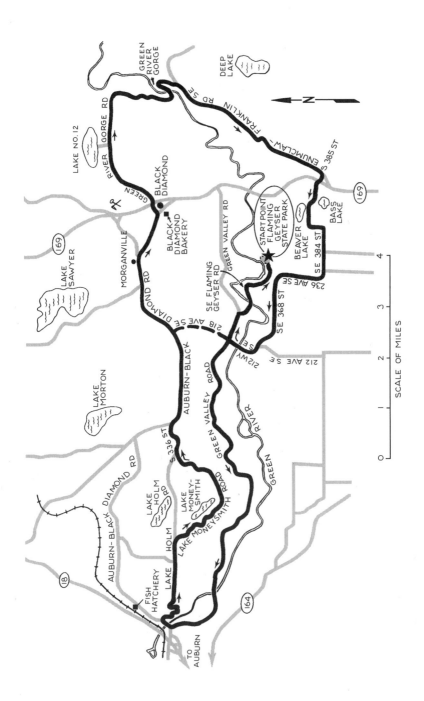

8 LANDSBURG–ENUMCLAW

STARTING POINT: Parking area by the north bank of the Cedar River on Issaquah-Ravensdale Road near Seattle Water Park (city of Seattle). Take exit 17 (Issaquah) from I-90 and go south on Issaquah-Ravensdale Road through Hobart to the Cedar River.

DISTANCE: 46 miles.
TERRAIN: Moderate; flat valley and rolling hills.
TOTAL CUMULATIVE ELEVATION GAIN: 1500 feet.
RECOMMENDED TIME OF YEAR: Any season.
RECOMMENDED STARTING TIME: 9 A.M.
ALLOW: 6 hours plus lunch.
POINTS OF INTEREST
Seattle Water Park and diversion
    dam
King County Fairgrounds, Enumclaw
Green River Gorge
Black Diamond Bakery

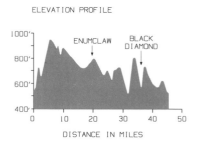

ELEVATION PROFILE

This is a fairly long and strenuous loop on paved backroads in southeast King County. The lunch spot at the King County park in Enumclaw comes near the halfway point. Interesting views of the farming communities, old coal mining areas, Mt. Rainier, and the Green River Gorge are afforded. The tour leaves the parking area, crosses the Cedar River, and heads over a hill. Dense forest attracts the Swainson's thrush, whose lovely song wafts through the trees during late spring and early summer. Livestock graze beneath power lines; damp weather makes these lines sizzle with corona discharge. The forested hills to the east of the Kanaskat-Kangley Road belong to the Seattle Cedar River watershed. No trespassing here.

The Green River is first crossed at the small towns of Palmer and Kanaskat. The 12 miles of river downstream of this crossing eventually will become the Green River Gorge Park, providing public access and facilities. Howard Hanson Dam is seven miles upstream at Eagle Gorge in the Tacoma watershed. The old coal-mining ghost town of Bayne slumbers two miles south of the Green River crossing, with only a few houses remaining intact. Cumberland is another small town along the way; it boasts a grocery store and a tavern.

Mt. Rainier towers over the nearby foothills as views change from forest-ed roadside to open farmland of the Enumclaw plateau. A King County park and several restaurants offer lunchtime possibilities when the route reaches Enumclaw. This is a crowded, busy place in late summer when the King County Fair is in progress.

Around Enumclaw several miles of flat valley road thread through subur-bia that is invading the dairy farms. Sixteen-hundred-foot Mt. Pete (Pinnacle Peak) rises out of the valley to the south. A few acres of grassland are given

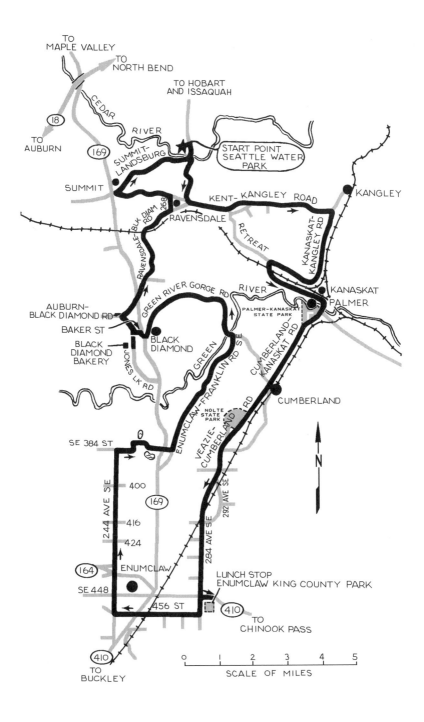

over to the airport along 244 Avenue S.E. and colorful balls strung along the power lines announce its presence. The farmland becomes rolling as the cyclist reaches little Beaver Lake and larger but marshy Bass Lake. The uninhabited forest is enjoyed before the whistling, freewheeling ride down to the Green River to view the gorge from the dizzy heights of the bridge. If the steep trail down to the water is taken, the climb back up will use up calories, but energy can be regained when Black Diamond is reached if the bakery is still open.

Black Diamond is headquarters for the Palmer Coking Coal Company, which operates an open-pit coal mine in the Franklin Hills east of town. The coal is trucked into Black Diamond, where it is processed. Most of the coal is sold to the state of Washington to be used for large state institutions, but the general public can buy coal from the stockpiles in Black Diamond. Red-colored mounds of burned coal-mine tailings are sold for gravel paths and landscaping.

When the cyclist returns to the Seattle Water Park, a tour of the diversion dam site just upstream is most interesting. The water is screened, monitored for quality and flow rate, then injected with chlorine and fluorides before being sent on its way to Lake Youngs reservoir southeast of Renton.

MILEAGE LOG

0.0 Parking area by the north bank of the Cedar River on Issaquah-Ra-vensdale Road near Seattle Water Park. Leave parking area, turn right, cross the Cedar River, and head uphill on **Landsburg Road S.E.**

1.6 Turn left on **S.E. Kent-Kangley Road**.

2.7 Keep left toward Selleck as Retreat-Kanaskat Road goes right to Kanaskat.

5.7 Turn right on **Kanaskat-Kangley Road S.E.** and head south.

8.5 Turn left across a bridge over the main-line tracks of the Burlington Northern Railroad on **Cumberland-Kanaskat Road S.E.** The route passes through the small towns of Kanaskat and Palmer and crosses the Green River at mile 9.6. Cumberland with tavern and grocery at mile 12.6. Valley farms and view of Mt. Rainier at mile 15.0. Continue south on **Veazie-Cumberland Road (284 Avenue S.E.)**.

19.0 Turn left on **State Route 410 (Roosevelt Avenue E.)**.

19.2 Turn right into Enumclaw King County Park picnic area. Restaurants nearby. After lunch, return along S.R. 410 to 284 Avenue.

19.4 Turn left (south) on **284 Avenue S.E.** King County Fairgrounds on left at mile 19.6.

19.8 Turn right on **S.E. 456 Street**. To the south, Mt. Pete rises out of farmland. Cross State Route 410 at mile 21.4.

22.2 Turn right (north) on **244 Avenue S.E.** Pass Enumclaw Airport and cross State Route 164 at mile 23.3.

26.6 Turn right on **S.E. 384 Street** and follow around little Beaver Lake and bigger Bass Lake as the road is renamed **252 Avenue S.E.**, **S.E. 380 Street**, and **S.E. 383 Street**.

28.3 Cross State Route 169 and turn left on **Enumclaw-Franklin Road S.E.** Head downhill to the Green River Gorge Bridge at mile 32.4 and begin the climb over the hill to Black Diamond.

36.5 Turn right on **State Route 169** in Black Diamond, then turn left on **Baker Street**. At the foot of this street and to the left on Railroad Avenue one block is the Black Diamond Bakery. The route turns right on **Railroad Avenue** and continues to Morganville.

37.8 Turn right (east) on **Auburn-Black Diamond Road** and cross State Route 169 at mile 38.5. Small coal-mining car is on display at this intersection. Continue on **Ravensdale-Black Diamond Road S.E.**

41.6 Cross railroad tracks, bear right with roadway, and turn left on **268 Avenue S.E.** in Ravensdale.

42.1 Turn left on **S.E. Kent-Kangley Road**.

43.8 Make a sharp right turn on **S.E. Summit-Landsburg Road**.

46.0 Bear left on **S.E. 252 Street** at a road fork.

46.3 Turn left on **Landsburg Road S.E.** and cross the Cedar River.

46.5 Turn left into parking area by entrance to Seattle Water Park; tour completed.

9 MUD MOUNTAIN DAM

STARTING POINT: King County Enumclaw Park on State Route 410.

DISTANCE: 15 miles.
TERRAIN: Flat to hilly.
TOTAL CUMULATIVE ELEVATION GAIN: 700 feet.
RECOMMENDED TIME OF YEAR: Late spring for best scenery.
RECOMMENDED STARTING TIME: Anytime.
ALLOW: 2 hours plus sightseeing and recreation at dam site.
POINTS OF INTEREST
Mud Mountain Dam
Views of White River

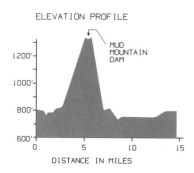

Construction of the Mud Mountain Dam was authorized by Congress in the Flood Control Act of 1936, but construction was not completed until after World War II. It is one of the highest dams of its kind (earth core and rock fill), and its sole purpose is to curtail floods in the fertile Puyallup Valley. Located on the White River at the border between Pierce County and King County, the reservoir is kept at low water to provide storage for spring runoff. The floodwaters thus are held and released gradually. Consideration is given to conservation of game fish on the White River. The Corps of Engineers collects salmon and steelhead in its trapping facilities near Buckley, puts them in big tanker trucks, and hauls them past the dam.

The bicyclist will find the round trip from Enumclaw to be a short but rather invigorating ride. The ride begins at the King County Enumclaw Park and turns south for three miles past rich farmland, with Mt. Pete rising out of the valley to the southwest. Reaching the Mud Mountain Road, the route begins a gradual, then steeper, climb to the dam site. Pillars of columnar basalt form a balustrade along the cliffy hillside. The Mud Mountain Road continues to busy State Route 410 but is left behind at the turnoff to Mud Mountain Dam. Signs at the entrance indicate the way to Vista Point. Just inside the entrance, a gigantic tower broods over neatly mowed lawns, picnic tables, shelters, restrooms, and an array of interestingly designed playground equipment. The tower is a support for the tramway used for the maintenance of the dam face. Vista Point affords views of the dam and reservoir on two sides. A trail leads down toward the water's edge.

On the return trip, good brakes are necessary to avoid runaway accidents on the steeply curving road. The loop around Mt. Pete includes forest, winding river road, and flat valley farmland. A gradual upgrade past the King County Fairgrounds brings the bicyclist back to the King County Enumclaw Park to complete this short ride.

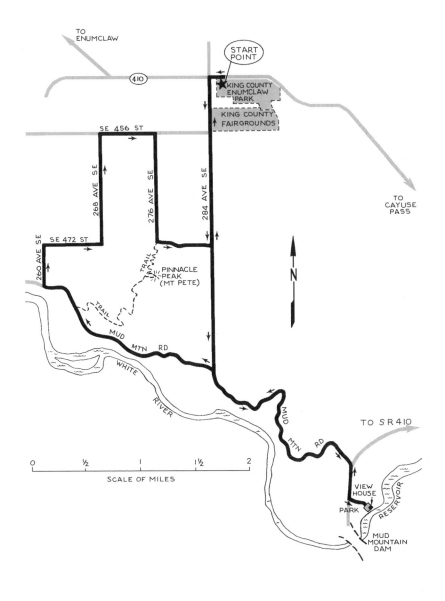

MILEAGE LOG

0.0 King County Enumclaw Park. Leave park and turn left (west) on **State Route 410**.

0.2 Turn left on **284 Avenue S.E.** at the Farman Pickle Factory. Continue straight ahead as S.E. 456 Street intersects from the right at mile 0.6.

2.6 Continue straight on **Mud Mountain Road** as it joins from the right. Start uphill at mile 3.0.

4.9 Turn right toward Mud Mountain Dam as Mud Mountain Road continues left to State Route 410.

5.0 Vista Point. Relax and take in the views, then freewheel back down the hill.

7.4 Turn left with **Mud Mountain Road** as 284 Avenue S.E. goes on.

9.2 Bear right on **260 Avenue S.E.**, which turns right and is renamed **S.E. 472 Street**.

10.1 Turn left on **268 Avenue S.E.**

11.1 Turn right on **S.E. 456 Street**.

11.6 Turn right on **276 Avenue S.E.** At mile 12.5, bear left along the north side of Mt. Pete (also called Pinnacle Peak).

13.0 Turn left on **284 Avenue S.E.** King County Fairgrounds on the right at mile 14.0.

14.5 Turn right on **State Route 410**.

14.7 Turn right into Enumclaw Park; tour completed.

Wet Brakes

10   UPPER SNOQUALMIE

STARTING POINT: Si View King County Park in North Bend. Take exit 31 from I-90 and follow North Bend Boulevard into North Bend. Cross the South Fork Snoqualmie River and turn right on Park Street, then right again on Healy Avenue toward Si View King County Park.

DISTANCE: 15 miles.
TERRAIN: Moderate to flat.
TOTAL CUMULATIVE ELEVATION GAIN: 300 feet.
RECOMMENDED TIME OF YEAR:
Good in all seasons except in snow conditions.
RECOMMENDED STARTING TIME:
10 A.M.
ALLOW: 3 hours .
POINTS OF INTEREST
Weyerhaeuser sawmill site
Salish Lodge
Puget Sound Power and Light Company, Snoqualmie Falls Park
Millpond
Puget Sound and Snoqualmie Valley Railroad
Snoqualmie Depot

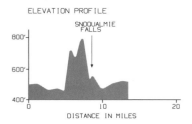

This short but scenic ride has a bit of everything: managed tree farms, productive farmlands, a state fish hatchery, a historical railroad museum with operating steam locomotives, a magnificent view of Snoqualmie Falls, plus picnic sites and excellent restaurants.

There is plenty of parking space at the Si View King County Park. Here also are picnic tables, playground apparatus, tennis courts, a baseball field, a gymnasium, an indoor swimming pool, and restrooms. The route heads west out of the park, then north through North Bend and out into the country past many homes with Mt. Si looming above. A holly farm, tucked in between two forks of the Snoqualmie River, shows bright red berries during late fall and winter. As the rider continues along Reinig Road, the North Fork, Middle Fork, and South Fork Snoqualmie River come together back among the trees and emerge as the Snoqualmie River. Occasionally, this river goes on a rampage and floods the valley below Snoqualmie Falls.

Just after the bicyclist passes under a canopy of sycamore trees and crests a hill, a panoramic view of the Weyerhaeuser sawmill site unfolds. Concrete foundations and landscaped yards gone wild are the only evidence of the former "company town" of Snoqualmie Falls. Bigleaf maple, buckeye, mountain ash, cedar, fir, and hemlock cover the hillside above the mill.

One isolated home is passed before the rider plunges downhill, crosses a logging artery, and enters a managed tree farm, where young Douglas fir tree plantings are carefully thinned and the competing brush suppressed.

This is a vivid demonstration of a modern timber company's dedication to perpetual-harvest forestry.

Salish Lodge, a popular place to dine, sits atop the cliff overlooking Snoqualmie Falls in the beautifully landscaped and maintained park of the Puget Sound Power and Light Company. Besides attractively designed picnic tables and shelters, this park provides a viewing platform cantilevered over the wall of the canyon for a spectacular view of the falls. The original hydroelectric plant here was completed in 1898 by Charles Baker and his Snoqualmie Falls Power Company, taken over a few years later by the firm of Stone and Webster (see Tours 52 and 53). The combine eventually became the Puget Sound Power and Light Company of today. Tours of the powerhouse are not offered to the general public, but special group tours can be arranged by appointment.

Near the falls, the blast of an air horn or the nostalgic echo of a steam locomotive chime whistle assails the ears on weekends when the Puget Sound Railway Historical Association operates the Puget Sound and Snoqualmie Valley Railroad between Snoqualmie and the depot at William Taylor Henry Railroad Park in North Bend. Passengers embark from the historic Snoqualmie Depot, listed in the National Register of Historic Places. A 1976 federal grant to the association provided funds for the restoration of the old depot to its original condition. The depot will also serve the Washington State Parks Department as their Snoqualmie Railroad Interpretive Center.

Around the shallow millpond of the now-defunct Weyerhaeuser sawmill, cattails, swamp dogwood, and other moisture-loving shrubs line the edge. An occasional duck scurries among the rushes. Pied-billed grebes quickly dive out of sight; only double-crested cormorants remain stationary atop their deadhead log.

The Mt. Si Golf Course spreads over many acres of the Upper Snoqualmie Valley, while across the road many acres of farmland lie dormant, acquired for open space in 1994 by the towns of Snoqualmie and North Bend. The outskirts of North Bend are again traversed before the ride is completed at Si View Park.

MILEAGE LOG

0.0   Si View County Park, North Bend. Leave park and head south (with the park buildings on the right) on **Orchard Avenue**. Road bends right immediately and is renamed **Healy Avenue S.**

0.2   Turn left on **E. Park Street**.

0.3   Turn right on **Main Avenue S.** and cross North Bend Way.

0.6   Turn right on **E. Sixth Street** as Main Avenue ends, then left on **Ballarat Avenue N.** and follow it out of North Bend. At the city limits, it becomes **420 Avenue S.E.**

1.0   Bear right with thoroughfare on **S.E. 108 Street**.

1.7   Turn left on **428 Avenue S.E.** Cross the Middle Fork Snoqualmie River at mile 2.6. Cross the North Fork at mile 3.0.

3.2   Route turns left on **S.E. Reinig Road**. *Note: A side trip can be taken here by proceeding straight ahead on 428 Avenue S.E., now called*

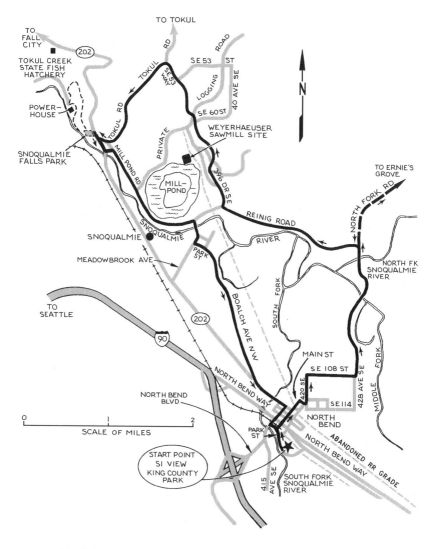

North Fork Road, for two miles to the little settlement of Ernie's Grove.

5.1   Bear right on **396 Drive S.E.** and proceed uphill, overlooking the old Weyerhaeuser sawmill, now converted to the production of horticultural pulp and kiln-dried lumber.

6.4   Bear left with 396 Drive S.E. as S.E. 60 Street goes on. Cross a logging road at mile 6.5. Keep right and head up a short, steep hill.

7.0   Follow left past a house at the top of the hill, then plunge downhill on

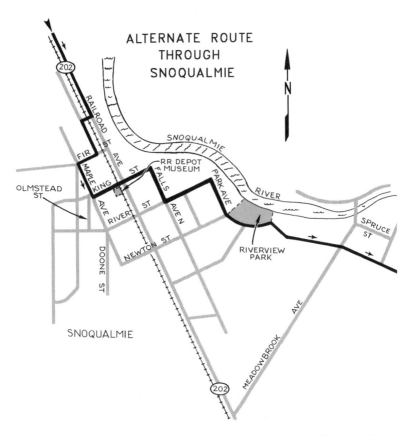

ALTERNATE ROUTE
THROUGH
SNOQUALMIE

N

SNOQUALMIE

S.E. 53 Way. Continue left on **Tokul Road** as it joins from the right.

8.5 Turn right on **State Route 202.** Puget Sound Power and Light Company's Snoqualmie Falls Park with tables, restrooms, shelters, cafe, and viewing platform at mile 8.7. After viewing the falls and perhaps stopping for a snack, head east (left) back along S.R. 202.

9.2 Turn left on **Mill Pond Road** just before S.R. 202 crosses a bridge over the Snoqualmie River. *Note: Those desiring a visit to the steam railway exhibit should continue into the town of Snoqualmie on S.R. 202. See Alternate Route next.*

10.7 Make a hard right turn on **Reinig Road**, cross the Snoqualmie River, and continue on **Meadowbrook Avenue** into the community of Meadowbrook.

11.0 Turn left on **Park Street** and follow it out into farmland. Pass Mt. Si Golf Course and restaurant at mile 11.7. Road changes name to **Boalch Avenue N.W.**

13.2 Turn left on **State Route 202 (North Bend Boulevard N.)**, cross the South Fork Snoqualmie River, and bear right with thoroughfare. Cross North Bend Way with traffic light at mile 13.8.

13.9   Turn left on **E. Park Street**.

14.4   Bear right on **Healy Avenue S.** and continue to Si View Park; tour completed.

ALTERNATE ROUTE

9.2   Continue on **State Route 202** across the Snoqualmie River and into the town of Snoqualmie.

9.6   Turn right just past the Snoqualmie entrance sign, cross the railroad tracks, and turn left through the public parking lot.

9.8   Turn right on **Fir Street** at T junction, then left again on **Maple Avenue**.

9.9   Turn left on **King Street** to Snoqualmie Depot; historic railroad depot, steam train excursions. Continue across Railroad Avenue on King Street.

10.0   Turn right on **Falls Avenue N.** as King Street ends.

10.1   Turn left on **River Street** by Snoqualmie City Hall. Road bends right and is renamed **Park Avenue**.

10.7   Cross Meadowbrook Avenue and continue on Park as the main tour route joins at mileage log 11.0.

"Ya can't kid me. They were all scrapped thirty years ago."

11 FALL CITY–SNOQUALMIE FALLS

STARTING POINT: Olive Taylor Quigley Park in Fall City on the Redmond-Fall City Road (State Route 202). Take exit 22 (Preston) from I-90; proceed through Preston to Fall City.

DISTANCE: 12 miles.
TERRAIN: Moderate with one long hill.
TOTAL CUMULATIVE ELEVATION GAIN: 780 feet.
RECOMMENDED TIME OF YEAR: Any season.
RECOMMENDED STARTING TIME: 10 A.M.
ALLOW: 2 hours plus lunch.
POINTS OF INTEREST
Tokul Creek State Fish Hatchery
Snoqualmie Falls

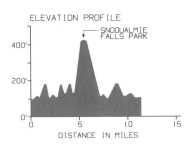

This ride from Fall City to Snoqualmie Falls is an easy one in spite of the hill on State Route 202 from the Tokul Creek fish hatchery to the Puget Sound Power and Light Company's park at Snoqualmie Falls. Although this is a long hill, its steady grade is not difficult for bicycles. By taking Fish Hatchery Road, the cyclist can avoid most of the highway traffic and get a close view of the Snoqualmie River. The powerhouse at the base of Snoqualmie Falls is the turn-around point at the end of the road. The big penstocks coming down over the hill to the powerhouse are not usually viewed by the motoring public. A trail leads around the back side of the powerhouse through fully enclosed chain link fencing and continues along the bank of the Snoqualmie River for 1/4 mile to a viewpoint below the falls. Another steep hiking trail begins near the powerhouse and leads uphill through the forest to Puget Power's park at the top of the falls.

The hatchery at Tokul Creek is another interesting place. Several varieties of trout hatch in shallow trays in the large shed, then are transferred to the long metal tanks, and finally to the outdoor concrete pools. At feeding time, the water erupts with hungry fish as an attendant distributes handfuls of food over the pools.

The beginning cyclist need not include the ride uphill to the falls, as a picnic lunch may be enjoyed along Tokul Creek or at the public access point on the Snoqualmie River. For the experienced rider, however, the uphill sprint to Puget Power's park is worth the effort. The park has picnic facilities, and the view of Snoqualmie Falls from the cantilevered platform is worth seeing over and over as the mood of the falls changes. A small cafe at the park is handy for those who would rather buy lunch.

The Upper Snoqualmie ride (Tour 10) to North Bend can be added to this Fall City-Snoqualmie Falls ride, making a total of 29 miles for the combination. Picnic tables at Si View Park or one of the several restaurants in North Bend can then be used for the lunch stop.

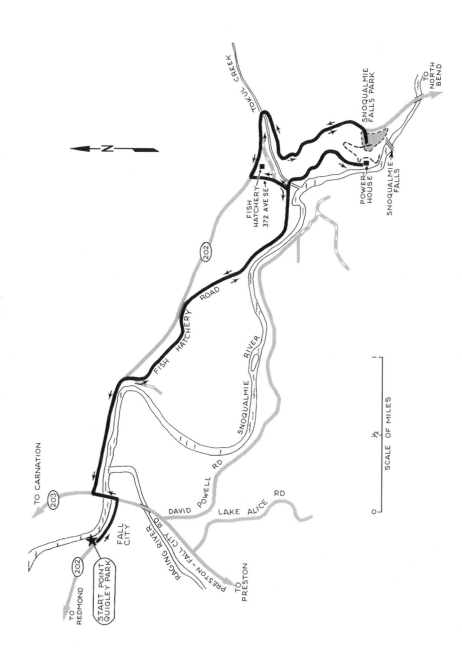

MILEAGE LOG

0.0 Olive Taylor Quigley Park in Fall City. Head east on **Redmond-Fall City Road (State Route 202)**.

0.2 Turn left with S.R. 202 and cross the Snoqualmie River.

0.4 Turn right (east) with S.R. 202 along the river.

1.2 Turn right on **Fish Hatchery Road**. Keep left on paved road as dirt road goes down to a golf course by the river. Road passes several homes, jogs close to S.R. 202, goes by a school, then descends to run along the river's edge. Public fishing access at mile 2.8 was donated by Emil Plum.

3.1 Turn right, cross Tokul Creek, and head uphill. A locked gate by automobile parking area at mile 3.6 is circumvented by a well-used path. Bicyclists and anglers may continue down a steep, paved road to Puget Sound Power and Light Company's powerhouse. A dirt trail continues to a viewpoint below Snoqualmie Falls. Return to Tokul Creek.

4.1 Cross Tokul Creek and turn right toward the fish hatchery on **372 Avenue S.E.**

4.3 Turn right on **State Route 202**. Pass Tokul Creek State Fish Hatchery at mile 4.5. Visit the hatchery, then continue up the long hill.

5.8 Snoqualmie Falls Park; tables in shelter, restrooms, cantilevered viewing platform. A small cafe provides a choice of lunch fare. Return to fish hatchery at mile 7.2.

7.4 Turn left on **372 Avenue S.E.** Keep right on **S.E. Fish Hatchery Road** at mile 7.6.

9.5 Turn left on **State Route 202**.

11.2 Keep left with S.R. 202 and over the bridge into Fall City.

11.4 Turn right with S.R. 202.

11.6 Back at Olive Taylor Quigley Park; end of tour.

12 FALL CITY–CARNATION

STARTING POINT: Olive Taylor Quigley Park in Fall City on the Redmond-Fall City Road (State Route 202). Take exit 22 (Preston) from I-90; proceed through Preston to Fall City.

DISTANCE: 16 miles.
TERRAIN: Almost flat.
TOTAL CUMULATIVE ELEVATION GAIN: 150 feet.
RECOMMENDED TIME OF YEAR: Any season.
RECOMMENDED STARTING TIME: Anytime.
ALLOW: 2 1/2 hours.
POINTS OF INTEREST
John MacDonald Memorial King
   County Park
Osprey nest

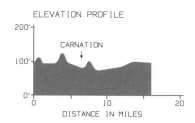

ELEVATION PROFILE

The Snoqualmie Valley seems to have resisted the creeping industrialization-urbanization that has beset so many of our fertile river valleys, and agriculture and recreation are still the principal land uses. Holstein-Friesian cows grace the pastures of the many dairy farms. Corn and rye are harvested for grain and silage, and orange pumpkins ripen in the fall. This is the flood plain of the Snoqualmie River, and evidence of past meanderings is seen in the many oxbow lakes decorating the valley. One of the unique wildflowers of this region is the wild *Clematis ligusticifolia*, or virgin's bower. In June or July, it trails in graceful loops with clusters of white starlike flowers over the bushes and trees. In August and even into the fall, the white plumy masses of silk-winged seeds make a showy sight.

Several golf courses rim the edges of the valley, with greens and fairways groomed from early spring to late fall. Kingfishers sound their rattling call by the river, plunging in when a fish is spotted. An osprey builds its nest of sticks atop an old snag in a wetland, its soaring glide high above the river suddenly interrupted as it spots a silvery glint near the surface. A momentary hover is followed by a sudden stoop and a headlong plunge into the water. The bird is not infallible, however, and it often goes away disappointed.

The 120-acre John MacDonald Memorial King County Park merits time for exploration. Located at the confluence of the Tolt and Snoqualmie rivers, the park is a favorite of steelheaders. Opened in 1974 as the Tolt River King County Park, it was renamed in 1976 for the late chairman of the park improvement committee of the Chief Seattle Council, Boy Scouts of America. The fruits of their labors may be seen by crossing the suspension footbridge to the west side of the Snoqualmie River and hiking the trails past a spacious picnic shelter with tables and barbecue pit; secluded, log sleeping shelters and several walk-in campsites. The contrast between these facilities and the "civilized" recreational vehicle campground on the east side of the river with its restrooms and hot showers is quite striking.

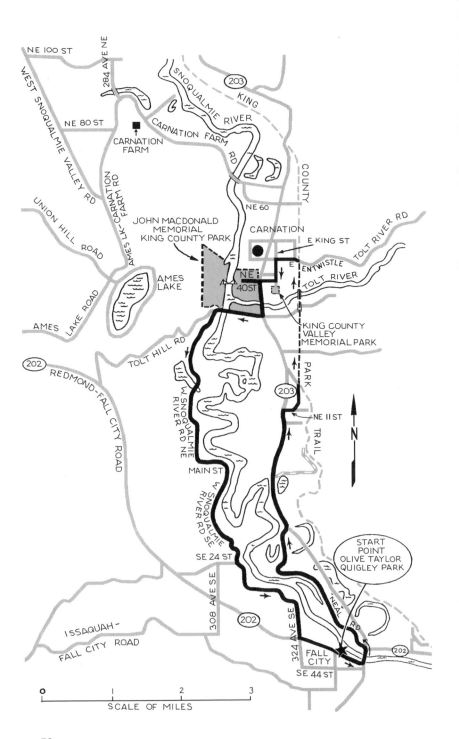

MILEAGE LOG

0.0   Olive Taylor Quigley Park in Fall City along the Snoqualmie River. Head east on **Redmond-Fall City Road (State Route 202)**.

0.2   Turn left with S.R. 202, cross the Snoqualmie River, and turn on **Carnation-Fall City Road (State Route 203)**.

0.4   Turn left on **Neal Road** past King County's Fall City Park, and bicycle along the Snoqualmie River.

3.7   Turn left on **State Route 203** as Neal Road ends.

5.2   Turn right on **N.E. 11 Street** toward Davidson Sawmill then left again on **324 Way S.E.** toward Camp Don Bosco.

5.6   Go past entrance to Camp Don Bosco and turn right on gravel drive as N.E. 16 Street goes left, then immediately turn left on **King County Park Trail** (unpaved). Cross the Tolt River on concrete-decked trestle at mile 5.9.

7.4   Turn left on **E. Entwistle**, then left on **E. King Street** in Carnation.

7.9   Turn right on **Blanche Street** as King Street enters Valley Park.

8.0   Turn left on **State Route 202**, then immediately right on **N.E. 40 Street**.

8.3   John MacDonald Memorial King County Park. Explore this delightful park, then return to S.R. 202 and turn right.

9.0   Cross the Tolt River and turn right on **Tolt Hill Road**.

9.7   Cross the Snoqualmie River, then immediately turn left on **West Snoqualmie River Road N.E.** as Tolt Hill Road continues on uphill. Warning signs with covered legends imply that water may cover this road during flood season. Deep ditches line the sides of the road, separating it from the thick marshland vegetation of alders, vine maple, salmonberry, skunk cabbage, spiraea, and occasional tall cedar trees. One old snag supports an osprey nest.

12.1   Road bends left and name changes to **E. Main Street**, then bends right and becomes **West Snoqualmie River Road S.E.**

13.8   Turn left on **S.E. 24 Street** as West Snoqualmie River Road ends. Changing its name at each turn, the road threads its way through the farmland along the river, finally turning right and becoming **324 Avenue S.E.**

15.6   Turn left on **Redmond-Fall City Road (State Route 202)** and continue on broad shoulder.

16.5   End of tour at Olive Taylor Quigley Park.

13 TOLT RIVER

STARTING POINT: King County Valley Memorial Park in Carnation. Take exit 22 (Preston) from I-90; proceed through Preston to Fall City. From Fall City, continue north on State Route 203 to Carnation. Sign along road indicates right turn to park on Blanche Street.

DISTANCE: 8 miles.
TERRAIN: Flat to moderate.
TOTAL CUMULATIVE ELEVATION
GAIN: 150 feet.
RECOMMENDED TIME OF YEAR:
Any season.
RECOMMENDED STARTING TIME:
Anytime.
ALLOW: 1 hour.
POINT OF INTEREST
Tolt River scenery

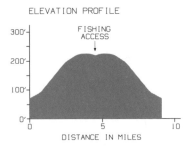

Although several homes appear along the road, much of this ride has the flavor of wilderness. A few log cabins heighten the impression. A well-maintained, oiled road with very little automobile traffic makes the riding carefree. At the road's end, a short path leads to the water's edge and winds along the river among rustic campsites. Water ouzels genuflect atop the boulders that dot the riverbed. The haunting song of the Swainson's thrush threads among the trees during summer months. The river, descending from the Seattle watershed, is the only water supply.

Those considering this too short a ride can combine it with the Fall City-Carnation tour (Tour 12), yielding a total of 24.2 miles—a good ride for the intermediate cyclist.

MILEAGE LOG

0.0 King County Valley Memorial Park in Carnation. Leave park and go north on **E. King Street** for three blocks, then turn right on **E. Entwistle** and head out of Carnation. This becomes the **Tolt River Road** after it leaves Carnation and heads uphill. Road name changes to **N.E. 80 Street** at mile 3.8.
4.2 Public fishing access on Tolt River, popular for fly fishing and picnicking. Look for water ouzels. Return along Tolt River Road.
8.4 Back at King County Valley Memorial Park.

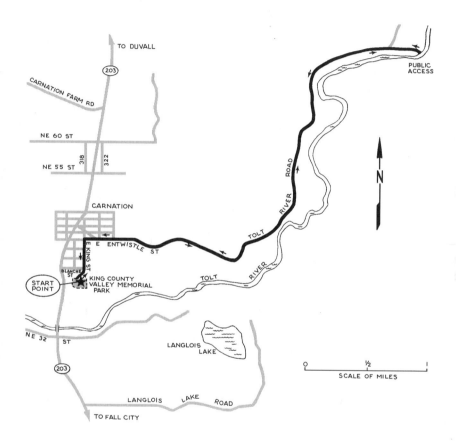

TO DUVALL

203

CARNATION FARM RD

NE 60 ST

318

322

NE 55 ST

CARNATION

E ENTWISTLE ST

TOLT   RIVER   ROAD

PUBLIC
ACCESS

N

E KING ST

BLANCHE
ST

START
POINT

KING COUNTY
VALLEY MEMORIAL
PARK

TOLT   RIVER

NE 32   ST

203

LANGLOIS
LAKE

0   ½   1
SCALE OF MILES

LANGLOIS   LAKE   ROAD

TO FALL CITY

59

14 UNION HILL–CARNATION

STARTING POINT: Emily Dickinson Elementary School parking lot (nonschool days only). Take State Route 520 (exit 168B from I-5 or exit 14 from I-405) to Redmond. Turn right at second traffic signal on Union Hill Road N.E. and continue for two miles. Turn right at top of hill on 208th Avenue N.E. to school on left.

DISTANCE: 27 miles.
TERRAIN: Hilly.
TOTAL CUMULATIVE ELEVATION GAIN: 1600 feet.
RECOMMENDED TIME OF YEAR: Any season.
RECOMMENDED STARTING TIME: 9 to 10 A.M.
ALLOW: 4 hours plus lunch.
POINTS OF INTEREST
Carnation Research Farm
John MacDonald Memorial King
  County Park
Remlinger Farms

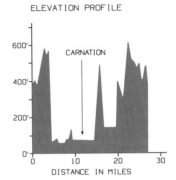

ELEVATION PROFILE

This ride frequents backroads through an area that once resounded to the whistles and puffing of the steam donkeys and locomotives of the Siler Logging Company. The roads, mostly graveled until a few decades ago, are now all paved and attracting suburban developers. Much of the route has been improved with the addition of wide, paved shoulders. The automobile traffic is light except at workday rush hour and allows a leisurely, relaxing ride. The very steep (15% grade) downhill run on the east end of Novelty Hill Road can be dangerous, however, so make sure your brakes are in good working condition.

An attractive setting for the photographer is provided by Carnation Research Farm, with its red-roofed, white buildings and lush green pastures, as seen from the overlook on the hill south of the farm. Self-guided tours of the barns are available from 10 A.M. to 3 P.M. April through October, except Sundays and holidays. Little Sikes Lake, left behind by the meandering of the Snoqualmie River, is visited by wintering waterfowl, such as scaups, baldpates, mallards, and shoveler ducks.

Carnation is still a small town, with little obvious distress from growing pains. Designation as flood plain has kept the developers at bay, although occasional flooding is an inconvenience to be endured. Cafes, a grocery, and a spacious King County park make Carnation an enjoyable lunch stop in any weather. An added attraction is the combination of cafe and produce and handicraft markets of Remlinger Farms.

The second crossing of the Snoqualmie River almost always yields sights of anglers fishing the confluence of the Tolt and Snoqualmie rivers. Beyond this, however, there are hills to climb. Tolt Hill is conquered only to dive back to the valley; a second climb brings cyclists to the summit of Union Hill and a sudden descent back to the starting point at Emily Dickinson School.

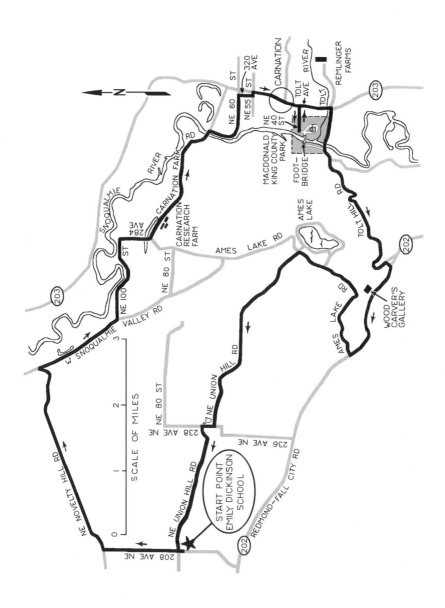

N

CARNATION

REMLINGER FARMS

203

NE 60 ST

NE 55 ST

320 AVE

TOLT AVE

TOLT RIVER

TOLT

NE 40 ST

MACDONALD KING COUNTY PARK

FOOT-BRIDGE

CARNATION FARM RD

SNOQUALMIE RIVER

CARNATION RESEARCH FARM

284 AVE

NE 80 ST

NE 100 ST

203

AMES LAKE RD

AMES LAKE

TOLT HILL RD

202

WOOD CARVER'S GALLERY

AMES LAKE RD

W SNOQUALMIE VALLEY RD

NE 80 ST

NE UNION HILL RD

SCALE OF MILES

3   2   1   0

238 AVE NE

NE 80 ST

236 AVE NE

REDMOND–FALL CITY RD

NE NOVELTY HILL RD

NE UNION HILL RD

208 AVE NE

202

START POINT
EMILY DICKINSON
SCHOOL

61

MILEAGE LOG

0.0 Parking lot of Emily Dickinson Elementary School. Leave parking lot and turn right (north) on **208th Avenue N.E.**, crossing N.E. Union Hill Road.

1.3 Turn right at stop sign on **N.E. Novelty Hill Road** and continue over the hill on a broad paved shoulder.

4.5 Turn right at the bottom of the hill on **W. Snoqualmie Valley Road N.E.**

6.0 Turn left on **N.E. 100 Street** and follow it as it bends along the Snoqualmie River. The road bends right at mile 7.4 and becomes **284 Avenue N.E.** Cross Sikes Lake on a narrow bridge.

8.0 Turn left on **N.E. Carnation Farm Road** and continue along Sikes Lake. Interesting tours available at Carnation Research Farm daily except Sundays and holidays at mile 8.5.

10.1 Cross the Snoqualmie River and immediately turn right on **310 Avenue N.E.** Road bends left at mile 10.7 and becomes **N.E. 60 Street**.

11.1 Turn right on **320 Avenue N.E.** as a stop sign appears ahead.

11.4 Turn left on **N.E. 55 Street** as 320 Avenue ends, then immediately turn right on **State Route 203**. Continue through Carnation business district (cafes, grocery) as the road acquires the name of **Tolt Avenue**.

12.2 Turn right on **N.E. 40th Street** toward John MacDonald Park. Entrance road ends by picnic area at mile 12.7. Restrooms in camping area near south end of park. After lunch return to **Tolt Avenue** and turn right.

13.6 Cross the Tolt River and turn right on **N.E. Tolt Hill Road** as N.E. 32 Street goes left to Remlinger Farms. Continue over Tolt Hill; summit at mile 15.7.

16.8 Turn right on **Redmond-Fall City Road (State Route 202)** at a small wye. Continue on paved shoulder. Wood carver's gallery on the right at mile 17.3.

18.5 Turn right on **N.E. Ames Lake Road** and climb hill.

20.8 Turn left on **N.E. Union Hill Road** and continue uphill. Top a summit at mile 22.5 and start a descent.

24.1 Turn right on **238 Avenue N.E.** as Union Hill Road ends at a stop sign.

24.4 Turn left on **N.E. Union Hill Road** near the top of a small rise. Continue over a summit, through a deep dip, and over another summit.

26.4 Turn left on **208th Avenue N.E.** at a 4-way stop.

26.6 Turn left into entrance to Emily Dickinson Elementary School for the end of the tour.

15   ISSAQUAH–SNOQUALMIE FALLS– FALL CITY

STARTING POINT: Parking area near Issaquah City Hall. Take exit 17 (Issaquah) from I-90 and enter Issaquah on Front Street. At traffic light, turn left on E. Sunset Way. Turn left or right into public parking area by historic railroad depot or by Issaquah City Hall.

DISTANCE: 25 miles.
TERRAIN: Hills.
TOTAL CUMULATIVE ELEVATION GAIN: 1400 feet.
RECOMMENDED TIME OF YEAR: March through November.
RECOMMENDED STARTING TIME: 9 A.M.
ALLOW: 4 hours.
POINTS OF INTEREST
Snoqualmie Falls
Fall City Herb Farm

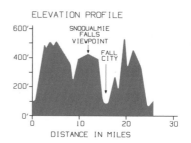

For many years since the construction of I-90, the community of High Point has been a remote peninsula for bicycles. The new highway, forbidden to cyclists, cut off all direct access from High Point to Issaquah. The 1980 decision of the Washington State Highway Commission to allow bicyclists on the I-5 shoulder between the High Point and Issaquah interchanges has redressed this grievance, opening up new possibilities for bicycle tour routes. This ride takes advantage of the connection to extend a previous short tour between Preston and Snoqualmie Falls, making it a full loop tour.

After the steady, mild upgrade along the East Fork Issaquah Creek on the I-5 shoulder, the route pays a brief visit to High Point and then plays hide-and-seek among the trees on the old High Point Road. Following an old railroad grade except for a missing trestle over the Raging River, the King County Lake Alice Park Trail provides an escape from automobile traffic. The trail has been extended past the Lake Alice Road to a point just short of a long, high trestle, where an overlook provides a great view of Snoqualmie Falls. The tranquil, flat trail ride is followed by a breath-taking, freewheeling ride down Lake Alice Road. A short stretch of busy road brings bicyclists to Fall City for another view of the Snoqualmie River from a small park where riders can lap ice cream cones purchased at nearby stores. The backroads out of Fall City lead to a delightful climb through deep forest to the edge of the Pine Lake plateau, followed by a precipitous plunge back to the Issaquah Valley.

63

MILEAGE LOG

0.0 Leave parking area and turn east on **E. Sunset Way**. Bear right through freeway entrance at mile 0.9 and ride the shoulder of I-90.

2.6 Bear right on **exit 20** (**High Point Way**).

2.9 Turn left on **270 Avenue S.E.**, go under freeway, and turn right on **S.E. High Point Way**.

5.1 Turn left to paved trail and continue on trail. Pass Lake Alice Trailhead by S.E. 87 Place and follow trail into forest. Turn hard right with pavement at mile 8.0 and dive down steep hill.

8.1 Cross Preston-Fall City Road, and turn right behind Jersey barriers.

8.2 Turn left on **68 Street** and cross the Raging River. Continue up to new roadway behind Jersey barriers, eventually climbing gravel switchbacks back up to railroad grade at mile 8.7.

9.7 Cross Lake Alice Road and continue on trail.

11.6 End of paved trail at chain link fence barrier. Park bicycles, walk short footpath to falls overlook, and enjoy the view. Return along Lake Alice Trail.

13.4 Turn right on **Lake Alice Road S.E.** Road name changes to **S.E. 47 Street** as it descends to the valley.

14.2 Turn right on **Preston-Fall City Road S.E.**

14.8 Turn left (west) at blinking red light on **State Route 202** (**Redmond-Fall City Road**) in Fall City. Olive Taylor Quigley Park is on the right along bank of Snoqualmie River.

15.0 Turn left on **335 Place S.E.**

15.2 Turn right on **S.E. 44 Place**.

15.4 Turn left on **332 Avenue S.E.** toward Issaquah-Fall City Road.

15.7 Road bends right and is renamed **S.E. Issaquah-Fall City Road**. Fall City Herb Farm on right at mile 16.0.

18.3 Turn left with Issaquah-Fall City Road as S.E. 40 Street goes right.

21.0 Turn left with Issaquah-Fall City Road as Duthie Hill Road goes right.

22.7 Bear left and downhill as Issaquah-Pine Lake Road forks right.

23.8 Bear left on **E. Lake Sammamish Parkway S.E.** and continue under I-5 and into Issaquah on **Front Street**.

24.9 Turn left on **E. Sunset Way**.

25.0 Back at parking area near city hall.

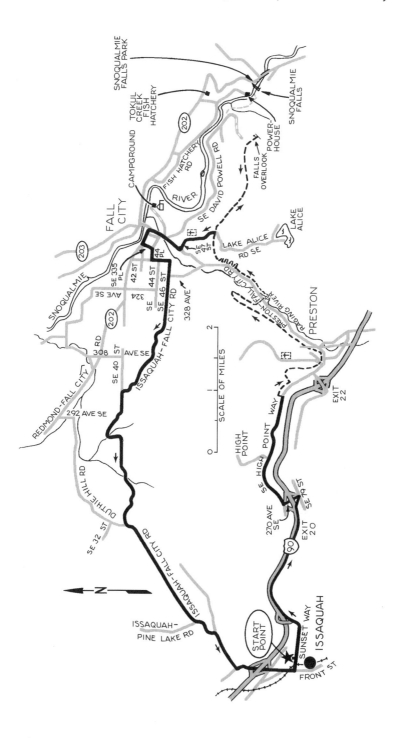

16 DUVALL–CARNATION

STARTING POINT: Cherry Valley Elementary School in Duvall. Take exit 22 (Preston) from I-90; proceed through Preston to Fall City. From Fall City, continue north on State Route 203 through Carnation to Duvall. At north end of Duvall, bear right and up the hill on N.E. Cherry Valley Road to Cherry Valley Elementary School. From the north, take exit 194 (U.S. 2) from I-5 in Everett to Monroe, then S.R. 203 south to Duvall. Follow Cherry Valley Road sharp left and uphill to the school.

DISTANCE: 25 miles.
TERRAIN: Moderate.
TOTAL CUMULATIVE ELEVATION GAIN: 660 feet.
RECOMMENDED TIME OF YEAR: Any season. Recommend Sunday following Mother's Day for Duvall Firemen's Breakfast before ride.
RECOMMENDED STARTING TIME: 8 A.M. to 3 P.M.
ALLOW: 3 hours.
POINTS OF INTEREST
Carnation Research Farm
John MacDonald Memorial King
    County Park

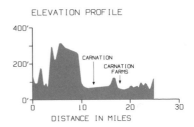

ELEVATION PROFILE

This is a relatively short and easy ride through the backroads of north-central King County. The beautiful farms of the lower Snoqualmie Valley pass in review. The self-guided tour of Carnation Research Farm is recommended. There is a lunch stop at the John MacDonald King County Park.

Cherry Valley Elementary School, the starting point of this tour, sits atop a hill overlooking its namesake, a small offshoot of the Snoqualmie Valley. Dairy cows graze on the lush, green pastures. The Cherry Valley Recreation Area stretches across the northwest part of the valley. Many small streams rush down the hillside on the right as the rider enters a typical lowland forest of Douglas fir, western red cedar, and western hemlock, with thick underbrush and many deciduous trees. In early spring, the yellow skunk cabbage flower exudes a distinctive aroma. The moist lowland also has stands of steeple bush (*Spiraea douglasii*) with fuzzy pink flowers that bloom in June. Red-tailed hawks perch on the tall trees and soar in wide circles. The broad, rufous tail and descending-scale scream identify this buteo.

Several roads take off into the forest before the cyclist crosses the Seattle Water Department's Tolt River right of way, but locked gates bar the way to travel on the graveled roads. The forest is left behind as the rider descends to the Snoqualmie River Valley on the steep Stillwater Hill. Traffic picks up along the valley road, but the scenery is rewarding. U-pick strawberry farms entice the cyclist to return after a late spring ride.

Named in memory of the Boy Scout leader who directed the scouts' building of the trails, amphitheater, and walk-in campsites as a bicentennial project, John MacDonald Memorial King County Park occupies many acres at the confluence of the Tolt and Snoqualmie rivers. The automobile camp-

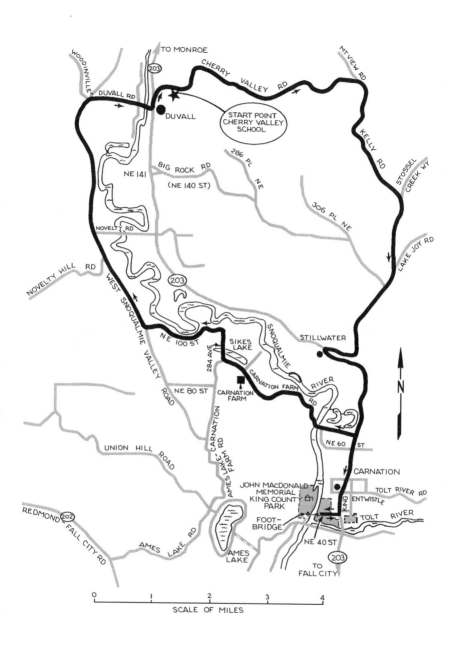

ing area on the east bank of the Snoqualmie River connects with the walk-in campsites on the west side via a suspension footbridge. Tables and log shelters mingle with an old orchard, and hiking trails lead up into the forest. During the summer, several varieties of swallows fly under the bridge, swoop low over the river, then rise high into the air in pursuit of insects.

The second leg of this ride visits Carnation Research Farm, where red-roofed, white buildings nestle against the forested hillside. The farm is open to visitors daily from 10 A.M. to 3 P.M. March through October, except Sundays and holidays. Allow at least 45 minutes for the tour.

Several dairy farms occupy the valley land along the Snoqualmie River. It is hard to visualize that these farmers had to clear the land of brush, trees, stumps, and fallen logs before they could have today's pastures. Extensive drain tile systems also had to be installed. Even now, the big river occasionally floods the valley.

On the return trip across the valley back into Duvall, Mt. Rainier looms large on the southern horizon and Mt. Baker rises to the north. These mountains will always be there; one can only hope that this valley of farms will be here also.

MILEAGE LOG

0.0 Cherry Valley Elementary School. Leave parking lot and head east (right) on **N.E. Cherry Valley Road**.

3.9 Road changes name to **Kelly Road N.E.** as it turns south and Mountain View Road (318 Way) goes left. Stossel Creek Way intersects on the left at mile 6.3. Pass Seattle Water Department's Tolt River pipeline right of way at mile 6.5. Lake Joy Road joins at mile 7.4.

7.9 Keep left with Kelly Road just after crossing a small creek, as Big Rock Road joins from the right. Plunge down Stillwater Hill.

9.4 Turn left on **State Route 203 (Fall City-Carnation Road)** at Stillwater Store. Enter Carnation at mile 12.0.

12.5 Continue through the center of Carnation (grocery, cafes) and turn right on **40 Street**.

12.8 John MacDonald Memorial King County Park. Enjoy a lunch at this unique park and return to S.R. 203.

13.1 Turn left on **State Route 203**.

14.2 Turn left on **Carnation Farm Road**. Cross the Snoqualmie River at mile 14.9. Carnation Research Farm at mile 16.8. Take a tour of this interesting facility, but remember it is closed Sundays and holidays.

17.2 Turn right on **284 Avenue N.E.** and cross Sikes Lake. As the road bends west away from the river, it becomes **N.E. 100 Street**.

19.2 Turn right on **West Snoqualmie Valley Road N.E.** Novelty Hill Road climbs uphill on the left at mile 20.6.

23.5 Turn right on **Woodinville-Duvall Road** and cross the valley. Cross the Snoqualmie River and enter Duvall at mile 24.5.

24.6 Turn left on **State Route 203** in Duvall, then almost immediately turn right and uphill on **N.E. Cherry Valley Road**.

25.1 End of tour at Cherry Valley Elementary School.

17 DUVALL–STOSSEL CREEK

STARTING POINT: Cherry Valley Elementary School in Duvall. Take exit 22 (Preston) from I-90; proceed through Preston to Fall City. From Fall City, continue north on State Route 203 through Carnation to Duvall. At north end of Duvall, bear right and up the hill on N.E. Cherry Valley Road to Cherry Valley Elementary School. From the north, take exit 194 (U.S. 2) from I-5 in Everett to Monroe, then S.R. 203 south to Duvall. Follow Cherry Valley Road sharp left and uphill to the school.

DISTANCE: 38 miles.
TERRAIN: Moderate to strenuous with 10 miles of rough gravel road.
TOTAL CUMULATIVE ELEVATION GAIN: 1530 feet.
RECOMMENDED TIME OF YEAR: March through September. Avoid this ride during hunting season in the last half of October and first half of November.
RECOMMENDED STARTING TIME: 9:30 A.M.
ALLOW: 5 hours plus lunch.
POINTS OF INTEREST
Youngs Creek Gorge and Falls
Swiss Hall

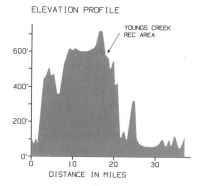

ELEVATION PROFILE

This is a rural, backwoods ride with much variation in scenery. The cyclist rides through dense forest, mountain scenery, and farmland along the Skykomish and Snoqualmie rivers. A lunch stop is made at a rushing mountain stream with waterfalls and gorge.

Good weather is a prerequisite for this tour. Although paved roads with little traffic mark the first 9 and the last 16 miles, the intervening unpaved roads can be messy in bad weather. Stands of second-growth forest nudge the scattered homesteads, accompanied by gardens, fruit trees, and a few animals. The forest closes in as the rider reaches Stossel Creek Way and shortly runs out of paved surface. A heavy gate may bar entry during high fire-danger conditions. Although rough at times, the compacted dirt and gravel road is well suited for bicycling. The old-growth trees were logged off many years ago, and the second-growth forest, now of considerable size, is being harvested and new trees replanted by Washington State Department of Natural Resources and the Weyerhaeuser Company. A number of cattail marshes are bisected by Stossel Creek Road, and a swamp-inhabiting warbler, the common yellowthroat, finds this environment to its liking. Ducks scurry into the pond weeds as bicycles approach. The sandy beach near the waterfalls at the gorge of Youngs Creek was once a very secluded place, but it has now been discovered. The bicyclist may have to share premises with horses, dogs, motorcycles, and their assorted owners. Water ouzels, the permanent residents of this cool and misty canyon, fly up and down the gorge seemingly oblivious to the uninvited guests.

Black-and-white Holstein-Friesian cows crop the pastures along the Sky-

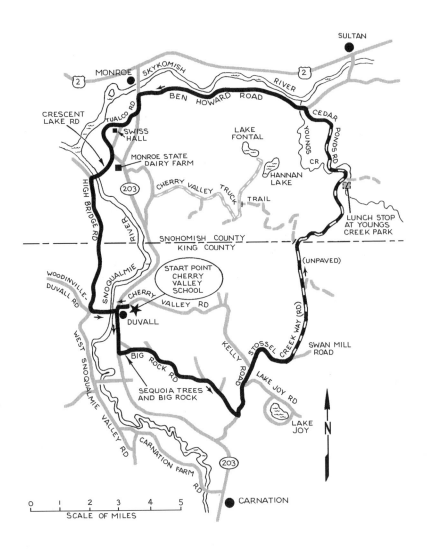

komish River by green cornfields. Blackberry vines encircle and take over abandoned buildings. Anglers break trails to the banks of the river, and a few small cabins sit next to one another near the water's edge.

The Tualco Valley Road winds through well-cared-for farms, from which summer breezes bring aromas of strawberries, new-mown hay, cows, silage, and flowers. A quick perusal of the mailboxes confirms that the majority of farmers of the Tualco Valley are of Swiss extraction. Every year on the Sunday before Mother's Day, they prepare a public banquet of ethnic food at their Swiss Hall. It has become a very popular event.

MILEAGE LOG

0.0 Cherry Valley Elementary School. Head west toward Duvall on **N.E. Cherry Valley Road**.

0.3 Turn left on **State Route 203**.

1.7 Turn left on **N.E. Big Rock Road**. Two large sequoia trees and a big rock mark this intersection.

6.8 Turn left on **Kelly Road N.E.** as Big Rock Road ends, and cross a small stream.

7.3 Keep left as Lake Joy Road goes right.

8.4 Turn right on **Stossel Creek Way N.E.** and enter dense forest. The oiled surface gives way to well-compacted dirt and gravel at mile 9.9 as the road is renamed **N.E. Stossel Creek Road**.

11.0 Bear left with main thoroughfare as unmarked track continues on. Pass roads ST1000 and ST2000 at crossroad. Clearcut areas sprout young Douglas fir plantings.

13.2 Bear left on lower road as road ST5000 forks right, and continue past marshy pond. Cross creek at mile 14.3.

14.5 Continue straight as a side road intersects from the left. Bear right as side roads fork left at 14.8 and 15.0.

15.6 Bear left as a side road goes right. Go over summit at mile 16.7.

18.1 Turn right into Youngs Creek picnic site. Upon leaving the park, do not turn right across the bridge but keep left on the **Cedar Ponds Road**.

"You hear something?"

20.2 Bear left at wye with main thoroughfare. Pavement resumes at mile 20.4.

21.5 Turn left on **Ben Howard Road**. Enjoy this paved road along the banks of the Skykomish River.

27.9 Turn left on **State Route 203**.

28.5 Turn right on **Tualco Road**.

29.3 Continue straight on **Tualco Loop Road** past Swiss Hall, site of annual Swiss Hall dinner.

31.8 Turn right on **Tualco Road** as Tualco Loop Road ends. Continue as road name changes to **Crescent Lake Road** and 203 Street S.E. goes left by the Monroe State Dairy Farm.

32.2 Cross the Snoqualmie River and turn left on **High Bridge Road**. Road changes name to **West Snoqualmie Valley Road N.E.** at the Snohomish-King County line.

36.5 Turn left on **N.E. Woodinville-Duvall Road** and cross the valley.

37.7 Cross the Snoqualmie River, enter Duvall, and turn left on **State Route 203**.

37.8 Turn right and uphill on **N.E. Cherry Valley Road**.

38.1 End of tour at Cherry Valley Elementary School.

"Look at those nuts out in the rain!"

18   REDMOND–WOODINVILLE

STARTING POINT: Marymoor Park (King County) in Redmond. Take State Route 520 (exit 168B from I-5 or exit 14 from I-405) east to the second Redmond exit, then south on West Lake Samammish Parkway to the park on the Sammamish River. From I-90, take exit 13 and proceed north along West Lake Sammamish Parkway to the park.

DISTANCE: 32 miles.
TERRAIN: Moderate with some hills and the flat Sammamish River Trail.
TOTAL CUMULATIVE ELEVATION GAIN: 1020 feet.
RECOMMENDED TIME OF YEAR: Any season.
RECOMMENDED STARTING TIME: 9 to 10 A.M.
ALLOW: 4 to 5 hours.
POINTS OF INTEREST
Chateau Ste. Michelle Winery
Sammamish River Trail

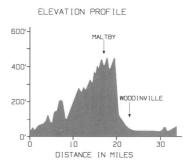

ELEVATION PROFILE

As the tour leaves Redmond, business parks are rapidly obliterating the pastures where horses used to graze. Nearby Bear Creek flows through the fields of a dairy farm, clinging to its existence as commerce nibbles at its edges. An extensive gravel operation presses on inexorably, soon to rip away the entire hill separating the valleys of Bear Creek and Evans Creek. Johnson and McWhirter parks, city of Redmond, spread across greensward and open forest of handsome fir and cedar trees.

During the fall spawning season, salmon seek out small, gravelly streams of Puget Sound, such as Bear Creek and its tributaries, and may be viewed from several bridges along the route. Mink Road and Paradise Lake Road still display the sylvan surroundings their names imply, giving bicyclists low-traffic backroads to enjoy.

Small industries near Woodinville are encountered before the route joins the Sammamish River Trail and travels up the Sammamish Valley. May 1980 saw the completion of the asphalt-paved, 9.3-mile Sammamish River Trail between Marymoor Park and Bothell. It is now linked with the Burke-Gilman Trail into Seattle.

A meticulously groomed green turf farm occupies many acres of the valley. Long strips of turf are regularly lifted from the ground, rolled into big bundles, and taken away to become "instant lawn." Other acres of the valley support truck farms and dairy and beef cattle. Horses romp in several fields, neighing at passing horseback riders who travel an unpaved parallel trail.

Near Woodinville, Chateau Ste. Michelle Winery, with its beautifully land-scaped and maintained grounds, invites visitors to picnic and explore the arboretumlike environment. It is open daily from 10 A.M. to 4:30 P.M. with frequent guided tours of the winery. During the fall and winter, many species of ducks and grebes ply the river waters keeping a wary eye on the persevering steelheaders along the banks. Canoeists skim the river during the warm summer months. The short-eared owl flies silently about in the daylight hours, looking for mice and rats in the open fields as meadowlarks sing from fence posts. Startled by the passing users of the trail, a great blue heron lifts off from the shallow edges of the river and, with huge wings flapping, slowly flies away to a distant treetop. Red-tailed hawks ride the high thermal updrafts back and forth across the valley, while northern harriers sweep low over the fields, competing for lift and airspace with hot air balloons, model airplanes, and gliders. Marsh wrens, red-winged black-birds, and common yellowthroat warblers regularly nest in the tall grasses, cattails, and tules along the Sammamish River.

A mile or so north of the Redmond City Hall, King County playing fields buzz with soccer and football. Additional playing fields receive constant use at Marymoor Park, terminus of the river trail. This park also boasts a velodrome for bicycle racing, a popular and growing sport in the Greater Seattle area.

MILEAGE LOG

0.0 Northwest parking lot in Marymoor Park. Exit the parking lot, cross the median strip, and turn left (east) on main park road.

1.0 Go out east entrance of park and bear right on **N.E. 65 Street**.

1.4 Turn left on **E. Sammamish Road N.E.** as 65 Street ends.

1.5 Get into rightmost left-turn lane and turn left at traffic signal, and then immediately turn right on **180th Avenue N.E.** Continue on marked bikeway as road curves left and is renamed **178th Avenue N.E.**

2.2 Turn right on **Union Hill Road N.E.** Ride past the United Parcel Service distribution center at mile 2.6 and the Cadman Gravel complex at mile 3.1.

3.4 Turn left on **196 Avenue N.E.**; pastures with horses and cattle.

4.2 Turn left on **N.E. 95 Street**. Cross Bear Creek.

5.0 Turn right on busy **Avondale Road N.E.** for a block, then right again on **Novelty Hill Road N.E.** Cross Bear Creek again.

5.4 Turn left on **Old Redmond Road** and continue uphill. McWhirter Park entrance on the left at mile 5.6.

6.8 Turn left on **N.E. 116 Street** as Old Redmond Road ends. Coast downhill and cross Bear Creek at mile 7.8.

7.9 Bear right on **Avondale Road**, then almost immediately turn right on **Avondale Place**.

8.3 Turn right on **Avondale Road** again. Endure this busy concrete highway for a few minutes.

9.0 Turn right on **N.E. 132 Street** and cross Cottage Lake Creek. Road bends left and becomes **Bear Creek Road N.E.** at mile 9.2.

10.5 Turn right on **Mink Road**.

12.1 Turn left on **Woodinville-Duvall Road N.E.**

12.3 Turn right on **204 Avenue N.E.** Road is renamed **N.E. 198 Street** and finally **Paradise Lake Road** as it enters Snohomish County at mile 13.9.

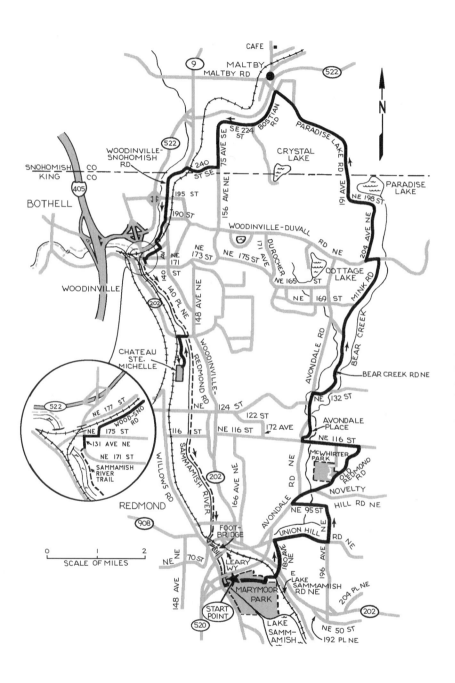

17.1 Turn left on **Bostian Road** just before S.R. 522 is encountered. *Note: Maltby Cafe on Maltby Road just north of S.R. 522 provides a good lunch stop.* Bostian goes uphill and is successively renamed **S.E. 224 Street** and **75 Avenue S.E.** as it executes bends to the left.

19.5 Turn right on **240 Street S.E.** Pedal through the Wellington Hills golf course and plunge steeply downhill.

20.2 Turn left on **Woodinville-Snohomish Road** as 240 Street ends. Reenter King County at mile 20.5.

21.4 Turn right on **139 Avenue N.E.** at second traffic light. Take the next left turn across the railroad tracks on **N.E. 181 Place** and turn right on **Woodinville-Snohomish Road N.E.** As the road enters Woodinville, it becomes **132 Avenue N.E.**

22.4 Turn right on **Woodinville-Duvall Road** (**N.E. 175 Street**).

22.5 Get into left-turn lane at next light and turn left on **131 Avenue N.E.**

22.8 Turn right into trail parking just past building N, across from building Q. Follow access trail to **Sammamish River Trail** and turn left.

24.5 Turn left off the trail, then turn right on the **State Route 202** bridge over the Sammamish River. Cross railroad tracks at mile 24.9.

25.0 Turn left into Chateau Ste. Michelle. Entrance to the winery at mile 25.2. Park bicycles, tour the gardens and winery on foot, and return to the Sammamish River Trail.

25.9 Turn left on **Sammamish River Trail** and continue south toward Redmond. Pass Redmond City Hall at mile 30.0.

30.7 Turn right with trail on footbridge over the Sammamish River, then turn right with trail and go under Leary Way.

31.7 Trail ends at Marymoor Park entrance road. Turn left and return to the parking lot to complete this tour at mile 32.1.

Pastoral Progress

19 REDMOND–HOLLYWOOD

STARTING POINT: Redmond's Anderson Park, in downtown Redmond. Take State Route 520 (exit 168B from I-5 or exit 14 from I-405) east to Redmond. Cross railroad tracks and turn left at first traffic signal on Redmond Way, then right at second traffic signal on 168th Avenue N.E., and right again on N.E. 79th Street. Park at edge of park along 79th Street.

DISTANCE: 25 miles.
TERRAIN: Partly hilly, mostly flat.
TOTAL CUMULATIVE ELEVATION GAIN: 1000 feet.
RECOMMENDED TIME OF YEAR: Any season.
RECOMMENDED STARTING TIME: 9 to 10 A.M.
ALLOW: 3 to 4 hours.
POINTS OF INTEREST
Old Red Brick Road
Bear Creek drainage system

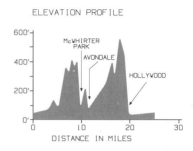

Redmond long ago ceased to be out in the country, but in a few places it still retains some of its country atmosphere. As Redmond is only a 30-minute drive from downtown Seattle via the Evergreen Point Bridge and I-405, it is surprising that it has not been completely swallowed up by creeping suburbanism. Many acres of forest are still visible, a reminder of Redmond's beginnings as a logging community on the old Sunset Highway between Snoqualmie Pass and the Kirkland-Madison Street ferry.

As the tour leaves urban Redmond, it circles a shopping complex that recently displaced a little-league ball diamond. A dairy farm, pasturing Jersey and Holstein-Friesian cows, clings to acreage along Union Hill Road, as commercial construction and manufacturing operations threaten to obliterate it. After crossing Evans Creek and turning on 196 Avenue N.E., the bicyclist bumps along the historic, picturesque, Old Red Brick Road. Threatened by obliteration with blacktop overlays, this road surface has been preserved through registration as a historic landmark, an action taken by local residents. Confronted by the determination of the community, King County now has restored the brick surface to near-original condition. The city of Redmond has acquired land for a park at this corner, but at present it is undeveloped. It bears the name of the late Arthur Johnson, one of the pioneers of Redmond.

The swampy lowland along Evans Creek floods regularly from heavy rains, and every ten years or so the Washington State Department of Wildlife must come in and literally bail out the residents, as a beaver colony periodically busies itself building new dams. Suburban farmers keep horses, cattle, and sheep on the moist pastureland of Happy Valley, where the sound of singing Pacific tree frogs is regularly heard in late winter and early spring.

Again the rider must follow State Route 202 a short distance before climbing out of the valley on a steep, circuitous road. Old farmhouses have been replaced by modern ones along 208 Avenue N.E. as the mixed deciduous and evergreen forests slowly give way to the land developer, but a large pond formed by an earthen dam attracts wild ducks and helps retain an appearance of the natural environment. Along Redmond Road, the 70 acres willed to Redmond in 1971 by the late Elsie Farrell McWhirter for a park contain a fine example of an open stand of second-growth fir and cedar trees. During autumn, salmon fighting their way upstream to spawn in the shallow, gravelly stream beds of Bear Creek and its tributary, Cottage Lake Creek, pass the bridges near Avondale, providing cyclists a chance to view a short portion of this incredible pilgrimage.

Rural, residential, and river-valley scenery predominate as Hollywood Hill is traversed, and the popular Sammamish River Trail is followed back to downtown Redmond.

MILEAGE LOG

0.0 Anderson Park in Redmond. Head east (away from 168th Avenue) on **N.E. 79th Street**.

0.1 Turn left on **Avondale Way N.E.** as 79th Street ends.

0.4 Turn right on **Union Hill Road** as Avondale Way is marked Local Access Only. Cross Bear Creek, cross Avondale Road at traffic signal, and ride past a dairy farm, United Parcel Service distribution center, and Cadman Gravel Company. Cross Evans Creek.

1.8 Turn right on **196 Avenue N.E. (Old Red Brick Road)**. Redmond's Arthur Johnson Park at this corner. Cross busy State Route 202 and Evans Creek at mile 3.1.

3.3 Turn left on **N.E. 50 Street**. This narrow, oiled road hugs the hillside for 1.6 miles, crossing busy Sahalee Way.

4.7 Turn left on **Redmond-Fall City Road (State Route 202)** and continue on paved shoulder.

5.8 Turn right on **204 Place N.E.**, which winds up a steep hill and is renamed **208 Avenue N.E.** as it levels out and heads north. Cross Union Hill Road at mile 7.1 by Missionary Alliance Church.

8.3 Turn left on **Novelty Hill Road** as 208 Avenue ends. Almost immediately, turn right on **206 Avenue N.E.**, marked Dead End. Pavement ends at mile 8.7.

8.8 Turn left on narrow lane along rail fence with brick corner post as road divides into narrow driveways.

9.0 Continue through bollards and downhill on narrow, asphalt-surfaced roadway past Overlake School campus. Road acquires name of **N.E. 106 Place**.

9.5 Turn left on **Redmond Road N.E.** as 106 Place ends, then take next right turn into Farrell McWhirter Park (city of Redmond). Continue past bollards on asphalt-surfaced trail through park. Restrooms and menagerie at mile 9.9, as trail continues.

10.2 Bear right through gate and up steep north entrance roadway.

10.3 Turn left on **196 Avenue N.E.** at park entrance.

10.6 Turn left on **N.E. 116 Street** as 196 Avenue ends. Cross Bear Creek at mile 11.2.

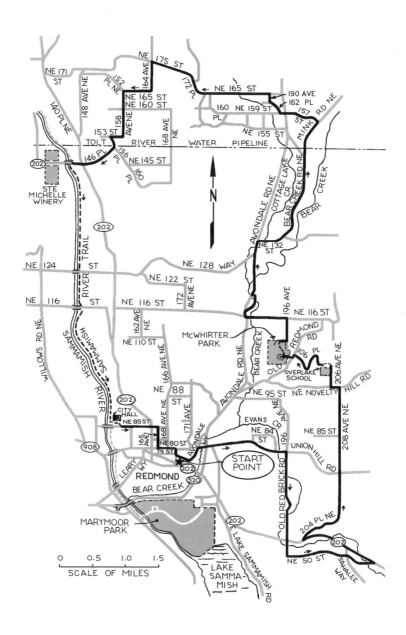

11.3 Turn right on **Avondale Road N.E.** by Avondale grocery, and continue right on **Avondale Place N.E.** Cross Bear Creek.

11.8 Continue on **Avondale Road N.E.** as it joins from the left.

12.4 Turn right on **N.E. 132 Street** and cross Cottage Lake Creek. Road changes name to **Bear Creek Road N.E.** at mile 12.6.

14.0 Bear right on **Mink Road N.E.**

14.5 Turn left on **N.E. 157 Street**, shortly renamed **N.E. 158 Street** and **N.E. 159 Street**. Cross Avondale Road N.E. and Cottage Lake Creek at mile 15.1.

15.2 Turn right on **N.E. 162 Place**.

15.4 Bear right on **190 Avenue N.E.** as N.E. 162 Street goes left.

15.6 Turn left on **N.E. 165 Street** as 190 Avenue ends. Road changes name to **N.E. 172 Place**.

17.4 Turn left on **164 Avenue N.E.** at stop sign. Road bends right at 17.8 and becomes **N.E. 165 Street**.

18.2 Turn left on **152 Place N.E.** as 165 Street ends. Road name changes to **158 Avenue N.E.**, **N.E. 153 Street**, and **155 Avenue N.E.** as it winds downhill. Seattle's Tolt River water pipeline passes overhead at mile 19.1.

19.2 Turn right on **N.E. 146 Place** at yield sign, and wind down creek canyon.

19.7 Continue on **N.E. 145 Street** (**State Route 202**) at stop sign. Grocery-deli, cafe-barbecue (open 11 A.M. on Saturday, noon on Sunday), bakery (closed Sunday) in shopping center on left.

19.9 Bear right on trail access and turn left under bridge on **Sammamish River Trail**. *Note: Chateau Ste. Michelle Winery, 0.5 mile farther on S.R. 202, offers a lovely picnic area, open to the public.*

24.0 Turn left on trail exit, just past Redmond City Hall, and continue on **N.E. 85th Street**.

24.5 Cross State Route 202 (164th Avenue N.E.) and turn right on **165th Avenue N.E.**

24.8 Turn left on **N.E. 80th Street** as 165 Avenue ends.

25.0 Turn right on **168th Avenue N.E.**

25.1 Turn left on **N.E. 79th Street** and return to starting point.

20 VASHON ISLAND

STARTING POINT: Lincoln Park in West Seattle. From I-5 in Seattle, take exit 163 or 163A (Spokane Street and West Seattle). Cross Duwamish Waterway to West Seattle, climb hill, and at traffic signal continue through on Fauntleroy Avenue (follow Vashon ferry signs). Park in north parking lot of Lincoln Park, three blocks north of Fauntleroy ferry terminal.

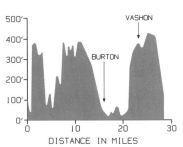

DISTANCE: 29 miles with options to 49 miles.

TERRAIN: Hilly.

TOTAL CUMULATIVE ELEVATION GAIN: Basic, 1800 feet; Burton, 200 feet extra; Point Defiance, 360 feet extra; Maury Island, 1200 feet extra.

RECOMMENDED TIME OF YEAR: All seasons except snow.

RECOMMENDED STARTING TIME: Consult current ferry schedule, but time should be between 8 and 10 A.M.

ALLOW: 5 hours for basic trip, 1 to 2 more hours if ferry to Point Defiance is taken, and 1 to 2 more hours if Maury Island is visited.

POINTS OF INTEREST
Point Defiance Park
Point Robinson Coast Guard
    Station

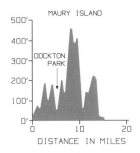

The basic 29-mile ride around Vashon Island passes many country homes with horses and cattle as well as forests thick with fir trees, madrona, and shiny evergreen huckleberry bushes. Traffic will be minimal on all but the Vashon Highway, which boasts generous shoulders for cyclists. The terrain is hilly for the most part, but the beautiful, flat ride along the shoreline at Portage and Ellisport offers close views of the waterfront. Goldeneye ducks are quite prevalent in winter, along with surf scoters, bufflehead ducks, and western grebes.

When the Burton Peninsula is added to the basic ride, it provides a spot on salt water at just the right time for a picnic lunch. The small King County Burton Acres Park is located halfway around the peninsula circle on Harbor Drive.

A second variation on this basic ride is to head for the southern tip of Vashon Island and take the little Washington State ferry to Point Defiance Park in Tacoma. Point Defiance Park is a fascinating place to visit on a bicycle, with its several miles of winding, blacktop roads leading to a zoo, an aquarium, Old Fort Nisqually, and a logging camp replica, but ferry schedules must be noted and the available hours considered. Just eating lunch at the park and exploring the waterfront can be rewarding.

Still another variation on the basic Vashon ride is to add the 12 to 14 miles around Maury Island. There will be more hilly terrain, but the many interesting places make it worthwhile. The King County park near Dockton has swimming, boat launching, picnic tables, and picnic shelters. Several radio stations have their transmitters on Maury Island.

At the easternmost tip of Maury Island, one of a dwindling number of manned Coast Guard light stations provides vital aid to the sailors of Puget Sound. Guided tours of the Point Robinson lighthouse are available from noon to 4:00 P.M. on weekends. Point Robinson King County Park next to the Coast Guard property provides picnic tables, trash barrels, and a trail leading to the beach. The park has no drinking water or restrooms.

Luana Beach Road, taken as the route leaves Point Robinson, is a lovely, twisting, narrow tunnel through the trees within sight of the water. There are private homes along here, but it is not densely settled. Even after dark, this can be an interesting ride as the lights of Seattle and the mainland twinkle across the channel. One last steep hill climb to the town of Vashon, followed by an exhilarating, freewheeling plunge to the ferry landing, completes this island getaway tour.

Yes, Vashon Island has become a popular place to get away from the city hustle for a week or a weekend, and the population of bed-and-breakfast establishments has virtually exploded. A partial listing of B&B's on Vashon and Maury islands is included in the B&B index in the back of this book.

MILEAGE LOG

0.0   Parking lot at Lincoln Park, Seattle.

0.5   Fauntleroy ferry landing; Vashon Island ferry landing. Put bicycle in low gear and head uphill on **Vashon Highway S.W.** At mile 1.5, do not turn on 103 Avenue S.W., but continue uphill past a fire station.

2.5   Bear right on **S.W. Cedarhurst Road** and head downhill as Vashon Highway bends left. View of Olympics and Kitsap Peninsula at mile 4.5. Road name changes to **Westside Highway S.W.**

5.4   Keep right with West Side Highway S.W. at a wye as 121 Avenue S.W. continues uphill to AYH home hostel.

8.6   Pass county dump and turn right with Westside Highway as Cemetery Road goes left.

10.4   Turn right on **S.W. 220 Street** as Westside Highway ends.

10.6   Turn left on **Wax Orchard Road S.W.** as 220 Street is marked Dead End. Wax Orchards at mile 11.2. Fresh pie cherries and apples in season; cider and berry juices.

14.1   Turn left on **Vashon Highway S.W.** *Note: Vashon Highway continues on to the Point Defiance ferry at Tahlequah. See Point Defiance addition.* Inspiration Point at mile 14.6; views toward Burton, Maury Island, and Tacoma. Enter the town of Burton at mile 17.2. Basic route continues north on the Vashon Highway. *Note: For a tour around Burton Peninsula, turn right on S.W. Burton Drive by grocery. See Burton Peninsula addition.*

18.1   Turn right on **S.W. Quartermaster Drive** toward Dockton, Quartermaster, Maury Island, and Point Robinson.

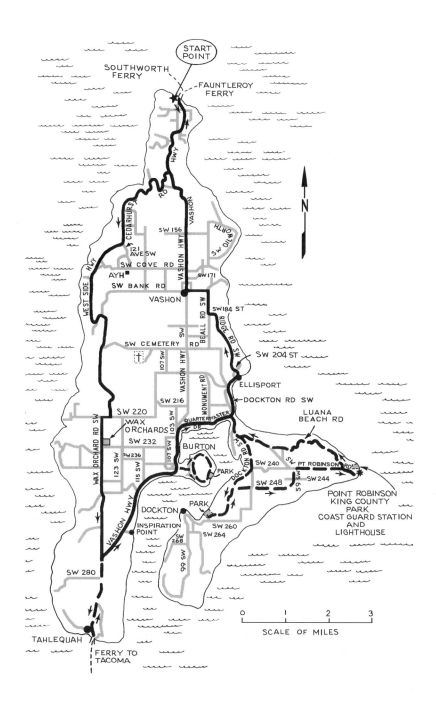

19.6 Basic tour turns left on **Dockton Road S.W.** toward Ellisport. *Note: For side trip to Maury Island, turn right instead. See Maury Island Loop.*

20.5 Keep right along the waterfront on **Chautauqua Beach Drive S.W.** and start uphill as Ellisport Road goes left.

20.9 Turn left on **S.W. 204 Street** and continue uphill and around several bends as the road is renamed **Ridge Road S.W.** and **S.W. 184 Street.**

22.7 Turn right on **Beall Road S.W.** as Ridge Road ends.

23.2 Turn left on **S.W. Bank Road** with main thoroughfare.

23.7 Turn right on **Vashon Highway S.W.** in the town of Vashon; restaurants, grocery stores. Vashon ferry landing at mile 28.6. Back to Lincoln Park at mile 29.1.

"There's a short hill just as you leave the ferry."

POINT DEFIANCE ADDITION

14.1 of the basic ride is mile 0.0 of side trip at the corner of Wax Orchard Road S.W. and Vashon Highway. Continue south and downhill on **Vashon Highway S.W.** for 2.0 miles to Tahlequah and the ferry to Point Defiance; 2.0 miles back uphill to the corner. An arbitrary number of miles can be cycled around Point Defiance Park.

BURTON PENINSULA ADDITION

17.2 of the basic ride is mile 0.0 of side trip at the corner of S.W. Burton Drive and Vashon Island Highway. Turn right on **S.W. Burton Drive** toward the peninsula.

  0.4 Turn right on **97 Avenue S.W.**, which bends left and is renamed **S.W. Bayview Drive** and **S.W. Harbor Drive**. King County Burton Acres Park at mile 1.2.

  2.1 Turn right on **Burton Drive S.W.** to complete the Burton Peninsula circle. Return to Vashon Highway at mile 2.5.

MAURY ISLAND LOOP

19.6 of the basic ride is mile 0.0 of side trip at the stop sign on Maury Island. Turn right on **Dockton Road S.W.**

  0.6 Pass KIRO transmitter and bear right with thoroughfare as S.W. Point Robinson Road continues up steep hill.

  1.6 Keep right with Dockton Road as 75 Avenue S.W. continues up steep hill. Pass golf course. Turn right into King County park at Dockton at mile 3.6. Enjoy lunch or a snack, and return along **Dockton Road S.W.**

  5.4 Turn right on **S.W. 248 Street** and proceed uphill past the golf course. Road bends left, is renamed **59 Avenue S.W.**, and descends hill.

  7.4 Turn right on **S.W. Point Robinson Road** as 59 Avenue ends. Steep downhill.

  8.5 Turn right with Point Robinson Road as S.W. Luana Beach Road goes left. Point Robinson King County Park at mile 8.8; picnic tables, trail to the beach. Continue through gate down steep driveway to the Coast Guard Station at mile 8.9. View or tour lighthouse and retrace route along Point Robinson Road.

  9.3 Continue on **S.W. Luana Beach Road** as Point Robinson Road turns left.

 11.9 Turn right on **S.W. Point Robinson Road** as Luana Beach Road ends. Plunge downhill.

 12.4 Continue on **Dockton Road S.W.** past KIRO transmitter as Point Robinson Road ends.

 13.1 Maury Island loop completed. Continue on basic tour.

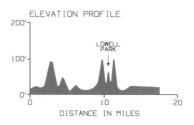

SNOHOMISH COUNTY

21 SNOHOMISH–LOWELL

STARTING POINT: Snohomish Airport, Snohomish. Take exit 23A (State Route 522) from I-405, then State Route 9 to Snohomish; or take exit 194 (U.S. 2) from I-5, then south on State Route 9. Exit S.R. 9 on Airport Way just south of Snohomish and proceed northerly to the airport. Park on the grass along the gravel road by the railroad track.

DISTANCE: 17 miles.
TERRAIN: Moderate.
TOTAL CUMULATIVE ELEVATION GAIN: 280 feet.
RECOMMENDED TIME OF YEAR: Any season.
RECOMMENDED STARTING TIME: Anytime.
ALLOW: 2 hours.
POINTS OF INTEREST
Snohomish Airport
Abel Johnson Park
Lowell Community Park

This is an easy, short ride with pleasant scenery and smooth roads. It follows the southern edge of the Snohomish River Valley from Snohomish to Lowell. The return route meanders along the river.

As it leaves the Snohomish Airport, the route heads south past the airfield and fertile farmland. At diminutive Abel Johnson Park, the big cedar snag has suffered several fires since the opening was cut through it and is now somewhat the worse for wear. The route bears left through well-kept dairy farms and climbs out of the valley to take in a panoramic view. Then the cyclist whistles downhill and across the highway to contour along the southern edge of the valley. A blueberry farm with its red and pink leaves adds a gorgeous touch of color in the fall. Beautifully landscaped homes are interspersed with barns and utility buildings. An abandoned schoolhouse now serves for hay storage where Marshland Road, coming across the valley, intersects the Lowell-Larimer Road. The Seattle Hill Road heads uphill to the left, connecting with Bothell and Silver Lake.

Radio station KRKO in Everett announces its transmitter location with signs and tall antenna towers just before the cyclist enters the community of Lowell. The Lowell Community Park illustrates modern design in playgrounds, restrooms, and picnic tables. After visiting the park, the bicyclist must retrace the 0.6 mile back to where Lenora intersects Second Avenue. A short, steep hill leads down to the valley floor, over the railroad tracks, and then south along the Snohomish River. A head gate and pumping station for flood control are decorated with informational signs. In December of 1975, a similar pumping station at the east end of the valley washed out, flooding the whole valley. The river also undercut its banks along Snohomish-Lowell River Road, taking out a significant stretch of the roadway. Rather than

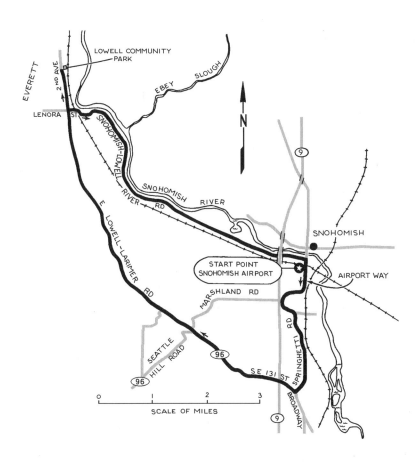

repairing the washout, road builders realigned the roadway beside the railroad tracks, leaving the remaining old sections for access to farmhouses along the river.

An occasional parachutist in a colorful parachute floats out of the sky into one of the fields, reminding watchers that the Snohomish Airport is the home of the Seattle Sky Divers. Snohomish-Lowell River Road is followed back to the airport. After the ride, a snack or a meal at the airport restaurant is a treat. Homemade soup and pies are a specialty there.

MILEAGE LOG

0.0 Snohomish Airport. Leave parking lot and turn right on **Airport Way**.

1.0 Turn left on **Springhetti Road** by big cedar snag in Abel Johnson Park. Continue across the valley and uphill past dairy farms.

2.7 Turn right on **Broadway** and start downhill. Cross State Route 9 and continue on **Lowell-Larimer Road**. Pass radio station KRKO transmitter at mile 9.0. As it enters Everett, the road name shortens to **Larimer Road**, then changes to **Second Avenue** and eventually to **Third Avenue**.

10.6 Turn right into Lowell Community Park for a rest stop and picnic lunch as desired. The park offers swings, slides, restrooms, and many novel recreational structures. Retrace route along Second Avenue.

11.2 Turn left and downhill on **Lenora Street**. As it leaves Everett, it is renamed **Snohomish-Lowell River Road**. Flood-control headworks on the right at mile 11.5.

17.0 Turn right at stop sign on **Airport Way**. Cross railroad tracks.

17.2 Turn right into Snohomish Airport parking lot; end of tour.

"Hit the brakes! Hit the brakes!"

22 SNOHOMISH–EBEY ISLAND

STARTING POINT: Snohomish Airport, Snohomish. Take exit 23A (State Route 522) from I-405, then State Route 9 to Snohomish; or take exit 194 (U.S. 2) from I-5, then south on State Route 9. Exit S.R. 9 on Airport Way just south of Snohomish and proceed northerly to the airport. Park on the grass along the gravel road by the railroad track.

DISTANCE: 18 to 32 miles; 24 miles nominal.

TERRAIN: Moderate; some flat, some hills.

TOTAL CUMULATIVE ELEVATION GAIN: 300 to 1300 feet; 940 feet nominal.

RECOMMENDED TIME OF YEAR: Any season.

RECOMMENDED STARTING TIME: 10 A.M.

ALLOW: 2 to 5 hours.

POINTS OF INTEREST
Flood control works by Snohomish
    River
Howarth Park in Everett

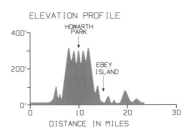

This is a pleasant, scenic ride from Snohomish along the south bank of the Snohomish River to Everett, where a number of parks give cyclists a choice of settings for a picnic lunch. The return trip traverses Ebey Island and follows the north bank of the Snohomish River back to Snohomish.

The managers of Snohomish Airport have graciously consented to allow bicyclists to park by the airport while touring in this area. The airport, which is the home of the Seattle Sky Divers, has a fine restaurant with good food, reasonable prices, and quick service. We recommend it. In return, bicyclists are asked to park on the grass and not take up airport and restaurant space.

As the route leaves the airport, it travels through dairy farms along the Snohomish-Lowell River Road to Everett. A flood-control headworks and pumping station help to keep the valley dry during spring runoff conditions and heavy fall rains. Swampy areas support nesting red-winged blackbirds and marsh wrens.

After passing through the community of Lowell, the route traverses busy streets to Mukilteo Boulevard where a designated bicycle lane eases traffic worries. Howarth Park, attractively designed and landscaped, provides bicycle parking and a foot trail to the beach. At Harborview Park, lawns lead to the edge of the bluff overlooking Possession Sound and Port Gardner, Everett's harbor. Gedney Island, alias Hat Island, pokes a rocky summit out of the water, while Whidbey and Camano islands stretch far into Puget Sound. Across the bay, the Tulalip Indian Reservation raises its forested crown. For the energetic, the alternate route continues down to Mukilteo, where the state park provides a beach with closer views of the water and restaurants feature Sunday brunch.

On the return leg of this tour, the route plays leapfrog with I-5 and follows the little-used streets of Everett's Riverside district. The Snohomish River, flowing beneath the sidewalk of the bridge on U.S. 2, provides a scenic waterscape with occasional boat traffic. Beyond the bridge, the sidewalk continues along the causeway, paralleling the giant pipeline that brings Everett's water supply from Lake Chaplain. Soon a side road descends to Ebey Island and cyclists have the road to themselves again, crossing the island and leaving via a concrete bridge over Ebey Slough.

As it wends its way along the river, the route surveys valley farmland and half-century-old homesteads. A former auction house stands along the road, which winds past a large cemetery decorated and attended by crowds of people on Memorial Day weekend. Soon the road enters Snohomish and the rider is back at the airport.

For the ambitious, this ride may be combined with Tour 23 by turning left on 85th Avenue S.E. by the G.A.R. Cemetery and following backroads to Ferguson Park. (See map.)

MILEAGE LOG

0.0   Snohomish Airport parking lot. Leave parking lot and head north (left) across railroad tracks on **Airport Way**.

0.2   Turn left on **Lowell-Snohomish River Road** just before Airport Way crosses the Snohomish River. Flood-control works appear on left at mile 5.5. Enter Everett at mile 5.9 as road changes name to **Lenora Street** and heads up steep hill.

6.0   Turn right on **South 2nd Avenue** and continue as it merges into **South 3rd Avenue**. Lowell Community Park on the right at mile 6.6.

7.2   Turn left on **41st Street** at interchange with I-5. *Note: To take short tour, continue on ramp to Smith Avenue and continue at mile 12.7 in mileage log.* Roadway bends left at mile 8.3, heads uphill, and is renamed **Mukilteo Boulevard**. Bike lane begins.

9.9   Turn right into Howarth Park on **Madrona Avenue**. The cyclist may take foot trails to beach from upper park. A pedestrian overpass over railroad tracks provides access to the beach. *Note: As an optional extension to the tour, continue on Mukilteo Boulevard 4.2 miles to*

Recycling Our Natural Resources

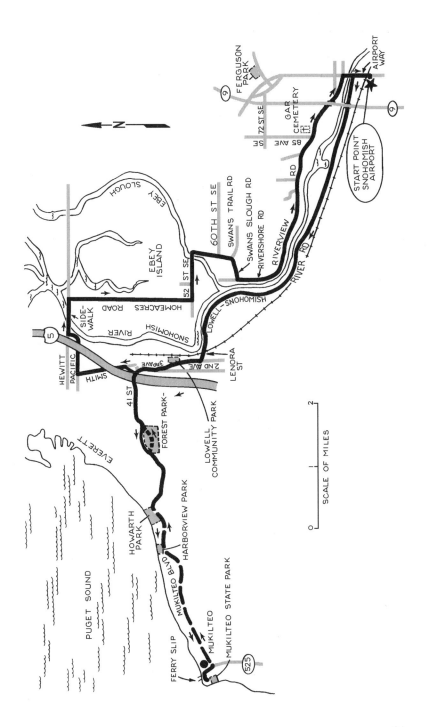

Mukilteo and return. Restaurants in Mukilteo. Return from Howarth Park along **Mukilteo Boulevard** and follow roadway back to freeway interchange. *Note: West entrance to Forest Park goes right at mile 10.7; steep climb, food concession in summer, menagerie, and return to Mukilteo Boulevard via east entrance.*

12.7   Turn left just past freeway entrance at foot of 41st Street. Follow ramp down as road is named **38th Street**, and immediately turn left on **Smith Avenue**. Continue north on Smith Avenue and go under I-5.

13.6   Turn right on **Pacific Avenue** at stop sign. Road goes under I-5, bends left, and becomes **Chestnut Street**.

14.3   Turn right on **Hewitt Avenue** for a block. Cross State Street, immediately turn left and lift bicycles up the step onto the sidewalk of the U.S. 2 bridge across the river. Be careful of glass on sidewalk.

15.0   Stop for curb step and turn right on **Homeacres Road (43rd Avenue S.E.)**

17.0   Turn left at T junction on **52nd Street S.E.** as 43rd Avenue ends. Cross Ebey Slough at mile 17.6 and continue with **Homeacres Road**.

18.4   Turn right on **Swans Slough Road** as Homeacres Road ends and Swans Trail Road continues straight and uphill. Follow thoroughfare left at mile 18.8 and continue on **Rivershore Road** along the river. As it goes up a hill past auction house and cemetery the road is renamed **Riverview Road**.

22.7   Go under State Route 9, climb a short hill, and bear right and downhill on **First Street**.

23.1   Turn right at stop sign on **Avenue D** in Snohomish. Cross Snohomish River and railroad tracks.

23.5   Turn right into Snohomish Airport parking lot; end of tour.

23 SNOHOMISH VALLEY

STARTING POINT: Monroe Riverside Park on State Route 203 by the Skykomish River. Take exit 194 (U.S. 2) from I-5 to Monroe and S.R. 203 to the park on the south edge of town; or take exit 23A (State Route 522) from I-405 to Monroe, then right on U.S. 2 and S.R. 203. Park cars on old concrete pavement near the river.

DISTANCE: 29 miles.
TERRAIN: Flat to moderate.
TOTAL CUMULATIVE ELEVATION GAIN: 950 feet.
RECOMMENDED TIME OF YEAR: All seasons.
RECOMMENDED STARTING TIME: 9 to 10 A.M.
ALLOW: 4 hours plus lunch.
POINTS OF INTEREST
Monroe State Dairy Farm
Old cedar tree by Snohomish Airport

This ride takes the bicyclist into territory seldom traveled by other than the local people. The roads are smoothly paved; the scenery is rural and unspoiled by commerce, industry, or suburbia. The Tualco Valley south of Monroe contains acres of strawberries, herds of dairy cows in lush pastures, and fields of corn. Every year around the last Sunday in April or first Sunday in May, the people of this area celebrate their Swiss heritage with a dinner at Swiss Hall and invite the public to sample their unique cuisine.

After a moderate climb, High Bridge Road provides a view across the confluence of the Snoqualmie and Skykomish rivers to steep-sided, 737-foot-high Bald Hill. The roadsides here are forested with firs and hemlock, interspersed with wild hazelnuts, so attractive to the Steller's jay. During early spring and late winter, the willow catkins decorate many branches, while the bigleaf maples provide shade in summer and attract the evening grosbeak to their seeds in autumn. The bridge over Evans Creek by Lake Beecher is a favorite summertime perch and flyway for swallows that wing their way through the willows in the swampy lowlands. Surface-feeding ducks search for food in the shallow, muddy waters of nearby ponds. On the second Sunday of every month, the members of the Horseshoe Grange in Cathcart, a short detour from the route, avail the public of a family-style dinner, a favorite with many bicyclists.

The town of Snohomish has atmosphere. At the airport restaurant, where homemade pies are a specialty, diners may watch sky divers putting on their aerobatic performances. Other interesting restaurants serve a growing clientele, and a small bakery sends forth delicious aromas just daring bicyclists to attempt to pass by. Snohomish boasts a Washington National Guard armory and two parks, with Ferguson Park offering overnight camping. Blackman's Lake, stocked with fish by the State Department of Wildlife, is fronted on the eastern shore by Hill Park, which has secluded picnic areas in a forest setting.

The Old Monroe-Snohomish Road runs along a valley carved out by glaciers; it is wide, fertile, and very productive. Skirting the forested hill on the western side of this valley, the Old Monroe-Snohomish Road offers views of the Washington State Twin Rivers Correction Center, standing like a white fortress atop a green hill above the entrance to Monroe.

MILEAGE LOG

0.0 Monroe Riverside Park near the Skykomish River on S.R. 203. Leave the park and head south across the river on **State Route 203**.

1.1 Turn right on **Tualco Road**. Keep straight past Swiss Hall at mile 1.9 on **Tualco Loop Road**.

3.4 Turn right on **Crescent Lake Road**, and pass the Monroe State Dairy Farm.

4.7 Cross the Snoqualmie River and turn right on **High Bridge Road**. Route goes under State Route 522 at mile 8.0. Road name changes to **Elliott Road**.

10.1 Bear right at stop sign with Elliott Road as Fales Road goes left and uphill. Cross Evans Creek at mile 10.3.

10.5 Keep right and uphill on **Connelly Road**. *Note: To take advantage of the Horseshoe Grange dinner offered on the second Sunday of every month, bear left with Elliott Road to Cathcart at the junction with Broadway. After dinner continue north on Broadway to Springhetti Road.* Kenwanda Golf Course at the top of the hill signals the end of the climb.

12.4 Turn right and downhill on **Broadway**.

12.8 Turn right on **Springhetti Road**. This turn comes in the middle of a downhill run, so don't miss it. Continue past Abel Johnson Park by the big cedar tree into Snohomish on **Airport Way**. The Snohomish Airport and restaurant appear on the left at mile 15.7.

16.0 Cross railroad tracks and the Snohomish River and continue north

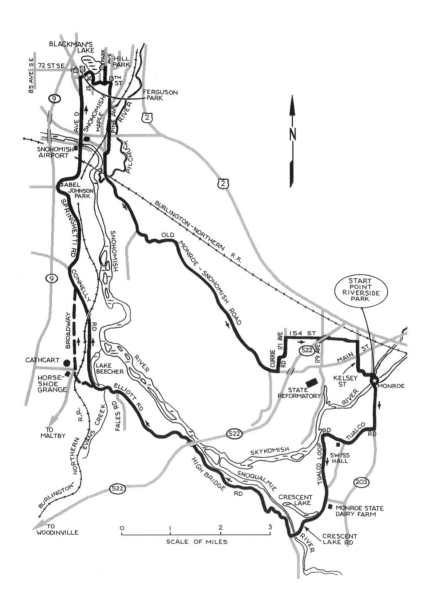

and uphill on **Avenue D** in Snohomish.

17.3 Turn right on **Ferguson Park Road** to Ferguson Park; tables, playground equipment, camping, restrooms. Park is open Memorial Day to Labor Day. Continue through bollards and follow **74 Street S.E.** down and around the southwest corner of Blackman's Lake. Public fishing access here.

17.9 Turn left on **13th Street**.

18.2 Turn left on **Park Avenue**.

18.4 Turn left into Hill Park (city of Snohomish); swimming during summer in Blackman's Lake. Tables, shelter, playground equipment. Retrace route to 13th Street.

18.8 Turn right on **Pine Avenue** and enjoy the downhill ride. Cross Second Street at mile 19.9 and continue downhill and right on **Center Street** to another stop sign. *Caution: Deep ditch between road and field at base of hill where road turns sharp right; descend hill with extra care.*

20.2 Turn left toward Monroe on **Lincoln Avenue**, which is promptly renamed **Old Monroe-Snohomish Road**. Keep left at Y intersection at mile 22.0.

26.1 Turn left on **Currie Road** as interchange with State Route 522 appears ahead. Road bends left at mile 26.7 and is renamed **171st Avenue S.E.**

27.0 Turn right on **154th Street S.E.** as 171st is marked Dead End. Go under State Route 522 at mile 27.6. Road name changes to **Blueberry Lane.**

28.2 Turn right on **N. Kelsey** as Blueberry Lane ends. Cross W. Main Street in Monroe at mile 28.7 and continue on **S. Kelsey**.

28.9 Turn left on **Terrace Street** as Kelsey ends.

29.0 Turn right on **S. Sams Street** as Terrace ends, then immediately turn left on **Sumac Drive**.

29.2 Cross State Route 203 (Lewis Street) and turn right into parking lot of Riverside Park. End of tour at mile 29.4.

24 MONROE–FLOWING LAKE–SNOHOMISH

STARTING POINT: Monroe Riverside Park on State Route 203 by the Skykomish River. Take exit 194 (U.S. 2) from I-5 to Monroe and S.R. 203 to the park on the south edge of town; or take exit 23A (State Route 522) from I-405 to Monroe, then right on U.S. 2 and S.R. 203. Park cars on old concrete pavement near the river.

DISTANCE: 34 miles.
TERRAIN: Moderate.
TOTAL CUMULATIVE ELEVATION GAIN: 1330 feet.
RECOMMENDED TIME OF YEAR: Memorial Day through Labor Day.
RECOMMENDED STARTING TIME: 9 to 10 A.M.
ALLOW: 4 1/2 hours plus lunch.
POINTS OF INTEREST
Leckies Flowing Lake Park (Snohomish County)
Snohomish County Centennial Trail

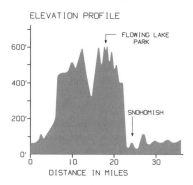

Even though Everett, the county seat, is a large, thriving metropolis, Snohomish County still has a beautiful, rural atmosphere in much of its environs. This ride takes the cyclist north of Monroe, along Woods Creek, which flows leisurely through a small valley. Several dairy farms are situated in this most picturesque setting. Rural living is at its best in the foothills east of Snohomish. Horses, gardens, and orchards are well cared for; open spaces and second-growth forest are everywhere.

Formerly a resort, Leckies Flowing Lake Snohomish County Park is located at just the right place on the tour for lunch. The shallow waters of the lake warm up in summer, making a before-lunch dip an inviting diversion. After leaving the park, the route descends to the Pilchuck River Valley, where the Snohomish County Centennial (railroad) Trail provides traffic-free, gentle grades all the way into Snohomish. After cutting a corner of the city of Snohomish, the route traverses the edge of a broad, green productive valley, a legacy of the glaciers of the last ice age. Several lovely homes stand out in this area. At the end of the valley, the Washington State Twin Rivers Correction Center near Monroe stands aloof on a knoll, stark and a bit foreboding. The road soon turns, however, and the sight of the old Carnation Company smokestack welcomes cyclists back to Monroe. A short detour through a residential area avoids city-center traffic and leads directly to the Riverside Park starting point.

MILEAGE LOG

0.0 Monroe Riverside Park on S.R. 203. Head north on **State Route 203 (Lewis Street)**.
0.5 Turn right on **Main Street** at traffic light.
0.9 Cross **U.S. 2** at traffic light and continue on **Old Owen Road**.
1.0 Turn left on **Oaks Street**.

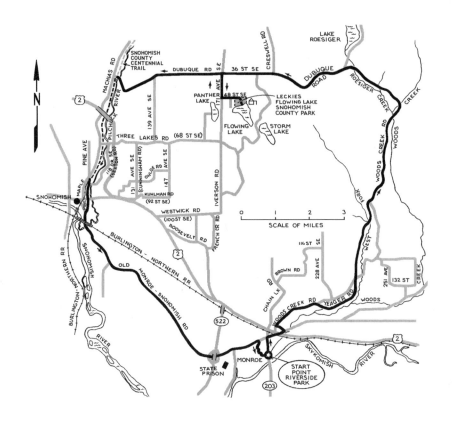

1.2 Turn right on **Woods Creek Road** as Oaks Street ends.

2.6 Keep right with **Yeager Road** as Woods Creek Road forks uphill to the left. Road name reverts to **Woods Creek Road** at mile 4.4. At mile 5.9, cross West Fork Woods Creek and start uphill through a forest of maple and alder.

11.8 Continue on **Dubuque Road** from Woods Creek Road as South Lake Roesiger Road goes right. The road descends a long hill, crosses a creek, and starts uphill again.

15.7 Turn left at top of hill on **171st Avenue S.E.** Excellent views of Cascade Mountains from this point.

16.5 Turn left on **48th Street S.E.** toward Flowing Lake County Park. This turnoff is just where 171st Avenue starts downhill, so watch for the park sign. Park entrance at mile 17.0. This is a large, attractive park with swimming pier, cleverly designed picnic tables, beach, restrooms, and overnight campsites. Return to 171st Avenue S.E. after lunch.

17.8 Turn right on **171st Avenue S.E.**

18.5   Turn left at 4-way stop on **Dubuque Road**. Cross Pilchuck River at mile 21.9.

22.1   Turn left on **Snohomish County Centennial Trail** just before Dubuque Road ends on busy Machias Road. Benches and picnic tables along the trail overlook the Pilchuck River.

25.2   Turn left on **Pine Avenue** as Bike Route (trail) ends and railroad rails continue. At mile 25.8, cross 2 Street (old U.S. 2) by shopping center and cafe and continue downhill and right on **Center Street** to another stop sign. *Caution: Deep ditch between road and field at base of hill where road turns right; descend hill slowly.*

26.2   Turn left toward Monroe on **Lincoln Avenue**, which is promptly renamed **Old Monroe-Snohomish Road**. Go under State Route 522 interchange at mile 32.3 and continue into Monroe on **W. Main Street**.

33.8   Turn right on **S. Kelsey Street**.

34.1   Turn left on **Terrace Street** as Kelsey ends, right on **S. Sands Street** as Terrace ends, and then immediately left with thoroughfare on **Sumac Drive** as Sands Street ends.

34.3   Cross State Route 203 and turn right into parking lot of Riverside Park. End of tour at mile 34.4.

*"You folded your spare tire in **half**?"*

25 MONROE–SULTAN

STARTING POINT: Veterans Memorial Park (city of Monroe). Take I-5 exit 194 (U.S. 2) to Monroe, or take I-405 exit 23A (State Route 522) to Monroe. Veterans Memorial Park sits beside U.S. 2 and near the tall, concrete smokestack.

DISTANCE: Loop A, 21 miles; Loop B, 18 miles.
TERRAIN: Moderate, some hills.
TOTAL CUMULATIVE ELEVATION GAIN: Loop A, 940 feet; Loop B, 620 feet.
RECOMMENDED TIME OF YEAR: Any season.

RECOMMENDED STARTING TIME: 9 to 10 A.M.
ALLOW: 2 to 3 hours for either loop.
POINTS OF INTEREST
Tall smokestack in Monroe
Views of Cascade Mountains

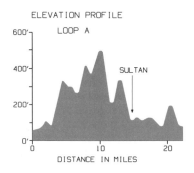

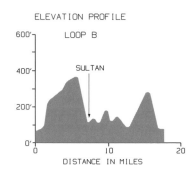

Monroe is of course best known for the Washington State Reformatory and the annual Evergreen State Fair, but it also is identified by a tall, singular smokestack that can be seen from miles away. According to natives, this monolith dates back to the early 1920s, when it was part of the Carnation Company's condensed milk plant. Although the plant was destroyed by fire in the 1920s and was never rebuilt, the smokestack was undamaged and remains to this day as a distinctive landmark. Monroe also has two of the prettiest entrance streets of any town around, as well as three small, well-maintained parks. These two Monroe-Sultan loop rides begin from Veterans Memorial Park, just east of the smokestack.

Actually, there are four ways to get from Monroe to Sultan without following U.S. 2, although one of these does cross it several times. Any two of the roads can be taken as a loop ride. The loops described here are 21 miles and 18 miles.

The first loop leaves Monroe on Woods Creek Road passing through the beautiful farmland northeast of the city. Dairy farms, specializing in Holstein-Friesian cattle, stretch along the banks of Woods Creek. As it leaves the valley, this route follows Bollenbaugh Hill Road past country places with gardens, horses, and cattle. One mile of gravel road takes the bicyclist down through a stand of young fir trees. A clearing at a road summit provides a distant view of Wallace Falls. After a thrilling downhill run, the rider crosses U.S. 2 just west of Sultan. The route crosses the Burlington Northern tracks

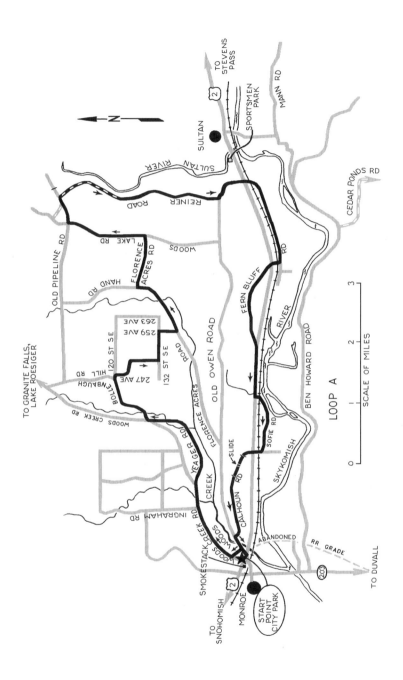

and turns west toward Monroe on the original Monroe-Sultan Road, which is now no more than a frontage road. The route follows this old road, crosses the present U.S. 2 several times, and is eventually forced onto the shoulder of the highway for 0.8 mile. The shoulder is wide and well surfaced for bicycle travel, so it presents little in the way of distress. Views of the Skykomish Valley are seen from the northern excursions of the road, while on its southerly meanderings, lush farmland along the river lies close at hand. As U.S. 2 is crossed for the fourth time, the road climbs a hill, crosses a slide area, and passes a cemetery before descending into Monroe.

The second loop takes Old Owen Road from Monroe to the edge of the town of Sultan. U.S. 2 then is followed east for a short distance across the Sultan River to the center of Sultan. Crossing the Skykomish River, the route returns to Monroe on the Ben Howard Road, following the south side of the Skykomish. Several dairy farms spread across the fertile land beneath Barr Mountain, where hang gliders frequently practice their daring sport.

Either loop can be completed without a lunch break, but on a leisurely trip, the Sportsmen Park on the Sultan River just west of Sultan makes an interesting stop. Grocery stores and cafes in Sultan are convenient for those who would rather not pack picnic materials from home.

MILEAGE LOG

LOOP A

0.0 Veterans Memorial Park, Monroe. Head east on **E. Main Street**, cross U.S. 2 at traffic light, and continue on **Old Owen Road**.

0.2 Turn left past shopping center on **Oaks Street**.

0.4 Turn right on **Woods Creek Road** as Oaks Street ends.

1.8 Bear right with **Yeager Road** as Woods Creek Road forks uphill to the left. York Farm on the right at mile 2.4.

3.6 Turn right on **Bollenbaugh Hill Road**.

4.7 Turn right on **120th Street S.E.** at top of hill as Bollenbaugh Hill Road forks left. Keep right at next road fork. Road is renamed **124th Street S.E.** and **251st Avenue S.E.** as it winds across the plateau.

5.7 Turn left on **132nd Street S.E.**

6.2 Turn right on **259th Avenue S.E.**

6.5 Turn left on **Florence Acres Road**.

7.6 Bear right with Florence Acres Road as Hand Road continues on.

8.5 Turn left on **Woods Lake Road** as Florence Acres Road ends.

9.8 Turn right on **Old Pipeline Road** (marked Private Road). Continue on **Reiner Road** as it enters from the left.

10.2 Bear right with Reiner Road as Lake Chaplain Road forks left. Head downhill as pavement ends. *Caution: Gravel road becomes steep in places.* Pavement resumes at mile 11.2.

13.3 Turn left and downhill as **Old Owen Road** joins from the right. Cross U.S. 2 and the Burlington Northern tracks at mile 13.9 and continue on **Fern Bluff Road**.

15.4 Cross railroad tracks and U.S. 2 and continue on Fern Bluff Road.

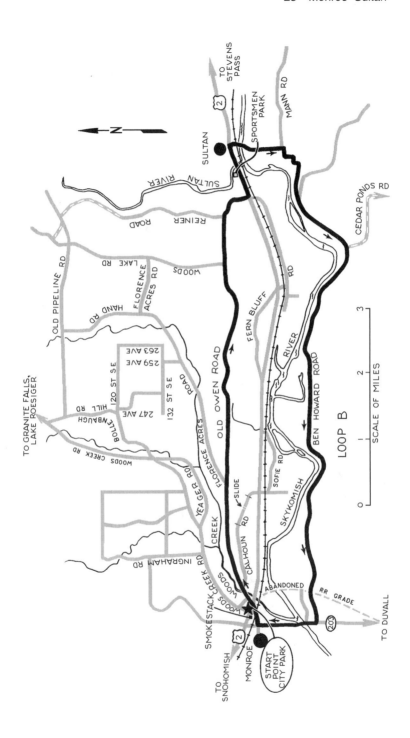

Views of valley.

17.0 Turn right on **U.S. 2**; wide shoulder.

17.8 Turn left on **Sofie Road**.

18.8 Cross U.S. 2 again and continue on **Calhoun Road** (marked Dead End). Go through Road Closed barrier at mile 19.1, walk/carry bikes through slide area and continue through upper barrier at top of hill at mile 19.5. Pass a cemetery.

20.5 Bear left on **Old Owen Road**. Cross U.S. 2 and continue into Monroe on **Main Street**.

20.9 Back at Veterans Memorial Park in Monroe.

LOOP B

0.0 Veterans Memorial Park, Monroe. Head east on **E. Main Street**, cross U.S. 2 at traffic signal, and continue on **Old Owen Road**. Keep left where Calhoun intersects on the right at mile 0.4.

1.9 Keep right with Old Owen Road as Florence Acres Road forks left. Reiner Road joins from the left at mile 6.2 as the route heads downhill.

6.8 Turn left on **U.S. 2** toward Sultan. Bridge over Sultan River with State Department of Wildlife fishing access at mile 7.3.

7.6 In the middle of the town of Sultan, turn right on **311 Avenue S.E.** and cross the Skykomish River and several sloughs, named Shingle Bolt, S. Sky, Sky River, and S. Slough.

8.4 Turn right on **Ben Howard Road**.

16.8 Turn right on **State Route 203**. Cross the Skykomish River and enter Monroe on **Lewis Street**.

17.7 Turn right on **Main Street** at traffic light.

18.0 Back at Veterans Memorial Park in Monroe.

*"You fold a tire like **this**!"*

26   NORTH FORK SKYKOMISH

STARTING POINT: Doolittle Pioneer Park in Index. From I-5 in Everett, take exit 194 (U.S. 2) 40 miles east to Index turnoff. After 1.0 mile, turn left over the North Fork Skykomish River into Index.

DISTANCE: 25 miles.
TERRAIN: Hilly.
TOTAL CUMULATIVE ELEVATION GAIN: 1300 feet.
RECOMMENDED TIME OF YEAR:
Any season except severe winter conditions. Avoid hunting season.
RECOMMENDED STARTING TIME:
9 A.M.
ALLOW: 4 to 5 hours plus lunch.
POINT OF INTEREST
Wild river scenery along North Fork Skykomish River

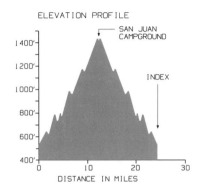

Although this is a beautiful ride in spring and summer, bright fall colors make it spectacular. The first week in October usually is best, when the vine maple has changed to muted pink, red, and yellow and the bigleaf maple is yellow and brown. Other deciduous trees display a bit of color if weather conditions are just right.

A well-maintained asphalt road takes the cycle tourist through several miles of national forest along the North Fork Skykomish River with its sparkling waters and many rapids. Along the route, rushing streams and ladderlike waterfalls provide a habitat to the liking of the drab, little water ouzel. Rough side roads lead to old mining areas with colorful names.

Two forest service campgrounds, located two miles apart at Troublesome Creek and San Juan Creek, provide the usual amenities—pit toilets, picnic tables, garbage cans, and campsites, although facilites at San Juan may be closed. Exploring the little town of Index before or after the tour along the North Fork Skykomish River offers interesting discoveries to the photographer, artist, or history buff.

The town's nearby namesake, Mt. Index, with its jagged snow-covered crags, rises to a spectacular point at 5979 feet. The towering rock and tree-covered cliffs to the north present subtle shades of green and gray until autumn's brisk days splash shades of red, orange, and brown.

The Bush Hotel, still in operation with rooms and a restaurant, dates back to 1898 and, although not truly a bed-and-breakfast house, is listed in our B&B Index. A modern grocery store does double duty as the post office for this little town tucked between the rushing rivers and snowy peaks of the Cascade Mountains.

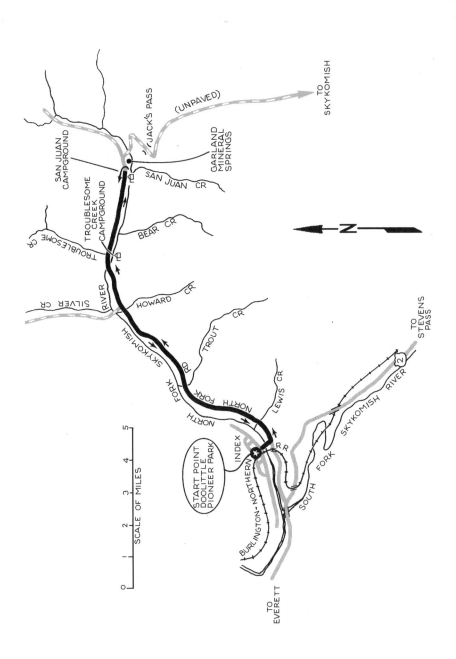

MILEAGE LOG

0.0 Doolittle Pioneer Park, Index. Head southeast across the North Fork Skykomish River and turn left on **North Fork Road**. Cross Lewis Creek at mile 1.8, Canyon Creek at mile 2.5, Bitter Creek at mile 3.3, Trout Creek at mile 5.4, and Howard Creek at mile 8.4. *Note: At mile 8.5, a gravel road goes left across the river to the old mining townsites of Galena and Mineral City. Trail from end of road leads over Poodle Dog Pass to Monte Cristo area.* Cross North Fork Skykomish River at mile 9.5. Troublesome Creek Campground on the right at mile 10.4; restrooms, picnic tables, overnight camping.

12.5 Turn right into San Juan Campground; restrooms, picnic tables, overnight camping. Enjoy a picnic lunch, then return to Index. It will be downhill most of the way.

Winter Rest Stop

27 SKYKOMISH–INDEX–JACK'S PASS

STARTING POINT: Skykomish, King County. Take exit 194 (U.S. 2) from I-5, 50 miles east to Skykomish turnoff. Park in parking area along railroad tracks near fire station.

DISTANCE: 46 miles; 8 miles of gravel forest service road; future paving planned.

TERRAIN: Alpine with steep gravel road. Recommend contacting Skykomish Forest Service for relative condition of roads and campgrounds.

TOTAL CUMULATIVE ELEVATION GAIN: 2600 feet.

RECOMMENDED TIME OF YEAR: Memorial Day to first weekend in October.

RECOMMENDED STARTING TIME: 8 A.M., Sunday preferred.

ALLOW: 6 to 8 hours.

POINTS OF INTEREST
Views of Mt. Index
Wild river scenery along Skykomish
    and Beckler rivers

ELEVATION PROFILE

If you have an aversion to bicycling on dirt and gravel roads, forget about this tour. If bicycling into the Cascades with views comparable to those received on hiking trails sounds appealing, however, this tour will prove interesting and exciting.

As the route leaves Skykomish and heads west along the South Fork Skykomish River, it travels a bypassed section of the Old Cascade Highway over Stevens Pass. Shortly after the old highway crosses Miller River, the Miller River Road goes left to the National Forest Service Miller River Campground. Tracks of the Burlington Northern Railroad run beside the old road, but eventually they cross to the north side of the river and play leapfrog with the present Stevens Pass Highway. Our route joins U.S. 2 near Money Creek and stays on the busy highway to the Index turnoff. An early morning departure from Skykomish avoids heavy traffic.

Grotto, the former site of the Northwestern Portland Cement Company, is still home to a few families. No evidence of the cement plant remains. The little settlement of Baring emphasizes the alpine character of its surroundings by the decor of *Der Baring Store und Post Office*. The 1935 date on the old concrete bridge over Barclay Creek shows that some of the sections of the present Stevens Pass Highway still follow the old Cascade route.

Continuing along U.S. 2, the route presents several viewpoints that tempt the cyclist to stop. Heybrook Lookout stands atop a ridge on the western horizon, but auto travelers barely have time to catch a glimpse of this wooden structure. The trail to the lookout leaves the highway 1.5 miles west of Baring, where waters of the South Fork Skykomish plunge over a series

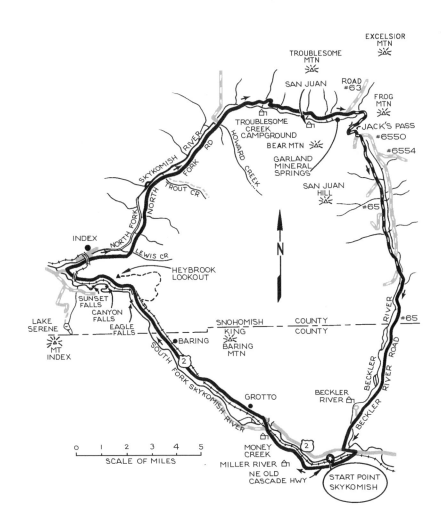

of spectacular falls. Mt. Index, with its Bridal Veil Falls, appears near the turnoff to Index, where the Bush Hotel restaurant offers breakfast for hungry cyclists.

The climb is gradual as the route heads upstream along the rushing waters of the North Fork Skykomish River, where summer cabins nestle among the deciduous and evergreen trees. Several small streams plunge down the hillside to join the river. Near one stream, a gravel road crosses the Skykomish and heads toward the old mining townsites of Galena and Mineral City and continues as a trail over Poodle Dog Pass to Monte Cristo. Two forest campgrounds at Troublesome Creek and San Juan Creek provide campsites beside the clear, rushing mountain streams.

As the climb to Jack's Pass begins in earnest, Troublesome Mountain and the peaks of the Monte Cristo group come into view. Alpine foliage on Frog Mountain takes on brilliant colors in the fall. Good brakes are needed for the descent from Jack's Pass, which is shown on most maps as Jack Pass, but all the old signs said Jacks, and at least one old-timer remembers it as Jackass Pass. Numerous smaller streams join the Beckler River and provide lovely alpine settings for a lunch break or just a stop to rest and enjoy the mountain scenery.

There will be some auto traffic on these narrow forest service roads, so they may be dusty or muddy depending on the weather, but most drivers are considerate and rather in awe of bicycles attempting these backroads. A campground on the Beckler River is passed just over a mile before the road joins U.S. 2, where another section of the Old Cascade Highway is followed back to the starting point in Skykomish.

MILEAGE LOG

0.0 Skykomish, King County; parking area near railroad tracks. Cross the railroad tracks and turn right on **N.E. Old Cascade Highway**. At mile 2.0, watch for acute-angled railroad tracks followed by steel bridge over the Miller River. Miller River Campground to the left on Miller River Road. Money Creek Campground on the right at mile 3.4.

3.5 Cross South Fork Skykomish River and turn left on **U.S. 2 (Stevens Pass Highway)**; two-foot shoulder. Community of Grotto at mile 4.3; Mt. View General Store at mile 7.6; Der Baring Store on the left at mile 8.2. Bridge over Burlington Northern Railroad tracks at mile 6.3 and again at mile 10.8. View of Eagle Falls at mile 10.3.

13.9 Turn right toward Index. *Note: Bridge over the North Fork Skykomish River goes left into Index at mile 14.8; Bush Hotel restaurant, grocery store, park.* Continue along the river on **North Fork Road**. Cross the North Fork Skykomish River at mile 24.1; Troublesome Creek Campground at mile 25.1; San Juan Campground at mile 27.2.

27.9 Continue uphill with thoroughfare toward Jack's Pass as side road goes right and downhill along river.

28.9 Continue on **Forest Road 65** toward Jack's Pass and Skykomish as pavement ends. Cross North Fork Skykomish River at mile 29.2 and start up long, steep hill, with switchbacks, to Jack's Pass.

31.3 Jack's Pass, elevation 2589 feet. Bear right with road 65. Note: *Road*

6550 continues on to a lower junction with road 65 but is poorly maintained and may present challenges. Road 65 is eventually re-named **Beckler River Road**. Pavement resumes at mile 36.9. Entrance to Beckler River Campground at mile 42.5.

43.9   Cross **U.S. 2** and turn left on the shoulder of the highway. Cross the South Fork Skykomish River.

44.4   Turn right on **Old Cascade Highway** toward emergency airfield, and cross railroad tracks.

45.7   Turn right across railroad tracks into downtown Skykomish.

45.8   End of tour at parking area.

... may present challenges ...

28 GRANITE FALLS–LAKE ROESIGER

STARTING POINT: Granite Falls, Snohomish County. Take exit 194 (U.S. 2) from
I-5, cross Snohomish River and bear left on State Route 204 to Frontier Village; then
turn north on State Route 9 to Mt. Pilchuck exit (State Route 92) to Granite Falls.
Park near the high school on Alder Avenue at the east end of town.

DISTANCE: 33 miles.
TERRAIN: Moderate.
**TOTAL CUMULATIVE ELEVATION
GAIN:** 1100 feet.
RECOMMENDED TIME OF YEAR:
Any season except in snow or icy
conditions.
RECOMMENDED STARTING TIME:
9 to 10 A.M.
ALLOW: 4 to 5 hours.
POINTS OF INTEREST
Hartford terminus of historic railroad
    to Monte Cristo
Mountain scenery

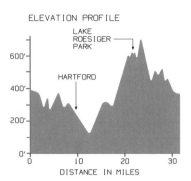

Although this tour and Tour 29 in the area south of Granite Falls have no
spectacular attractions, we have enjoyed them over and over. Perhaps this
is so because of peaceful scenery, the scarcity of automobile traffic, and the
network of backroads that allows the cyclist to vary the route on each trip.

These two rides in the Pilchuck River basin cover most of the available
roads and are about the longest nonrepetitive tours possible without branch-
ing out into some of the other rides in adjacent areas. Several minor loops
starting from Lake Roesiger Park (Snohomish County) or Granite Falls are
obvious and are left to the ingenuity of the reader.

Depending upon the direction taken, or the starting time from Granite
Falls, the cyclist may enjoy a picnic at Lake Roesiger Park or a meal at a
cafe in Lake Stevens. Views of Mt. Pilchuck and Three Fingers Mountain
form an impressive backdrop in the northeast.

MILEAGE LOG

0.0 High school parking area on S. Alder Avenue (Mountain Loop Highway). Leave parking area and head south on **S. Alder Avenue**.
0.2 Turn right on **E. Stanley Street**. **State Route 92** begins at mile 0.4.
0.8 Turn right on **Jordan Road** (**187 Avenue N.E.**).
1.1 Turn left on **100th Street N.E.** (**Burn Road**).
2.7 Turn left on **163rd Avenue N.E.**
2.9 Turn right on **96th Street N.E.** (**Goebel Hill Road**). Follow it past
abandoned farms. Continue uphill, then downhill as road bends left
and is named **147th Avenue N.E.**
4.5 Turn right on **84th Street N.E.** as Goebel Hill Road ends.
6.0 Turn left on **123rd Avenue N.E.** Views of Mt. Pilchuck and Three
Fingers Mountain. Road bends left on **44th Street N.E.** at mile 8.6.

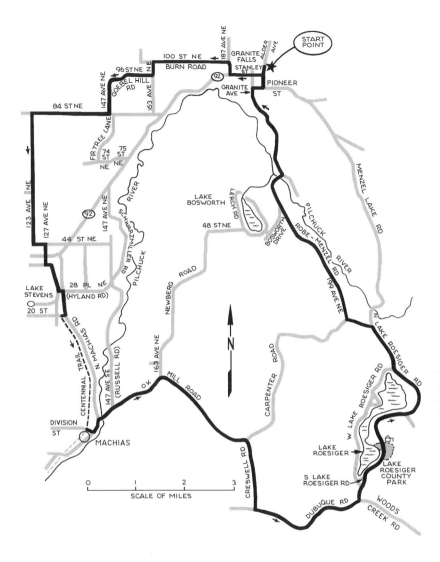

8.8   Turn right on **127th Drive N.E. (Ridel Road)**. Cross State Route 92.

9.2   Turn left on **36th Street N.E.**, which bends right and becomes **Old Hartford Drive**.

9.9   Turn left at stop sign on **28th Place N.E.** *Note: For food services, continue on Hartford Drive into Lake Stevens business district and return.* On left is a Boy Scout Troop 43 historical sign commemorating the beginning of the historic railroad to Monte Cristo built in 1891-93.

10.0   Turn right on **N. Machias Road**. Site of old town of Hartford. Cedar shingle mill on the right at mile 10.1.

10.5 Turn right on **20th Street N.E.**, then immediately left on **Centennial Trail**.

13.1 Turn left on **Division Street** by Machias rest area, then left at stop sign on **N. Machias Road**. Pass Machias Grocery.

13.7 Turn right on **OK Mill Road** and cross the Pilchuck River.

17.5 Turn right on **Creswell Road** as Carpenter Road goes on.

18.8 Turn left on **Dubuque Road** (36th Street S.E.).

21.3 Turn left on **South Lake Roesiger Road** as Dubuque Road is renamed Woods Creek Road and starts downhill.

21.5 Keep right with South Lake Roesiger Road as West Lake Roesiger Road goes left.

22.7 Turn left into Lake Roesiger County Park; picnicking, swimming, and camping facilities available. Campsites are on the east side of the road away from the lake. Return to South Lake Roesiger Road and continue north along the lake after lunch. Keep right and downhill as West Lake Roesiger Road intersects from the left at mile 25.3.

26.3 Turn left on **Carpenter Road** at a wye as Menzel Lake Road continues on.

26.8 Turn right on **Robe-Menzel Road** at a wye. Cross Pilchuck River at mile 30.2. Enter Granite Falls at mile 31.9.

32.2 Turn right on **E. Pioneer Street** toward Menzel Lake Road.

32.4 Turn left on **S. Alder Avenue**. Cross E. Stanley Street at stop sign at mile 32.6. End of tour at high school at mile 32.8.

Man's Best Friend

29   GRANITE FALLS–LAKE BOSWORTH

STARTING POINT: Granite Falls, Snohomish County. Take exit 194 (U.S. 2) from I-5, cross Snohomish River and bear left on State Route 204 to Frontier Village; then turn left on State Route 9, then right at Mt. Pilchuck exit (State Route 92) to Granite Falls. Park near the high school on Alder Avenue at the east end of town.

DISTANCE: 40 miles.
TERRAIN: Hilly.
TOTAL CUMULATIVE ELEVATION GAIN: 1600 feet.
RECOMMENDED TIME OF YEAR: Any season except in snow or icy conditions.
RECOMMENDED STARTING TIME: 9 A.M.
ALLOW: 6 hours.
POINTS OF INTEREST
Lake Bosworth
Lake Roesiger County Park

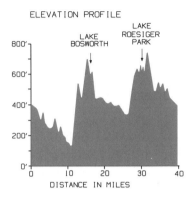

This visit to Snohomish County roams the rural highways and byways. Automobile traffic will be scarce; scenery, magnificent. Early fall is the best time for this ride, but it can be taken at any season. Fall often brings flamboyant colors and blue skies. The Cascades, particularly Mt. Pilchuck and Three Fingers Mountain, stand out when they have received a light dusting of snow. Autumn rides find an abundant fallout of apples and pears. In early October, Granite Falls celebrates Railroad Days with parades and games. Two lakes are visited: small and quiet Lake Bosworth, and Lake Roesiger, the site of a Snohomish County park. Swimming at the park in summer makes this trip a good choice for hot weather.

The bird watcher is likely to receive several thrills on this ride as grouse are flushed along the backroads. Great blue herons frequent the shallow waters near Lake Roesiger County Park, and ducks tantalize, just far enough away to be impossible to identify without binoculars.

MILEAGE LOG

0.0 High school parking area on S. Alder Avenue (Mountain Loop Highway). Leave parking area and head south on **S. Alder Avenue**.

0.1 Turn right on **E. Stanley Street**. **State Route 92** begins at mile 0.4.

0.8 Turn right on **Jordan Road**.

1.0 Turn left on **100 Street N.E. (Burn Road)**.

2.5 Turn left on **163rd Avenue N.E.**

2.8 Turn right on **96 Street N.E. (Goebel Hill Road)**. Continue uphill, then downhill as road bends left and becomes **147th Avenue N.E.**

4.3 Turn left on **84th Street N.E.**, then almost immediately turn right on **Fir Tree Lane**.

5.0 Turn left on **Sleepy Hollow Road (74th Street N.E.)** as Fir Tree

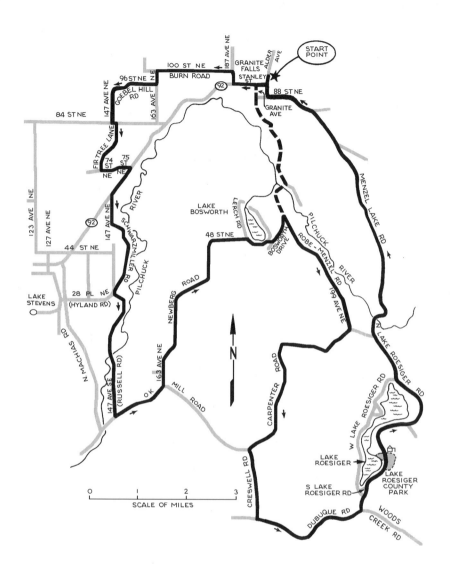

Lane ends at stop sign.

5.6 Turn right on **State Route 92** as Sleepy Hollow Road ends.

6.7 Turn left on **147th Avenue N.E. (Schwarzmiller Road)** and continue down the Pilchuck River Valley. Views of Mt. Pilchuck and Three Fingers Mountain.

8.7 Bear left on **147th Avenue N.E. (Tanner Road)** as Schwartzmiller Road ends.

8.8 Continue as road name changes to **Russell Road** and Hyland Road goes right. *Note: For food services, turn right at this intersection on Hyland Road for one mile, then left on Hartford Drive to Lake Stevens city center. Return to this intersection.* Cross Pilchuck River at mile 10.2; Machias Elementary School appears at mile 11.3.

11.5   Turn left on **O.K. Mill Road** as Russell Road ends.

12.7   Turn left on **Newberg Road** (**163 Avenue**) and head up a long, steep hill toward Lake Bosworth.

17.0   Turn right on **Lerch Road** as Newberg Road ends. Follow along south end of Lake Bosworth.

17.5   Bear right with thoroughfare on **Bosworth Drive** at southeast corner of Lake Bosworth.

18.2   Turn sharp right on **Robe-Menzel Road**. *Note: Those desiring only a 21-mile ride turn left and return to Granite Falls. See map.*

20.9   Turn right on **Carpenter Road**.

25.0   Turn left on **Creswell Road**.

26.5   Turn left on **Dubuque Road** (**36 Street N.E.**) and proceed gradually uphill.

28.8   Turn left on **South Lake Roesiger Road** toward Lake Roesiger at crest of hill.

29.0   Keep right with South Lake Roesiger Road.

30.0   Turn left into Lake Roesiger County Park; picnicking, swimming, camping. Relax and then continue north along the lake. West Lake Roesiger Road intersects at mile 32.5.

33.5   Keep right toward Granite Falls on **Menzel Lake Road** as Carpenter Road goes left. Cross Pilchuck River at mile 34.0.

39.5   Turn right on **S. Alder Avenue** in Granite Falls toward Mountain Loop Highway. Cross E. Stanley Street at mile 39.7. Return to starting point at mile 39.8; end of tour.

30 LOWER STILLAGUAMISH

STARTING POINT: Business district of east Stanwood, Snohomish County. Take exit 212 (State Route 532) from I-5 to the second Stanwood turnoff by Viking Village on 88 Avenue N.W. Turn right on 271 Street N.W. Turn left on Florence Road by railroad tracks to public parking area behind shops.

DISTANCE: 31 miles.
TERRAIN: Flat to moderate.
TOTAL CUMULATIVE ELEVATION GAIN: 550 feet.
RECOMMENDED TIME OF YEAR: Any season.
RECOMMENDED STARTING TIME: 10 A.M.
ALLOW: 4 hours.
POINTS OF INTEREST
Stillaguamish Pioneers Hall
Haller Park in Arlington

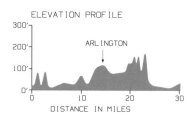

The lower Stillaguamish Valley, like many alluvial valleys in northwestern Washington, is characterized by multiple channels or sloughs forming large islands. The islands of the Stillaguamish are not accorded names, and without a map the cyclist would hardly be aware of being on an island. Two of these islands are visited on this tour, harboring towns of Silvana and Florence.

The route taken on the first leg of the journey from east Stanwood winds through the intensely farmed valley. Its curving, sometimes bumpy surface slows what little traffic has not been diverted to the fast, straight State Route 532. An old fairground and meeting hall nestle back among the trees. Ripe silage, animal manure, cottonwood trees, new-mown hay, and drying river-bank mud all add to the scents that greet the bicyclist. A deer, surprised at the two-wheeled contraptions, bounds into a nearby copse.

Upon crossing the rumbling freeway, traffic speeds up and becomes more persistent. The bicycle route escapes almost immediately by taking a side road and climbing the edge of a small bluff to the south. Views of the valley sift through the trees in winter but are screened by summer foliage. At the Stillaguamish Pioneers Hall, many tools of the early logging industry are displayed. A section of an old fir log, protected from the weather by a shelter, has its rings dated back through several centuries.

The rider arrives abruptly at Arlington and proceeds along another high-way to Haller Park beside the Stillaguamish River. Just east of the park lies the confluence of the two main forks of the Stillaguamish River. There are good views from rocks north of the highway bridge. The park itself is well appointed, with restrooms, shelter, tables, spring horses, and chair swings along the riverbank.

The first leg of the return route climbs out of the valley to traverse backroads over the neighboring upland. After crossing Pilchuck Creek, which is the drainage of Lake Cavanaugh (see Tour 35), another hill is surmounted, followed by a delightful plunge down a small canyon to the

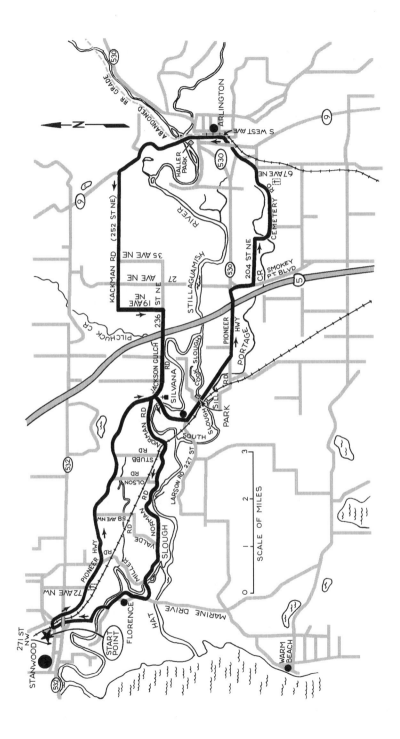

open river valley. From here, the twisting riverfront roads are followed back to Stanwood as cows stare curiously at bicyclists. Kingfishers rattle from the trees, while a great blue heron lifts ponderously from the riverbed and rabbits scurry into the shrubbery. Following a short detour on an old concrete roadbed through the community of Florence, bicyclists run the risk of meeting livestock tethers stretched across the road. The river is crossed for the last time and the ride ends in Stanwood.

MILEAGE LOG

0.0 Leave public parking area on Florence Road. Turn east (left) on **271st Street N.W.** and cross railroad tracks. Bear right and uphill on **Triangle Road** and continue out of town on **Pioneer Highway**. Cross State Route 532 at mile 0.3. Pass cemetery at mile 0.6 and proceed along the northern edge of the lower Stillaguamish Valley.

6.4 Keep right with Pioneer Highway at center of figure 8 loop of tour. Cross the Stillaguamish River on concrete bridge with a walkway set off by Jersey barriers. Old historic church on hill to the left. Enter Silvana. Original Silvana school bell (circa 1890) displayed along the main street. Cross Stillaguamish River again at mile 8.0. Public fishing access park maintained by Snohomish County Parks and Recreation Department. Cross I-5 on overpass at mile 10.3. Several restaurants at this intersection.

10.6 Bear right on **Old 99 (Smokey Point Boulevard)** at a wye.

11.1 Turn left on **Cemetery Road (204th Street N.E.)** At mile 12.1, the road leaves the valley, climbs a hill, and runs along a bluff.

13.9 Turn left on **67th Avenue N.E.** at a traffic light. Cemetery at this corner. Stillaguamish Pioneers Hall is on the left at mile 14.2.

14.5 Keep left on **S. West Avenue**. Cafes to the right and left in Arlington's business district.

14.8 Cross State Route 530 at stop sign and continue north on **State Route 9**. Haller Park in Arlington on the left at mile 15.6. After visiting the park, cross the Stillaguamish River and continue north and uphill on S.R. 9.

17.7 Turn left on **252nd Street N.E. (Kackman Road)**. At mile 20.3, the road bends left and is marked **19th Avenue N.E. (Kackman Road)**.

21.4 Turn right at T junction on **236th Street N.E.** Cross I-5 at mile 22.0, proceed downhill, cross Pilchuck Creek, and climb uphill on **Jackson Gulch Road**, then plunge downhill again.

23.5 Turn right on **Pioneer Highway** at center of figure 8 loop, then immediately turn left on **Norman Road (239th Street N.W.)**. Cross Stillaguamish River at mile 27.7.

28.1 Turn right on **Marine Drive (76th Avenue N.W.)**.

28.5 Bear right on **Florence Road** through Florence for 0.5 mile, then rejoin **Marine Drive**. Road is renamed **Florence Road** as it enters Stanwood.

30.6 End of ride in east Stanwood.

31 GRANITE FALLS–ARLINGTON

STARTING POINT: Granite Falls, Snohomish County. Take exit 194 (U.S. 2) from I-5, then north on State Route 9 to Mt. Pilchuck exit (State Route 92) to Granite Falls. Park near the high school on Alder Avenue at the east end of town.

DISTANCE: 30 miles.
TERRAIN: Moderate.
TOTAL CUMULATIVE ELEVATION GAIN: 1150 feet.
RECOMMENDED TIME OF YEAR: Any season.
RECOMMENDED STARTING TIME: 10 A.M.
ALLOW: 4 hours.
POINTS OF INTEREST
Jordan Footbridge and Park
American Legion Cemetery
River Meadows Regional Park (Snohomish County)

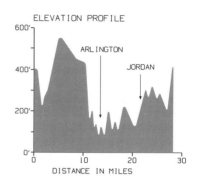

Although this ride follows the South Fork Stillaguamish most of the way, little is seen of the river at first. Dense forest, interrupted occasionally by small farms and country homes, provides an uneventful but pleasurable ride with very little automotive traffic. Haller Park at the halfway point is an attractive location for lunch. A short hike east from the park, over or under the railroad tracks, gains an unusual view of the confluence of the two forks of the Stillaguamish River. Gravel bar foliage provides forage for the deer that are occasionally glimpsed along the water's edge. On the return leg of the tour, the road undulates over the hills and valleys, repeatedly giving the cyclist tantalizing views of flat gravel bars and sparkling waters. Except at low water in late summer, however, the cyclist will always find a swift channel between the bank and the gravel bar.

River Meadows Regional Park, one of Snohomish County's newer parks, provides the first available public access. A steep, unpaved entrance road leads downhill to a broad, open meadow lined with trees along the river. Although the park is designated for both day and overnight use, a pit toilet provides the only sanitary facility.

At the little community of Jordan, a new, rebuilt suspension footbridge spans the South Fork Stillaguamish River, leading to a delightful little county park by a gravel bar along the river. The bridge also allows cyclists to make a figure-eight loop of this ride or shorten it appreciably.

Impressive cliffs line the valley's edge approaching Granite Falls. The river is crossed again near the southern terminus of the ride and a long, steep grade leads up out of the valley, ending at the American Legion Cemetery. Another mile takes the cyclist back to Granite Falls, where spirits can be revived at any of several refreshment concessions. For the novice or intermediate cyclist, this ride by itself is a good tour; the advanced rider may combine it with Tour 32 for a total distance of 46 miles.

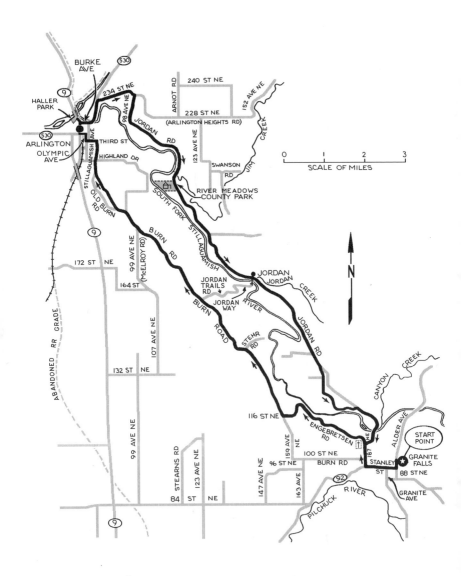

MILEAGE LOG

0.0 High school parking area on S. Alder Avenue (Mountain Loop Highway) in Granite Falls. Leave parking area and head south on **S. Alder Avenue**.

0.1 Turn right on **E. Stanley Street (State Route 92)**.

0.8 Turn right on **Jordan Road (187 Avenue N.E.)**.

1.4 Keep left with **Engebretsen Road** past American Legion Cemetery, then downhill along the South Fork Stillaguamish River. At mile 3.4, the road turns left up two successive short, steep hills.

4.0 Turn right at stop sign on **Burn Road** as Engebretsen ends. *Note: At mile 7.5 Jordan Trails Road goes right to a county park and a suspension footbridge to rejoin route at log mile 22.1. This may be used to shorten route by 13 miles.* Continue through forest of alder and evergreen trees past Bonneville Power Administration Murray Substation. Enter open valley alongside State Route 9, then climb a hill and enter Arlington on **Stillaguamish Avenue** at mile 12.1.

12.6 Turn left on **E. 3rd Street** as Stillaguamish ends, and plunge downhill.

13.0 Turn right on **N. Olympic Avenue** at stop sign at bottom of hill; cafes, stores.

13.3 Turn left on **W. Division Avenue** as Olympic ends.

13.4 Turn right on **N. State Route 9 (N. West Avenue)**.

13.6 Turn left into Haller Park. Restrooms, shelter, picnic tables, and chair swings by the river. After lunch, retrace route 2 blocks south on S.R. 9 and turn left across the railroad tracks on **Burke Avenue**. Join **State Route 530** at mile 14.2 and proceed east out of Arlington. Cross South Fork Stillaguamish River.

15.1 Turn right on **Arlington Heights Road (234 Street N.E.)** toward Jordan Road.

16.1 Turn right on **Jordan Road (98 Avenue N.E.)** toward Granite Falls. River Meadows Regional Park on the right at mile 19.1. Picnic areas and campsites along river in meadow. Public access to river beach at Jordan via picturesque suspension footbridge at mile 22.1.

25.7 Bear right on **Chappel Road** for a short diversion from the main road.

27.2 Turn right on **Jordan Road** as Chappel Road ends. Cross bridge over South Fork Stillaguamish at mile 28.1.

28.6 Keep left with Jordan Road at T junction by American Legion Cemetery.

29.3 Turn left on **W. Stanley Street (State Route 92)** in Granite Falls.

29.9 Turn left on **S. Alder Avenue**.

30.0 Back to high school parking lot; end of ride.

32 ARLINGTON–JIM CREEK

STARTING POINT: Haller Park in Arlington. Take exit 208 (Arlington, State Route 530) from I-5. In Arlington, proceed 0.3 mile north on State Route 9 to park on left just before S.R. 9 crosses the Stillaguamish River.

DISTANCE: 22 miles.
TERRAIN: Moderate.
TOTAL CUMULATIVE ELEVATION GAIN: 630 feet.
RECOMMENDED TIME OF YEAR: All seasons.
RECOMMENDED STARTING TIME: Any hour.
ALLOW: 3 hours.
POINTS OF INTEREST
Old schoolhouse at Trafton
Jim Creek Naval Radio Station

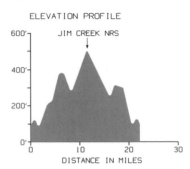

ELEVATION PROFILE

Although not long, this tour explores interesting backroads where a long-wavelength, ultra-low-frequency radio transmitter spreads its antenna the length and breadth of an entire valley.

As the route leaves Arlington, the moderately heavy automobile traffic along State Route 530 will be annoying, but the wide, paved shoulder is adequate and alleviates the dangers associated with highway riding. After only a few miles, a small roadside grocery in Trafton offers a few snacks. At the turnoff to Jim Creek Naval Radio Station, an old two-story schoolhouse, complete with bell, is a picturesque landmark. Colorful pictures in the windows and interesting playground structures show that the school still serves its original purpose in contrast to the abandoned schoolhouses in so many rural areas. A steep grade near the base of Ebey Hill reaches a summit where green pastures stretch across many acres. As the route proceeds downhill between forest and pastures, the snow-laced crags of Three Fingers Mountain present a surprising panorama.

Towers march along the tops of ridges as the route continues up the gentle grade along Jim Creek Road to the wrought-iron portal proclaiming the Jim Creek Naval Radio Station. A sentry bars entry to visitors that have no active or retired military credentials or otherwise have not prearranged a tour with the base commander. Several miles of roads and trails as well as picnic and camping areas invite those who are allowed through the gate. The view through the gate reveals expansive lawns, several buildings, and a vast spider web of antenna structures spanning the valley between the ridge-top towers. For information on arranging access, call (206) 435-2162 or 1-800-734-1123, or write to: Outdoor Recreation, Jim Creek Naval Radio Station, 21027 Jim Creek Road, Arlington, WA 98223-8599.

Back at the first bend in the road, a broad gravel bar along the creek invites cyclists to stop. A water ouzel dips on top of a rock, jumps into the water, and comes out again to thrash a small fish against the rocky shore. When the fish is thoroughly limp and unresisting, down it goes with a gulp

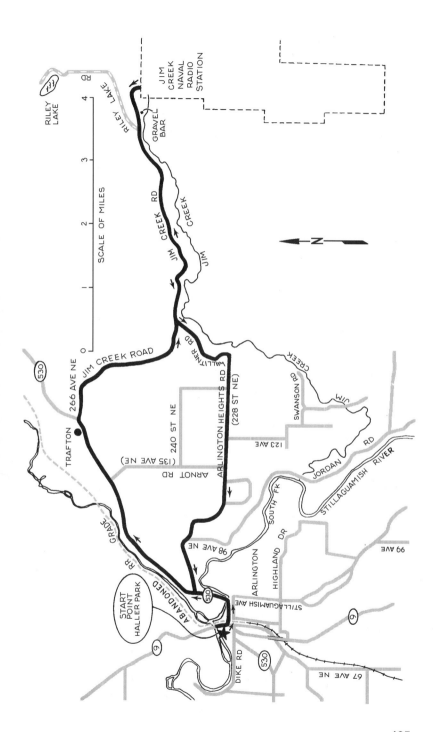

and the bobbing dance continues. The ride back to Arlington under a canopy of maple trees and over a winding, parklike road is uneventful but pleasant. Eventually, the road descends with a swish to the South Fork Stillaguamish, and the final mile leads back to Arlington.

MILEAGE LOG

0.0 Haller Park in Arlington. Leave park and head south on **N. West Avenue (State Route 9)**.

0.2 Turn left on **Burke Street (Avenue)**; cross railroad tracks. Continue straight ahead on **State Route 530** at stop sign as Broadway Street crosses at mile 0.4. Bridge over South Fork Stillaguamish River at mile 0.7. Trafton grocery and service station on left at mile 4.3.

4.5 Turn right on **Jim Creek Road (266 Street N.E.)**. Old Trafton school-house at this turn.

7.3 Keep left with Jim Creek Road as Wallitner Road goes right. Pass gravel bar at mile 10.5.

11.4 Entrance gate to Jim Creek Naval Radio Station. Turn around and return along Jim Creek Road.

15.4 Keep left on **Wallitner Road**. Road bends right and becomes **228 Street N.E. (Arlington Heights Road)**. Jordan Road intersects from the left at mile 19.9.

20.9 Turn left on **State Route 530**. Cross bridge over Stillaguamish River and enter Arlington on **E. Burke Avenue (Street)**.

21.7 Keep straight ahead on Burke Street as S.R. 530 turns left on Broadway Street N.

21.8 Turn right on **State Route 9 (N. West Avenue)** as Burke Street ends.

22.0 Back at Haller Park; end of tour.

33   LAKE CASSIDY

STARTING POINT: Jennings Memorial Park in Marysville. Take Marysville exit 199 (State Route 528) from I-5 and proceed through Marysville on S.R. 528 (4th Street). Turn left on 47th Street (Liberty) and follow thoroughfare to the park.

DISTANCE: 24 miles.
TERRAIN: Hilly.
TOTAL CUMULATIVE ELEVATION GAIN: 950 feet.
RECOMMENDED TIME OF YEAR: Any season.
RECOMMENDED STARTING TIME: 10 A.M.
ALLOW: 3 hours.
POINTS OF INTEREST
Jennings Memorial Park
Northwest Waterfowl Game Farm
   and Wildlife Preserve

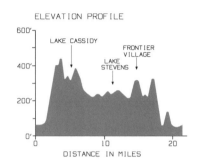

ELEVATION PROFILE
DISTANCE IN MILES

Why do we call this ride Lake Cassidy? The avid bird watcher will understand. Just imagine identifying canvasback, redhead, pintail, hooded merganser, shoveler, green-winged teal, bufflehead, wood, ruddy, golden-eye, scaup, ring-necked, baldpate, and other ducks on ponds near the marshy southern end of Lake Cassidy. This tour offers such an opportunity.

Although this is a relatively short tour, it is vigorous. The rider climbs the hill east of Marysville in steps before topping the summit and following backroads to Lake Cassidy. Our duck area is the Northwest Waterfowl Game Farm and Wildlife Preserve, licensed by the state and federal governments. The ducks have it made. They receive ample food in complete safety. Grass, reeds, and tules supply the shelter and natural material for the ground-nesting ducks, while boxes are provided for those ducks preferring a hole in which to nest. Occasionally, wild ducks fly into the pond and hobnob with the permanent residents, freeloading on the chow line. Canada, snow, Ross, and emperor geese are also raised at this farm.

The roads east of Lake Cassidy have views of Mt. Pilchuck and the Cascade foothills, with little traffic to dilute the enjoyment. Near Lake Stevens, traffic will pick up a little, but the roads are paved and the speed limit is low. East Lake Stevens Road takes the cyclist along the shoreline, where coots paddle away as they prepare for takeoff. Seagulls perch on piers and logs and generally ignore the bicyclist. Kingfishers sit atop sailboat mastheads, ready to plunge after any fish that catches the eye. Grebes scurry away on the surface of the water, or dive and disappear.

Wyatt Park on the west side of Lake Stevens has all the conveniences for a summer picnic, and although its restrooms are not open in fall and winter, a toilet is always available. A sandy swimming beach is surrounded by a pier with takeoff slots for water-skiers. Lifeguards preside in warm weather.

Houses crowd the shorelines and march up the hillside along Davies and Vernon roads. The freewheeling ride down Soper Hill Road is pleasant; then superb and unusual views of Everett and the Snohomish River delta fill the

127

western horizon as the rider proceeds along Sunnyside Boulevard into Marysville and back to Jennings Memorial Park.

Jennings Park is certainly one of the nicest for the bicycle tourist. The land was part of an old homestead donated to the city of Marysville in 1961 by the children of the original owners, Wilbur and Tilly Jennings. They asked that it be made a memorial park to their parents. The community has supported the project; garden clubs give many hours of service and others have donated equipment. The WSU Extension Service Demonstration Garden, old steam donkey, restored pioneer home, military field piece, ravine, and duck pond are worthy of examination. The park is open all year and the heated restrooms are welcome in cold, wet weather. This park deserves considerate treatment by cyclists.

MILEAGE LOG

0.0   Jennings Memorial Park, Marysville; heated restrooms. Leave park and turn right on **Armar Avenue.**

0.3   Turn right on **Grove Street** and follow it out of town.

1.3   Turn right on **67th Avenue N.E.** as Grove Street ends.

2.1   Turn left on **64th Street N.E.** and head up the terraced hillside.

3.2   Turn right on **83rd Avenue N.E.**

4.3   Turn left on **E. Sunnyside Road**. Cross State Route 9 at mile 4.8 and continue on **42nd Street N.E.**

"Dear—uh—I'm getting wet. Uh—can't we go now?"

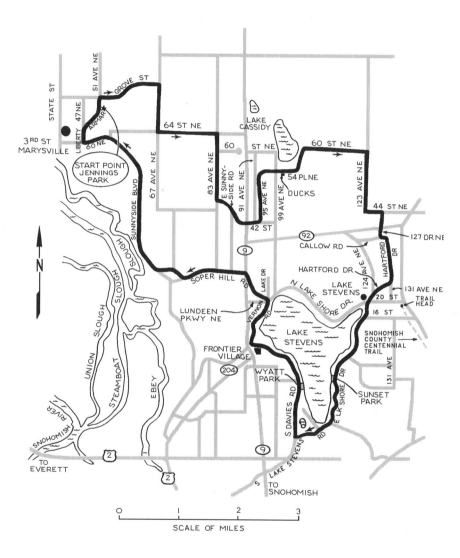

SCALE OF MILES

5.2 Turn left on **95th Avenue N.E.** Road bends right at mile 6.0 and is renamed **54th Place N.E.** At mile 6.5, stop at Northwest Waterfowl Game Farm and see how many ducks you can identify. Continue east on 54th Place N.E. as it bends around the south end of Lake Cassidy and is renamed **105th Avenue N.E.** and **60th Street N.E.**

8.2 Turn right on **123rd Avenue N.E.** as 60th Street N.E. ends.

9.2 Turn left with thoroughfare on **44th Street N.E.**

9.5 Turn right on **127th Drive N.E.** and cross State Route 92.

9.9 Turn left on **36th Street N.E.**, which bends right and becomes **Old Hartford Drive**, and finally **Hartford Drive**.

10.7 Turn right with Hartford Drive as 131st Avenue continues on.

11.3 Turn left on **124th Avenue N.E.** by Lake Stevens City Hall as North Lake Shore Drive continues on. Road is promptly renamed **E. Lake Shore Drive**. Sunset Park of the Snohomish County Park Department at mile 12.7. Concrete steps lead down to pier and pebbly beach. As the road continues south, it becomes **South Lake Stevens Road**. Tiny Stitch Lake is separated from the bigger lake by a bouncy peat bog.

14.4 Sharp right turn on **Davies Road** toward county park and boat ramp. Snohomish County's Millard A. Wyatt Park at mile 15.4; swimming, pier, shelter, tables, and restrooms. Continue on Davies Road and head uphill. Entrance to Frontier Village (cafe) at mile 16.5.

16.6 Turn right on **Vernon Road** and head downhill along the lake.

17.5 Cross Lundeen Parkway at stop sign and continue straight on **Soper Hill Road**. Almost immediately, turn left with Soper Hill Road as Lake Drive continues on. Cross State Route 9 at mile 18.3, continue uphill past the landscaped Hewlett Packard plant, then plunge down the other side of Soper Hill.

19.6 Turn right on **Sunnyside Boulevard** as Soper Hill Road ends on the edge of the valley east of Marysville. Enter Marysville on **60th Street N.E.** at mile 22.7.

22.8 Turn right on **47th Avenue N.E.** alias **Liberty** alias **Armar Road** and follow it back to Jennings Memorial Park at mile 23.6.

34   SNOHOMISH–MARYSVILLE

STARTING POINT: Snohomish Airport, Snohomish. Take exit 23A (State Route 522) from I-405, then State Route 9 to Snohomish, or take exit 194 (U.S. 2) from I-5, then south on State Route 9. Exit S.R. 9 on Airport Way just south of Snohomish and proceed northerly to airport. Park on the grass along road by the railroad track.

DISTANCE: 34 miles.
TERRAIN: Moderate to hilly.
TOTAL CUMULATIVE ELEVATION GAIN: 1250 feet.
RECOMMENDED TIME OF YEAR: Any season.
RECOMMENDED STARTING TIME: 9 to 10 A.M.
ALLOW: 5 hours.
POINTS OF INTEREST
Snohomish County Centennial Trail
Jennings Park
Snohomish Historic District

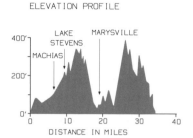

ELEVATION PROFILE

With the completion of the Snohomish County Centennial Trail from Snohomish to Lake Stevens in 1994, bicycling between these two cities becomes a pleasure. Plans have been made to extend the trail northward along the old abandoned railroad grade to Arlington and beyond, starting late 1996. Along the trail, two trailheads with parking area have been established, and picnic tables have been placed at convenient points for those who would like to picnic or just sit and enjoy the scenery. The Pilchuck River flows along the trail for much of its length, providing attractive views.

At Lake Stevens, bicyclists may enjoy a meal at one of several cafes and shorten the tour by riding along the eastern and southern shores of Lake Stevens, or continue along the lake's northern edge and over the hill to Marysville. Either way, the lake scenery includes several opportunities to watch the native waterfowl and the water sports enthusiasts.

At Marysville, a number of food services are offered in the city's shopping district, but Marysville's Jennings Park provides an unusually enjoyable setting for a picnic lunch. A demonstration garden maintained by Washington State University's Extension Service volunteer Master Gardeners offers many tips for successful gardening. Picnic tables along Allen Creek and the pond formed by a small dam provide opportunities to share a picnic lunch with the local waterfowl.

On the return to Snohomish, low-traffic roads offer views of the estuarial Snohomish River and its several sloughs before climbing over the hill to the edge of the city of Snohomish. On the way, the route passes through the base of a power line tower. With dates of their construction proudly displayed on their porches, homes in the historic old residential district of Snohomish provide glimpses of past architecture before the tour returns to the Snohomish airport.

MILEAGE LOG

0.0 Leave the Snohomish Airport, turn left on **Airport Way**, and cross railroad tracks and the Snohomish River, where the road is renamed **Avenue D**.

0.3 Turn right on **First Street**.

0.8 Cross railroad tracks and turn left on **Willow Avenue**.

0.9 Cross Lincoln Avenue and bear right on **Wood Street**. At the next intersection, turn left on **Pine Avenue**. Cross Second Street (old U.S. 2) at stop sign.

1.6 Bear right on bikeway (**Centennial Trail**) as Pine Avenue crosses Maple Avenue. A trailhead with toilets is on the left at mile 3.2. Picnic tables under the U.S. 2 overpass provide comfortable shelter in inclement weather. Another trailhead with toilet facilities in the community of Machias at mile 6.4.

9.0 Turn left on **20th Street N.E.**

9.5 Cross Little Pilchuck Creek and turn left on **124th Avenue N.E.** in downtown Lake Stevens. Food services.

9.6 Turn right on **N. Lakeshore Drive (Vernon Road)** and ride along the lake. *Note: Ride may be shortened by 14 miles by continuing along 124th Avenue, E. Lakeshore Drive, and S. Lake Stevens Road to rejoin route at log mile 27.6.*

11.2 Turn left on **Lundeen Parkway** as Vernon Road ends.

11.7 Go past 99th Avenue and turn right on **Soper Hill Road**. Almost immediately turn left and uphill with Soper Hill Road as Lake Drive continues on.

12.4 Cross State Route 9 with traffic light and immediately turn right on short, faint trail to paved, dead-ended **Densmore Road**.

13.4 Turn left on **E. Sunnyside School Road** as Densmore Road ends.

13.8 Turn left on **83rd Avenue N.E.** as Sunnyside School Road ends.

13.9 Turn right on **44th Street N.E.** and charge up and down hills. The road bends right at mile 14.9 and is renamed **67th Avenue N.E.**

15.4 Turn left at bottom of hill on **52nd Street N.E.** Turn right on **Sunnyside Boulevard** as 52nd Street ends. As it enters Marysville the road is renamed **Old Pacific Highway** and **61st Street N.E.**

17.0 Turn right at stop sign on **Liberty Street**. Continue with thoroughfare as it bends left on **Armar Road N.E.** A marked bikeway begins. Jennings Memorial Park, the nominal lunch stop, on the right at mile 17.6.

17.8 Turn right at stop/yield signs on **Grove Street**.

18.6 Cross Allen and Munson creeks and turn right on **64th Avenue N.E.**

18.9 Turn left on **71st Street N.E.**, then immediately right at stop sign on **65th Avenue N.E.**

19.1 Turn right on **69th Street** as 65th Avenue ends. The road immediately bends left and becomes **64th Drive N.E.**

19.4 Turn left at stop sign on **64th Street N.E.** as 65th Drive ends, then take the next right turn at traffic light on **67th Avenue N.E.**

20.3 Turn right on **52nd Street N.E.**, then left on **Sunnyside Boulevard** as 52nd Street ends.

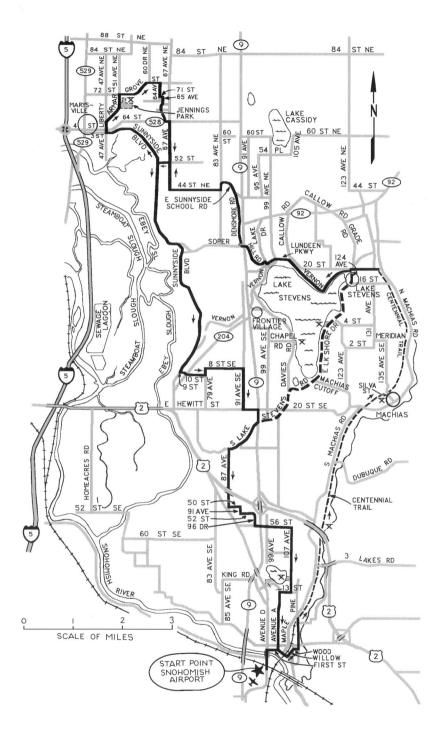

24.9 Turn left on **9th Street S.E.** at top of small rise and crank up steep hill. Cross State Route 204 and continue uphill on **10th Street S.E.**

25.5 Turn left on **79th Avenue S.E.** as 10th Street ends. Bend right with thoroughfare on **8th Street S.E.**

26.3 Turn right on **91st Avenue S.E.** as 8th Street ends.

27.1 Cross **20th Street S.E. (Hewitt Avenue)** and turn left on broad shoulder.

27.2 Turn right at traffic light on **State Route 9** and continue on shoulder.

27.6 Turn right on **S. Lake Stevens Road (23rd Street S.E.**).

28.4 Turn left under power lines on **87th Avenue S.E.** Go under power line tower and U.S. 2.

29.5 Turn left on **50th Street S.E.**, then right on **91st Avenue S.E.** as 50th Street ends. The road bends left and right and is renamed **52nd Street S.E.** and **96th Drive S.E.**

30.4 Turn left at stop sign on **56th Street S.E.** Cross State Route 9 and continue past drive-in cafe. The road bends right at mile 31.1 and becomes **107th Avenue S.E.** Enter Snohomish at mile 31.4. Hill Park is on the right at mile 32.1 as the road is renamed **Park Avenue.**

32.4 Turn right on **13th Street** at stop sign.

32.6 Turn left on **Avenue A** and proceed through the Snohomish historic residential area.

33.7 Turn right on **First Street** at stop sign at bottom of hill.

33.9 Turn left on **Avenue D** at stop sign. Cross the Snohomish River and railroad tracks.

34.2 Turn right into Snohomish Airport; end of tour.

SKAGIT COUNTY

35 ARLINGTON–ROCKPORT

STARTING POINT: Arlington, Snohomish County. Take Arlington exit 208 (State Route 530) from I-5. Park in public parking lot behind Rome Restaurant between 3rd and 4th streets on Olympic Avenue.

DISTANCE: Total, 109 miles: first day, 49 miles; second day, 60 miles.
TERRAIN: Flat to moderate.
TOTAL CUMULATIVE ELEVATION GAIN: 2100 feet: first day, 900 feet; second day, 1200 feet.
RECOMMENDED TIME OF YEAR: May, June, and September to avoid heaviest North Cascade Highway traffic.
RECOMMENDED STARTING TIME: 8 to 9 A.M. each day. This is a two-day ride with overnight camping at Rockport State Park, or motel or bed-and-breakfast lodging.
ALLOW: 2 days.
POINTS OF INTEREST
River and mountain scenery
Exhibits of old ferry barge and Indian dugout canoes at Steelhead Park in Rockport (Skagit County)
Washington State Department of Fisheries fish trap on the Baker River at Concrete

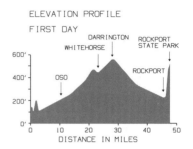

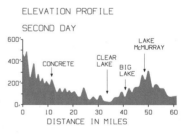

This rural ride starts at Arlington in Snohomish County, proceeds to Darrington in the foothills of the Cascades, then follows the Sauk River Valley to Rockport State Park in Skagit County for the night. The route east out of Arlington on State Route 530 follows the valley of the North Fork Stillaguamish River. Frailey Mountain makes an imposing, green backdrop to the north as the tour approaches the town of Oso. Farther along, 6820-foot Whitehorse Mountain reveals its impressive glaciers and snowfields. Squire Creek Snohomish County Park provides shade, shelter, and water for a picnic lunch, while Darrington caters to those who prefer restaurant fare.

Out of Darrington, the route follows the Sauk River, which has the characteristic gray-green color of silt from active glaciers on Glacier Peak to the southeast. The nearby foothills, however, rise too steeply to allow a view of this magnificent peak. Uninhabited forests offer occasional glimpses of wildlife; we have had a male ruffed grouse attack us from the underbrush, hiss, then fly back to a stump to strut. The Skagit River flows by just before the route enters the little town of Rockport, where a Skagit County park by the river offers fishing, picnicking, and camping. Exhibits of old Indian dugouts and the ferry barge that preceded the present bridge make this worth a stop. Rockport State Park, one mile west on State Route 20, has 62 campsites that include 12 walk-in sites, Adirondack shelters, a group camp, picnic area, and restrooms with hot showers. Several hiking trails in this 447-acre park await those who have not had enough exercise.

From Rockport State Park, the route follows State Route 20 along the Skagit River toward Concrete. At the confluence of the Baker River and the Skagit River, the Department of Fisheries has an unusual fish trap. Walkways for viewing and descriptive posters invite the visitor to stop. Little is left now of the old Portland cement-manufacturing plant just west of Concrete. Gray was the color of everything during its existence, as the fine powder settled on trees, flowers, lawns, and buildings. A pleasant mile of valley road separates Concrete from the Skagit River, where small streams lined with ferns make their way down the hillside and foxgloves grow in profusion, their tall, lavender spikes sparkling in the summer sun. Deer may quite unexpectedly appear along this road.

Leaving the river level, the rider goes up to the small settlement of Day Creek, where the store provides snacks. Again following the Skagit, the route intersects State Route 9 just south of Sedro Woolley and follows it most of the way back to Arlington. At Clear Lake, several small grocery stores may be open. At Big Lake, the roads on either side of the lake may be taken, but the west side enjoys better views and has less traffic. A corner grocery at the north end of the lake is open all week. Lake McMurray and a small settlement of the same name come into view at mile 97.0. The return to Arlington is completed through open valley farmland and forested countryside.

MILEAGE LOG

FIRST DAY

0.0   Arlington, Snohomish County. Turn right (north) from public parking lot behind Rome Restaurant on **N. Olympic Avenue**.

0.2   Turn right on **State Route 530 (Division Street)** and follow it as it bends left and right on **Broadway Street** and **Burke Avenue** and crosses the South Fork Stillaguamish River. Ryan Falls, spectacular in springtime, on the right at mile 7.0.

11.5   Turn right in the small town of Oso by the Oso General Store on **Oso Loop Road**. Turn left at T junction after crossing the river. Rejoin **State Route 530** after 2.0 miles. Whitehorse grocery and service station at mile 23.0. Squire Creek Snohomish County Park with picnic tables, restrooms, water, and campsites at mile 24.0.

28.0   Enter Darrington; cafes, motels and grocery, small fenced city park. Turn north with State Route 530 (**Randall Street**) along the Sauk River toward Rockport.

36.2   Cross the Sauk River and keep left with S.R. 530. Right fork of the road goes to the Suiattle River hiking trails. *Note: Alternative route to Concrete and Day Creek for those not planning to stop at Rockport State Park goes left across the Sauk River on Concrete-Sauk Valley*

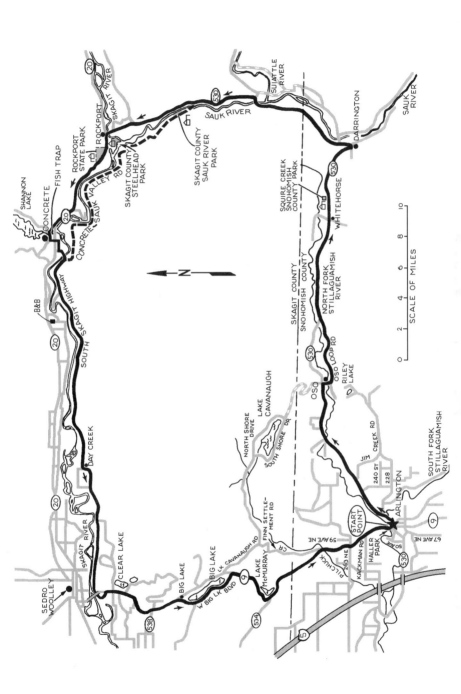

Road at mile 40.0. Skagit County Sauk River Park, with primitive campsites, just across bridge.

47.5 Cross the Skagit River and pass Howard Miller Skagit County Steelhead Park in Rockport; cafe, motel, grocery. Old Skagit ferry and Indian dugout canoes on display in park; picnic area, campground, restrooms with hot showers. Continue toward State Route 20.

47.8 Turn left on **State Route 20** as S.R. 530 ends.

49.0 Turn right into Rockport State Park for overnight camping.

SECOND DAY

0.0 Leave Rockport State Park, turn right, and continue west along the Skagit River on **State Route 20**.

7.0 Go past motel and turn right on **Everett Avenue**, then left on **Main Street** on old highway. State Fisheries Department trap on Baker River at mile 7.3. Cross Baker River on **Thompson Street** into town of Concrete. Small city park on the left with shelter at mile 7.7.

7.8 Turn right on **Main Street** and continue through Concrete.

8.2 Turn left on **Superior Avenue**, descend hill, and cross S.R. 20. *Note: Motel and cafe 1.2 miles right on S.R. 20; bed-and-breakfast, 6 miles right.*

8.6 Turn right on **Cedar Street** as Superior heads uphill toward high school.

8.8 Turn left on **Concrete-Sauk Valley Road** at stop sign as Dalles Road goes on.

9.7 Cross the Skagit River and turn right (west) along south side of the river on **South Skagit Highway** as Concrete-Sauk Valley Road goes left to Darrington. Day Creek community and store at mile 24.4.

33.9 Turn right on **State Route 9** just after passing under this highway south of Sedro Woolley. Go through Clear Lake at mile 35.2.

40.5 Turn right on **West Big Lake Boulevard** and follow around the west side of Big Lake.

44.9 Turn right on **State Route 9**. Pass Lake McMurray (grocery) at mile 48.7 and continue on S.R. 9 into Arlington.

59.2 Turn left on **Division Street** in Arlington, then right on **N. Olympic Avenue**.

59.5 Turn left into public parking area behind Rome Restaurant; end of tour.

36 ARLINGTON–LAKE CAVANAUGH

STARTING POINT: Haller Park in Arlington. Take exit 208 (Arlington, State Route 530) from I-5. In Arlington, proceed 0.3 mile north on State Route 9 to park on left just before S.R. 9 crosses the Stillaguamish River.

DISTANCE: 48 miles; 5 miles unpaved.
TERRAIN: Mountainous.
TOTAL CUMULATIVE ELEVATION GAIN: 1550 feet.
RECOMMENDED TIME OF YEAR: June through mid-October.
RECOMMENDED STARTING TIME: 8 to 9 A.M.
ALLOW: 6 hours.
POINTS OF INTEREST
View of Three Fingers and Whitehorse mountains
Arlington Trout Hatchery

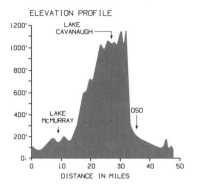

Five miles of this tour are on dirt or gravel roads, into the hinterland north of Frailey Mountain in Skagit County. An exceptionally steep hill on gravel must be negotiated, so this ride is not recommended for bicycles with narrow tubular tires. Two-wheel brakes are mandatory. The territory explored will give the feeling of being away from it all, deep in the heart of the forest.

The first part of this trip follows busy State Route 9 north out of Arlington through rural countryside where cattle graze in lush pastures. Managed tree farms, harvested a decade ago, are now covered with young Douglas fir trees, the replanting having been very successful. The small community of Lake McMurray enjoys a quiet, rural existence until the first day of fishing season brings in urban sport fishing enthusiasts by the score. As the route turns toward Lake Cavanaugh, the country homes soon disappear and the dense second-growth forest closes in on the narrow road, punctuated with new clearcuts. Occasionally, Pilchuck Creek pulls alongside with its splashing rapids and deep cauldrons. Not until the road widens near the junction of Northshore and Southshore drives around Lake Cavanaugh does civilization with its summer homes, people, and sounds reappear. Only one short interval along Northshore Drive is too steep and precipitous to allow even a cabin along the shoreline. Power boats and water-skiers crisscross the lake on a warm summer day, while on cold, rainy days, well-stoked wood stoves fill the air with the pleasant smell of burning fir and alder wood. Dense forest surrounds the rider as the route continues up the steep slopes east of Lake Cavanaugh. One false summit and an ensuing dip precede the true peak and the precipitous plunge down to the Stillaguamish Valley. Continue cautiously down the steep, gravel road. Logged clearings are numerous, but the rider will be much too busy watching the rough roadway to notice them. The resumption of the pavement near Oso is most welcome.

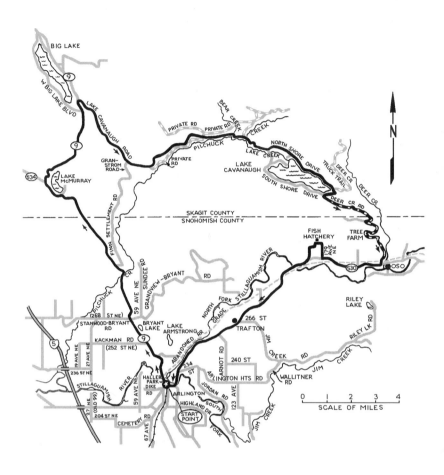

A visit to the fish hatchery near Arlington provides an informative side trip. Houses are slowly but surely creeping toward the Cascade foothills along the Stillaguamish Valley. This becomes most obvious as the rider returns to Arlington via State Route 530.

MILEAGE LOG

0.0 Haller Park in Arlington, Snohomish County. Head north on **State Route 9** and cross the Stillaguamish River. Cross Pilchuck Creek on a narrow bridge at mile 5.1. At mile 5.4, ignore Finn Settlement Road as it is marked on the right to Lake Cavanaugh. Enter Skagit County at mile 7.9. Public fishing access road on Lake McMurray at mile 9.0. Lake McMurray Store at mile 10.2.

10.4   Keep right with S.R. 9 as State Route 534 goes left to Mt. Vernon.

14.7   Turn sharp right on **Lake Cavanaugh Road** as S.R. 9 executes an uphill S curve.

25.2   Keep left on **Northshore Drive** as Southshore Drive goes right. Lake Cavanaugh, Three Fingers Mountain, and Whitehorse Mountain are visible between summer homes that crowd the shoreline.

29.3   Turn left and uphill on **Deer Creek Road** at a small wye just short of a fire station and a grocery. Pavement ends at mile 29.5. Crank over the first summit and drop 150 feet that must be recovered again in the climb up a very steep hill to the final summit at mile 31.6. Start steeply

"Steep gravel? I can handle it!"

downhill. Road levels out and paved surface begins at mile 34.4.

35.1 Turn right on **State Route 530** near bridge over Deer Creek in the small town of Oso. Oso General Store is to the left 0.2 mile on S.R. 530. No shoulders on S.R. 530.

37.7 Turn right on **179th Avenue N.E. (McGovern Road)** toward fish hatchery. Ride through Arlington Trout Hatchery grounds at mile 38.4.

39.4 Turn right on **State Route 530** and continue; shoulder is mostly paved. Trafton General Store at mile 43.8. Cross the South Fork Stillaguamish and enter Arlington on **Burke Avenue**.

47.8 Continue on Burke Avenue as S.R. 530 turns left on Broadway.

47.9 Cross railroad tracks and turn right on **State Route 9**.

48.0 Turn left into Haller Park; end of tour.

"I think they're trying to tell us something."

37   SKAGIT FLATS

STARTING POINT: Edgewater Park, Mt. Vernon. Take exit 226 (Mt. Vernon, State Route 536) from I-5. Proceed through Mt. Vernon on S.R. 536. After crossing the Skagit River, turn left on Ball Street or Baker Street, 0.2 mile to the park.

DISTANCE: 32 miles.
TERRAIN: Flat.
TOTAL CUMULATIVE ELEVATION GAIN: 170 feet.
RECOMMENDED TIME OF YEAR: Any season.
RECOMMENDED STARTING TIME: Anytime.
ALLOW: 3 to 4 hours.
POINTS OF INTEREST
La Conner
Flowering bulb fields (in season)

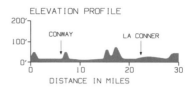

This is a ride with practically no hills, wandering through the rich farmland of Fir Island, formed by the North Fork and South Fork of the Skagit River, to La Conner, a quaint fishing village along the Swinomish Slough. The roads are paved and the traffic minimal. In summer, meadowlarks sing from the fence posts and fields. In spring and fall, ducks and geese wing across the sky. The Skagit Wildlife Recreation Area is a great place to see the migrating waterfowl, or just to ride the loop trails through this wetlands river delta.

The tour begins at Edgewater Park on the west bank of the Skagit River, crosses the river, and skirts the Mt. Vernon business district. After following a wandering slough, the road straightens out by a tall river dike and heads for the settlement of Conway, where the first hill, in the form of a concrete bridge, spans the South Fork Skagit River to Fir Island. Just beyond the bridge, a sharp right turn takes the rider north along the Skagit, beside another dike. This is flat country, and the dikes keep the river from flooding the farmland during heavy rains and spring runoff.

The junction of the two forks of the Skagit River was for many years the limit of navigable water for flat-bottomed river steamers, and Skagit City sprang up to handle the resulting regional freight and commerce. The notorious *Skagit Belle*, one of the last of the river steamers to ply these waters, was favored to become a floating restaurant but ended up being dredged piecemeal from the bottom of Elliot Bay near Pier 53 in Seattle.

Many dairy farms dot the valley; corn is grown for silage and canning and cabbage, broccoli, peas, and other vegetables flourish in the fertile delta. Solid rock hillocks that the glaciers could not grind away remain as forested knobs sprinkled here and there across the valley. Stone quarries and rock crushers now are slowly accomplishing what the glaciers failed to do.

From the top of one of the rocky knolls, an impressive, large-steepled church presides over the town of La Conner, nestled between the high rock and the Swinomish Slough. Many outstanding old homes are open for inspection during La Conner's annual Historic Home Tour. The Harvest

143

Hoedown and celebration also bring visitors to town to view the wares of local artisans. Several of the old homes are available for lodging as bed-and-breakfast inns. (See B&B Index.)

The return ride to Mt. Vernon takes roads through cornfields, farmyards, and colorful tulip fields. Suddenly, a side road appears, and for the first time the route runs along the top of the levee, presenting a view of the Skagit River and Mt. Vernon. A few houses spring up along the dike and the ride ends back at Edgewater Park.

MILEAGE LOG

0.0   Edgewater Park, Mt. Vernon. Leave park and turn right on **Ball Street**.

0.2   Turn right on **Division** and cross the Skagit River into downtown Mt. Vernon.

0.4   Sharp right turn on **Main**.

0.6   Turn left and downhill on **Kincaid**, then immediately right on **1st**, promptly renamed **Cleveland**.

1.0   Turn right on **Hazel**. Road bends left at mile 1.3 and is renamed **Britt Road**. Continue on Britt Road at mile 1.7 and follow along Britt Slough as Dike Road goes right.

3.4   Turn left on **Dike Road** as Britt Road ends.

7.4   Turn right on **Fir Island Road** in Conway onto the bridge over the South Fork Skagit River to Fir Island.

7.6   Turn sharp right on **Skagit City Road** by white church with tall steeple and ride along the dike beside the west side of the South Fork Skagit River. *Note: Turning left on Mann Road by church leads 3.7 miles to the Skagit Wildlife Recreation Area.* At mile 10.8, a side road leads over the dike 0.2 mile to a public fishing access on a sandy beach. Skagit City of bygone days lined the river here. Road bends left at mile 11.6 and becomes **Dry Slough Road**, following the base of the high dike along the North Fork Skagit River. Cross Moore Road at mile 11.8.

14.0   Turn right on **Polson Road** past a nursery.

15.5   Turn left on **Moore Road** and pedal along the dike.

16.4   Turn right and uphill on **Chilberg Road** and cross the North Fork Skagit River. Corner grocery on right at mile 17.0.

17.4   Turn left on **Dodge Valley Road**. Keep left as Valentine Road goes right at mile 18.5.

20.6   Turn left at stop sign on **Chilberg Road** toward La Conner as Dodge Valley Road ends.

21.4   Keep left on **Morris** into La Conner at the intersection with La Conner-Whitney Road. Monument to pioneers in center of traffic wye. Visit the waterfront along the Swinomish Slough; interesting shops, cafes. Retrace route back to the Pioneer Monument at the northeast end of town.

23.4   Continue east on **Chilberg Road** past dairy farms and around a hill.

25.6   Turn left on **Rudene Road**, then left again on **Best Road**.

26.0   Turn right on **Calhoun Road** and ride through fertile farmland. In April, acres of brilliant spring bulbs bloom near Bradshaw Road.

29.7   Road bends left and is renamed **Penn Road** and continues along a dike by the Skagit River.

30.9   Bear right onto the dike on **Behrens-Millett Road**. Views of the river as it flows past Mt. Vernon.

32.0   Back to Edgewater Park.

38 CAMANO ISLAND

STARTING POINT: (Weekends and bank holidays only.) Bank parking lot near island directory, Camano Island. Take exit 212 (State Route 532, Camano, Stanwood) from I-5. Go through Stanwood, over West Pass and Davis Slough to Camano Island. Turn left at wye by island directory sign on East Camano Drive, right on Sunrise Boulevard as S.R. 532 ends, then right into the bank parking lot.

DISTANCE: 24 to 41 miles.
TERRAIN: Hilly.
TOTAL CUMULATIVE ELEVATION GAIN: 2400 feet.
RECOMMENDED TIME OF YEAR: Any season.
RECOMMENDED STARTING TIME: 9 A.M.
ALLOW: 5 hours plus lunch or overnight.
POINTS OF INTEREST
Camano Island State Park
Views of Saratoga Passage

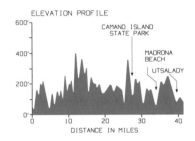

This is a scenic, hilly ride around Camano Island with a lunch stop at Camano Island State Park. Although it is a fairly strenuous ride of 41 miles, it can be shortened by taking any of several cross-island roads.

Every turn brings a new view as the cyclist pedals along the paved side roads of Camano Island. Houses shoulder each other along coves and beaches facing Port Susan as Mt. Baker and the northern Cascades dominate the eastern horizon. Tree-lined lanes wander through the older developments, while open clearings mark more recent plats. A summit is gained just as the rider rounds the south end of the island, followed by an exhilarating, long freewheel ride past steep driveways that head down to beach homes. Views of Saratoga Passage and Whidbey Island open up to the west. South Camano Island Grange, located just south of Elger Bay Grocery, is noted for the annual salmon bake held in July. For information on date of this event, call (360) 387-2312 or -2299. Traffic picks up at the Elger Bay Grocery as the direct route from the mainland causeway to the state park joins from the right. A very long, steep hill blocks the way, but once this summit is conquered the rest is easy.

Camano Island State Park has an extensive beach that yields clams at low tides; a short, wooden stairway leads from the picnic area to the beach. The eastern section of the park is reserved for camping, including coin-operated hot showers and a large group camp. Farther on, another contact with the beach can be made at Madrona and Sunset beaches. Mt. Baker comes into view as the rider rounds the north end of the island near Utsalady. The view is soon blocked by the headland, so enjoy it while you can. A short climb and a curving descent lead suddenly to the close of the ride.

MILEAGE LOG

0.0 Parking lot of Camano Branch of Whidbey Island Bank (nonbanking days only). Leave parking lot, turn left, cross East Camano Drive, and continue on **Sunrise Boulevard**.

2.4 Turn right on **Russell Road**.

3.1 Turn left on **Barnum Road**, then right on gravel road, and follow close to the water. Salt marsh stretches out into the bay to the east.

3.5 Turn left on **Lehman Drive** as gravel road ends.

5.2 Turn left on **East Camano Drive** for 0.5 mile.

5.7 Turn left and downhill on **Cavelero Road**.

6.2 Turn left on **Country Club Drive** as Cavelero Road ends.

6.5 Turn left on **Beach Drive** as Country Club Drive goes steeply uphill.

7.4 Turn left on **Country Club Drive** as Beach Drive ends.

8.0 Turn left on **E. Camano Drive** as Country Club Drive ends.

8.4 Turn left on **Cascade View Drive**. *Note: Turning right at mile 8.8 on Mt. Baker and continuing on Mountain View Road shortens the ride by 15 miles.* Continue straight at 9.1 as road name changes to **Highland Drive**. Road changes to a narrow, tree-lined lane.

10.0 Turn left on **East Camano Drive**. Grocery at mile 13.5. Round southern tip of Camano Island at mile 16.3 as road name changes to **West Camano Drive**. South Camano Island Grange at mile 24.0; site of annual salmon feed in July.

24.2 Turn left with West Camano Drive by Elger Bay Grocery and cafe, last refueling stop before the park. Freewheel down to the valley, then charge up "superhill."

Youth

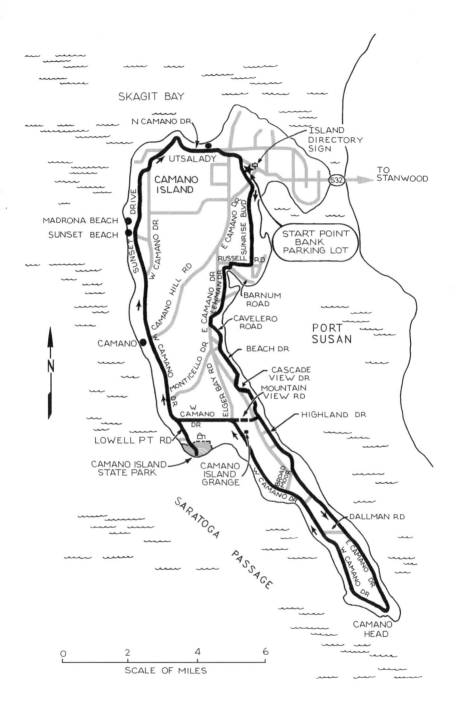

26.2 Turn left on **Lowell Point Road** toward Camano Island State Park. Keep right and downhill to the picnic grounds at mile 27.3. Stairway leads to the beach; water, tables, and pit toilets. After lunch, pedal uphill out of the park.

28.4 Turn left on **West Camano Drive**.

32.8 Keep left on **Sunset Drive** for a visit to Madrona Beach and Sunset Beach.

37.0 Turn left on **West Camano Drive**. As road turns east by grocery at mile 37.2, it becomes **North Camano Drive**.

40.5 Turn right on **Sunrise Boulevard**, then left into bank entrance.

40.7 End of ride at bank parking lot.

... mostly hilly with some flat.

39 LOPEZ ISLAND

STARTING POINT: Ferry landing at Upright Head on Lopez Island. Ferry leaves Anacortes, Skagit County. Take exit 230 (State Route 20) from I-5 and proceed west to Fidalgo Island. Follow signs to Anacortes and the ferry landing.

DISTANCE: 30 miles.
TERRAIN: Moderate.
TOTAL CUMULATIVE ELEVATION GAIN: 1600 feet.
RECOMMENDED TIME OF YEAR: Any season.
RECOMMENDED STARTING TIME: Early morning ferry from Anacortes; consult current ferry schedule.
ALLOW: 1 or more days. This can be the first stop of an island-hopping tour through the San Juan Islands.
POINTS OF INTEREST
Spencer Spit State Park
Views at Outer Bay

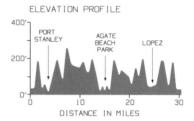

ELEVATION PROFILE

Although the white man has lived on Lopez Island since the 1850s, it is still rather sparsely settled and a single school in the center of the island houses kindergarten through grade 12. Farming was an important livelihood of the islanders during the 1930s, and exports included cream, eggs, meats, and grains. A few large farms remain today with acres of pastureland supporting beef cattle and herds of sheep. Lopez is not as hilly as the other major Puget Sound islands, a fact that is certainly a plus for bicycling.

Lopez Island boasts two San Juan County parks. Odlin Park, at the north end of the island, has overnight camping, while Agate Beach at the south end is limited to picnicking. Spencer Spit State Park, on the northeast part of the island, has campsites including several walk-in tent sites with tables among the young fir trees. A small group camp is available with running water and pit toilets. There is also a shelter near the end of the spit, where small boats can tie up at moorage facilities. Several miles of beach invite exploration, and numerous waterfowl along Spencer Spit entice the bird watcher. Birders will thrill at the sight of bald eagles soaring overhead or perching on the limbs of tall trees to survey their island habitat. Red-tailed hawks also occupy an important niche in the island's ecology.

The scenic ride along MacKaye Harbor to Outer Bay stays close to the water. Three bed-and-breakfast opportunities are offered at the southern end of the island, the one at MacKaye Harbor providing dinner meals. The Town of Lopez offers a grocery and a cafe, and resorts around Fisherman Bay welcome tourists.

Bicyclists should budget their time for this trip. A leisurely ride of around 30 miles or more can be completed easily in the ten hours between the mid-morning ferry arrival and early evening departure. If an extended cycling

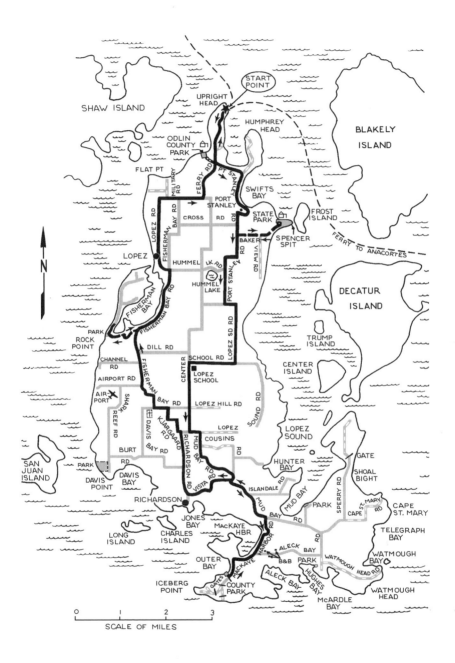

SHAW ISLAND

BLAKELY ISLAND

START POINT

UPRIGHT HEAD

HUMPHREY HEAD

ODLIN COUNTY PARK

FLAT PT

SWIFTS BAY

FROST ISLAND

PORT STANLEY

STATE PARK

SPENCER SPIT

FERRY TO ANACORTES

CROSS RD

BAKER VIEW RD

LOPEZ

HUMMEL

LK RD

HUMMEL LAKE

DECATUR ISLAND

FISHERMAN BAY RD

MILITARY RD

FERRY RD

PT STANLEY RD

LOPEZ RD

PORT STANLEY RD

LOPEZ SD RD

TRUMP ISLAND

CENTER ISLAND

PARK

ROCK POINT

DILL RD

CENTER SCHOOL RD

SCHOOL RD

CHANNEL RD

AIRPORT RD

AIR-PORT

SHARK REEF RD

DAVIS BAY RD

KJARGAARD RD

BURT RD

LOPEZ SCHOOL

LOPEZ HILL RD

SOUND RD

LOPEZ SOUND

SAN JUAN ISLAND

PARK

DAVIS POINT

DAVIS BAY

RICHARDSON

LOPEZ COUSINS RD

MUD BAY RD

RICHARDSON RD

VISTA RD

ISLANDALE

HUNTER BAY

MUD BAY RD

MUD BAY RD

PARK

SPERRY RD

CAPE RD

GATE

SHOAL BIGHT

ST. MARY RD

CAPE ST. MARY

LONG ISLAND

JONES BAY

CHARLES ISLAND

MACKAYE HBR

MACKAYE HARBOR

ALECK BAY

B&B

PARK

WATMOUGH HEAD RD

TELEGRAPH BAY

WATMOUGH BAY

OUTER BAY

ICEBERG POINT

GATES

COUNTY PARK

ALECK BAY

HUGHES BAY

McARDLE BAY

WATMOUGH HEAD

N

0   1   2   3

SCALE OF MILES

151

sojourn in the San Juan Islands is desired, convenient ferry-departure times on the following morning make island-hopping with bicycles an enjoyable experience.

MILEAGE LOG

0.0   Ferry landing at Upright Head, Lopez Island. Leave ferry and immediately begin uphill climb on **Ferry Road**.

1.3   Turn left on **Port Stanley Road**. Odlin County Park is on the right 0.4 mile. *Note: At mile 3.8, Baker View Road goes left 1.2 miles to Spencer Spit State Park; picnicking, camping, hiking, beachcombing.*

5.7   Turn left on **Lopez Sound Road** as Port Stanley Road turns right.

7.2   Turn right on **School Road** as Lopez Sound Road turns left.

8.2   Turn left on **Center Road** as School Road ends by Lopez Island School.

9.7   Turn left on **Mud Bay Road** as Center Road ends. Vista Road joins from the right as Mud Bay Road heads uphill at mile 11.5.

12.6   Turn right on **MacKaye Harbor Road** by fire station and bicycle rest area with mowed lawn, picnic table, water and pit toilets.

14.4   Agate Beach County Park, southern terminus of basic loop tour; picnic tables and pit toilets. Retrace route to Mud Bay Road.

16.2   Turn left on **Mud Bay Road**.

17.3   Turn left on **Vista Road** in the middle of a downhill run.

18.6   Turn right on **Richardson Road** as Vista Road ends.

20.0   Turn left on **Kjargaard Road** as Richardson Road turns right.

20.8   Turn left on **Fisherman Bay Road** as Kjargaard Road ends.

21.1   Turn right with Fisherman Bay Road as Davis Bay Road goes on past a large cemetery. Head downhill toward the bay at mile 22.6. Resorts along the bay shore. *Note: Optional, 1.5-mile side trip to the west side of the bay turns left on Bayshore Road at mile 23.0.*

24.8   Turn left on **Lopez South Road**. Lopez Village Market, cafe, bakery, post office, and deli at mile 25.0. As it turns right at mile 25.3, the road is renamed **Lopez North Road**. Continue on **Military Road** at mile 26.7 as it joins from the left.

26.9   Turn left on **Fisherman Bay Road** as Military Road ends.

27.3   Continue on **Ferry Road** with thoroughfare as Center Road goes right. Odlin County Park is on the left at mile 28.2. Continue over hill to the ferry landing at mile 29.6.

40 ORCAS ISLAND

STARTING POINT: Orcas ferry landing on Orcas Island. Ferry leaves Anacortes, Skagit County. Take exit 230 (State Route 20) from I-5 and proceed west to Fidalgo Island. Follow signs to Anacortes and the ferry landing.

DISTANCE: Basic route 49 miles; options to 80 miles.
TERRAIN: Numerous steep hills.
TOTAL CUMULATIVE ELEVATION GAIN: 4900 feet.
RECOMMENDED TIME OF YEAR: Any season.
RECOMMENDED STARTING TIME: Early morning ferry from Anacortes; consult current ferry schedule.
ALLOW: 1 to 3 days on the island.
POINTS OF INTEREST
Moran State Park
Mt. Constitution observation tower
Rosario

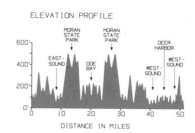

Shaped like a jagged horseshoe, Orcas, the largest of the San Juan Islands, is quite a challenge to the touring bicyclist. Close to 80 miles of roads, the majority of which are paved, traverse this rugged island. Several rides may be taken, depending on the time spent here. Moran State Park, on the east side of the horseshoe, is the most obvious place to camp. Walk-in campsites at Doe Bay and at Washington State Department of Natural Resources (DNR) Obstruction Pass Park provide camping alternatives. For those who do not wish to carry camping gear, hotels at Orcas and Eastsound, and resorts at Doe Bay, West Beach, and Deer Harbor offer rooms or cabins. The Doe Bay Resort also features American Youth Hostel accommodations. Bed-and-breakfast opportunities are listed in the B&B Index.

Beauty abounds. In spring, wild roses, hawthorns, madronas, and fruit orchards all are in blossom. In fall, each has a distinctive and colorful fruit. Several varieties of cattle, including the unusual white Charolaise, graze the grassland of valley farms, and herds of sheep roam across many acres. The chocolate-brown sheep occupy a special place of importance, as their wool is prized by hand weavers.

The nine-mile ride from Orcas to Deer Harbor proceeds through forested hills and valleys, skirts the waterfront at Westsound, and contours along the rocky cliffs above the sound before climbing a forested hillside and descending to Deer Harbor. Along the cliffs, madrona trees with red berries, peeling red bark, and large evergreen leaves are strikingly silhouetted against a blue fall sky. Oregon white oak also grow on the rocky hillside, accompanied by Douglas fir and lodgepole pine. In the fall, large flocks of waterfowl seek out the sheltered waters of West Sound: western grebe and bufflehead ducks, to name a few. Pairs of common loons, in full breeding plumage, peruse the waters in spring before ascending to their nesting sites on high mountain lakes. Bald eagles find the San Juan Islands suitable for their nests, placed in high trees near large bodies of water.

American kestrels occasionally accompany the bicyclist along the 8.5-mile ride from Orcas to Eastsound, where several flat, paved roads invite investigation. A ride to the beach on the North Beach Road is suggested. Continuing on the Horseshoe Highway past Eastsound, a long, steady uphill grade leads to Moran State Park. Here at a 350-foot elevation, Cascade Lake shimmers in a peaceful forest setting. Hiking trails offer a diversion; the strong and low-geared may enjoy the bicycle ride to the top of 2409-foot Mt. Constitution.

Two miles along the route past Mt. Constitution, a side road leads a mile to the turnoff on a dirt road to the DNR Obstruction Pass Park. The trailhead, with parking lot and pit toilets, is an additional mile beyond. Bicycles must be walked or carried an additional half mile to the campsites above the beach; there are tables, fire pits, garbage cans, and pit toilets but no potable water. Mooring buoys for boats indicate that this park is intended for the water-borne public. A store at the marina at the end of Obstruction Pass Road offers groceries. Doe Bay, three miles from the Obstruction Pass side road, is the turn-around point for our basic tour of Orcas Island. Beyond Doe Bay the road surfaces gradually deteriorate into gravel, and all roads lead to private property. Resort facilities at Doe Bay include dormitory, cabin, camping, and duplex motel-unit accommodations, all with kitchens or kitchen privileges, and hot tubs fed by local hot springs. The cafe is open spring and summer months only.

Just before the western entrance to Moran State Park, a short, steep side road leads down to Rosario, the former Moran estate, now converted into a plush resort. A number of residences and country estates hug the hill above the resort. A "boatel" brings in the boating fraternity. Varied concert programs at the resort are open to the public.

One other road not to be overlooked is the one to West Beach. Continuing south toward Westsound along the edge of Crow Valley, the road runs along the ridge as the valley panorama passes beneath. Beautiful, creamy-white plumes of the oceanspray will greet the June and July bicyclist. Its straight young shoots were used for arrows by the native Indians.

The remaining major road on the island proceeds east out of Orcas toward Dolphin Bay and Killebrew Lake. The first two miles are paved, but the remaining six are not. The hills are steep, numerous, and forested. There are no rewarding views of the sound, unless an obscure dirt side road to Dolphin Bay is taken. This road is not recommended unless the rider feels very energetic.

MILEAGE LOG

0.0 Ferry landing at Orcas, Orcas Island. Turn left past Orcas Hotel and head uphill on the **Horseshoe Highway**. Deer Harbor Road goes left to Westsound and Deer Harbor at mile 2.6. Island directory sign at mile 5.2. Continue through Eastsound at mile 8.3; cafes, drive-in, grocery store. Road traverses a short, steep hill and returns to water level along Crescent Beach, where cultured oyster beds appear at low tide.

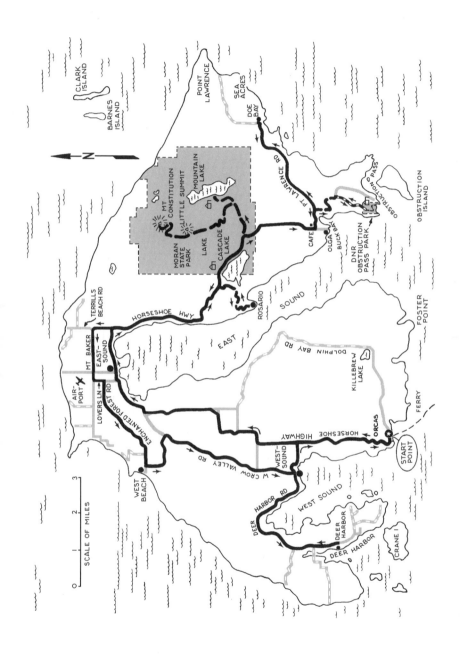

9.4 Turn right with Horseshoe Highway as Terrills Beach Road goes left. Pass a cafe at mile 9.8 and begin a strenuous climb up a mile-long grade. *Note: Side road to Rosario on right at mile 12.5.* Enter Moran State Park at mile 12.6. Campgrounds along Cascade Lake at miles 13.1, 13.4, and 13.6. Foot trails encircle the lake.

14.0 Basic route continues right with main road. *Note: Road to left goes uphill to campgrounds at Mountain Lake and to the top of Mt. Constitution, a vigorous side trip.*

16.0 Turn left with thoroughfare by cafe as Olga Road continues to Olga. *Note: Optional side trip on the right to DNR Obstruction Pass Park and Obstruction Pass marina and store at mile 16.5.*

19.4 Doe Bay, turn-around point for basic tour. Return back along route toward Eastsound.

29.3 Continue on **Terrills Beach Road** as Horseshoe Highway turns left to Eastsound.

29.8 Bear left with thoroughfare on **Mt. Baker Road** as Terrills Beach Road turns right.

31.0 Pedal past Eastsound Airport and turn left with thoroughfare on **Lovers Lane**.

31.3 Turn right on **Enchanted Forest Road** and crank up a steep hill toward West Beach.

33.6 Turn left on **West Beach Road** as Enchanted Forest Road continues on to West Beach. Woodlawn Cemetery on the left at mile 34.3.

34.8 Turn right on **W. Crow Valley Road** and proceed along the south side of Crow Valley.

38.4 Turn right on **Deer Harbor Road** as Crow Valley Road ends in Westsound. Pedal along cliffs overlooking West Sound. Reach Deer Harbor at mile 42.1; cafe. Return to Westsound at mile 45.8 and continue along the waterfront.

46.7 Turn right toward Orcas on **Horseshoe Highway**.

49.3 End of tour at ferry landing in Orcas.

Whale Watching

41   SAN JUAN ISLAND

STARTING POINT: Ferry landing at Friday Harbor on San Juan Island. Ferry leaves Anacortes, Skagit County. Take exit 230 (State Route 20) from I-5 and proceed west to Fidalgo Island. Follow signs to Anacortes and the ferry landing.

DISTANCE: Basic loop, 30 miles; options to 55 miles.
TERRAIN: Hilly to strenuous.
TOTAL CUMULATIVE ELEVATION GAIN: Basic loop, 2500 feet; options to 4500 feet.
RECOMMENDED TIME OF YEAR: Any season.
RECOMMENDED STARTING TIME: Early morning ferry from Anacortes; consult current ferry schedule.
ALLOW: 2 to 3 days. As the drive to Anacortes and the ferry ride to San Juan Island take several hours, we strongly advise making the San Juan Island tour at least a two-day weekend. The following accommodations are available:
1. Motels, hotel, and AYH hostel in Friday Harbor.

2. Bed-and-breakfast opportunities at various locations on the island.
3. Lakedale campground, 4.5 miles northwest of Friday Harbor at junction of Roche Harbor Road and Egg Lake Road.
4. San Juan County Park, with designated bicycle camping area.
   The San Juan national historic parks at American Camp and English Camp do not have camping facilities, nor does Lime Kiln Point State Park or the county park at Cattle Point.
5. Pedal Inn Bicycle Camp by False Bay.

POINTS OF INTEREST
American Camp
English Camp
Lime Kiln Point State Park
Cattle Point Light

ELEVATION PROFILE

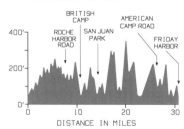

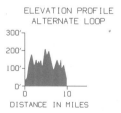

Back in the 1850s, it was unclear whether Britain or the United States owned San Juan Island, and the people living there were divided in their allegiance. When a prize English pig uprooted an American potato patch and the American shot the pig, a heated argument began. Sides were taken and a full-fledged battle nearly developed as both the British and the Americans moved in soldiers and supplies and set up armed garrisons. Cooler heads prevailed and a boundary commission was appointed to settle the dispute. After 12 years of deliberation, the commission failed to come to an agreement, and the dispute was brought to the arbitration of Kaiser Wilhelm I of Germany. In 1872, he decided in favor of the Americans, fixing the boundary as Haro Strait, west of San Juan Island. The British garrison moved out, and the remaining settlers swore allegiance to the United States.

Today, both the English and American camps are part of San Juan Island National Historic Park, with park headquarters at American Camp on the barren, wind-swept southeast tip of the island. At American Camp, two original buildings have survived and the remains of the redoubt, the principal defense work, are well preserved. The interpretive shelter, containing an exhibit that describes the historical background of the American-British boundary dispute, marks the head of a self-guided interpretive trail.

English Camp, recently renamed British Camp and established on the broad, sheltered cove of Garrison Bay, boasts three original buildings—barracks, blockhouse, and commissary—that have been restored to their original condition. The small, formal gardens have also been restored and are maintained beside the broad, grassy beach. Large cedar and maple trees, along with an old orchard complete the picturesque scene. No wonder the early-day soldier considered this a choice duty post.

Friday Harbor, county seat of San Juan County, fronts on a deep-water bay on the eastern side of San Juan Island. The Washington State ferries dock here after a two-hour run from Anacortes. With the exception of a food concession at Roche Harbor, all the island's commercial, governmental, and educational facilities are located in Friday Harbor.

The University of Washington's Oceanographic Laboratories are across the bay from Friday Harbor on 484 acres of land, given to the university by an act of Congress in 1921. The land, formerly a military preserve, was ceded to the the university specifically for a marine laboratory. The site is preserved as a biological preserve and no hunting is allowed. Although the laboratories are active all year, the major work and study programs are carried on in summer.

Marine views are superb from a number of places on San Juan Island. Near San Juan County Park on Smallpox Bay, ships ply Haro Strait on their way to Vancouver, British Columbia, while Vancouver Island, with Victoria at its southern point, lies across the strait. The broad expanse of water to the southwest is the Strait of Juan de Fuca, with the Olympic Peninsula beyond. When a fog bank rolls in, the spectacular view disappears, and the fog horn at Lime Kiln Lighthouse, just south of San Juan County Park in the new Lime Kiln Point State Park, begins sounding its mournful warning. Whale-watching platforms lie at trail's end in this state park, popular during whale migration season, June through September. From American Camp, not only are the Strait of Juan de Fuca, the Olympic Peninsula, and Haro Strait discernible, but also Cattle Point at the tip of San Juan Island with Lopez Island across the channel. If visibility is exceptionally good, Shaw and Orcas islands can be seen. From Cattle Point Park, the southern portion of Lopez Island appears across the San Juan Channel. Old concrete buildings, the remnants of a military installation, provide shelter for picnic lunches, but the water supply, although potable, has a pungent aroma.

If cyclists return to Friday Harbor with extra time before the ferry departure, they may want to ride the ten-mile, center-island loop into Beaverton Valley. Here farmers make good use of rainfall by constructing ponds to catch the runoff, conserving water for the dry summer season.

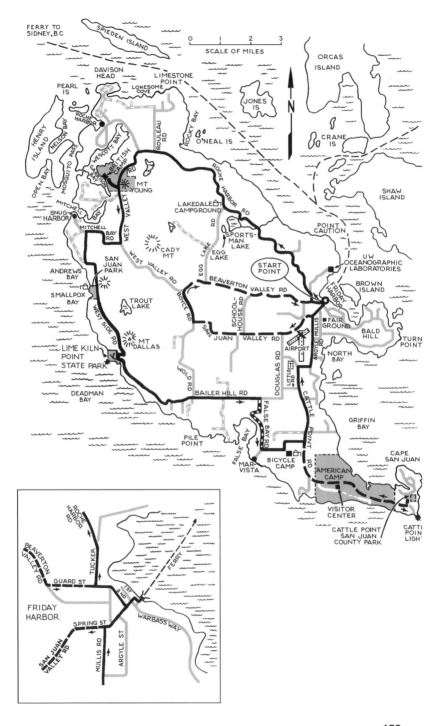

MILEAGE LOG

0.0 Ferry landing, Friday Harbor, San Juan Island. Leave ferry and head uphill on **Spring Street**.

0.2 Turn right on **Second Street**.

0.4 Turn left on **Guard Street**, then right on **Tucker Street**, which becomes **Roche Harbor Road** as it leaves Friday Harbor. Lakedale Campground on left at mile 4.5.

8.5 Turn left on **West Valley Road** as Roche Harbor Road continues on to Roche Harbor. Entrance to British (English) Camp National Historic Park on the right at mile 10.1.

11.6 Turn right on **Mitchell Bay Road** toward West Side Road and San Juan Park, as West Valley Road continues on to Friday Harbor. As road bends left at mile 13.0, it changes its name to **West Side Road**. San Juan Park on right at mile 14.8; camping. Lime Kiln Light and Lime Kiln Point State Park on right at mile 17.8. Road is renamed **Bailer Hill Road** at mile 19.1.

22.2 Turn right on **False Bay Road** (unpaved). Pavement resumes as road bends left at mile 24.0 and is renamed **False Bay Drive**. Pedal Inn Bicycle Camp at mile 24.8.

25.6 Turn left on paved **Cattle Point Road** as False Bay Road ends. *Note: Optional side trip turns right 1.9 miles to American Camp. Cattle Point Light and Cattle Point Park (San Juan County) are an additional 2.8 miles beyond.* Road name changes to **Argyle Road** at mile 28.2 and to **Mullis Road** at mile 29.0.

29.4 Turn right on **Spring Street** in Friday Harbor as Mullis Road ends. Follow thoroughfare back to ferry landing at mile 30.0.

OPTIONAL CENTER LOOP

0.0 Ferry landing. Head out of Friday Harbor on **Spring Street**. As it leaves Friday Harbor, it is renamed **San Juan Valley Road**.

4.4 Bear right on **Boyce Road** as San Juan Valley Road ends and Wold Road goes left.

5.4 Turn right on **Beaverton Valley Road** as Boyce Road ends and West Valley Road goes left.

9.0 Turn left on **Guard Street** in Friday Harbor.

9.6 Bear right on **Second Street**.

9.8 Turn left on **Spring Street**.

10.0 Back at ferry landing.

KITSAP COUNTY

42   BAINBRIDGE ISLAND

STARTING POINT: Washington State ferry terminal at Pier 52, Seattle. Take ferry to Winslow on Bainbridge Island.

DISTANCE: 20 to 39 miles.
TERRAIN: Hilly.
TOTAL CUMULATIVE ELEVATION GAIN: 3000 feet.
RECOMMENDED TIME OF YEAR: All seasons.
RECOMMENDED STARTING TIME: Early morning ferry; consult current ferry schedule.
ALLOW: 8 hours including lunch and ferry.
POINTS OF INTEREST
Frog Rock
Kane Cemetery and old homes in
    Port Madison

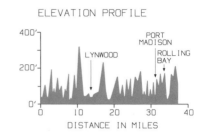

ELEVATION PROFILE

Many miles of road run along the fascinating salt-water harbors and beaches of Bainbridge Island. At Winslow, protected Eagle Harbor shelters many boats and for a century has been the home of timber-processing industries.

Interesting marine views toward Seattle are afforded along Country Club Road with little Blakely Rock in the foreground. It is easy to appreciate what a spectacular view of Mt. Rainier Captain Vancouver had when he landed at Restoration Point in 1792. Here also the calm waters of Blakely Sound attract flocks of wintering ducks such as baldpate, bufflehead, goldeneye, and scoters.

From Fort Ward State Park, the views of Rich Passage and the Kitsap Peninsula north of Port Orchard are panoramic, and the old gun emplacements look down on the water with a 240-degree sweep of the horizon. Be careful of poison ivy patches in this area. Although park facilities here are limited, future development is planned. The beach at Fort Ward State Park is inviting on warm, summer days. In winter, jet-black cormorants line up on linear remains of old piers that now serve as cormorant drying racks.

The beach road west of Lynwood gives the bicyclist a view of Sinclair Inlet and the Kitsap Peninsula beyond. The area around Fay Bainbridge State Park offers beach walks and views of the shipping lanes through the sound. Along Manitou Beach, the road is squeezed between the water's edge and a row of waterfront homes.

Although located in Kitsap County with land ties to Bremerton, Bainbridge Island serves as a bedroom community for Seattle. Many retired people live here the year round; others occupy homes during the summer. Arts and crafts are very popular pursuits here and are attractively displayed at the center in Winslow.

This island is rather typical of islands in Puget Sound in that the roads usually go up and down, sometimes quite steeply, with level stretches being a rarity. Madrona trees are prevalent, as is the evergreen huckleberry. Ivy, escaped to the wild, grows over bushes and trees; around Port Madison, the narrow, twisted roads are lined with tall firs and cedars that have ivy twining up their trunks for many feet. Also near Port Madison, the old cemetery will appeal to the historian and tombstone buff. Frog Rock, an appropriately painted boulder, greets the traveler at a major intersection south of Port Madison.

On a cool day, the distinctive aroma of burning driftwood fills the air as the island residents use their stoves and fireplaces to take the chill out of their houses. Bainbridge Island has its own flavor—a slower, more relaxed atmosphere than that of the metropolis to which it is connected by Washington State Ferries.

The two state parks are suggested as picnic sites. Lunch provisions may be purchased at groceries in Winslow, Lynwood, Island Center, and Rolling Bay. There are cafes in both Winslow and Lynwood. Cyclists wishing a shorter ride than the 36-mile overall island loop can take a southern tour of approximately 20 miles or a northern tour of approximately 20 miles. These route modifications are obvious from the map. An optional trip to Battle Point Park, formerly a naval communications installation, adds three miles and a very steep hill to the basic loop tour.

MILEAGE LOG

0.0 Coleman Ferry Terminal, Pier 52, Seattle; Winslow ferry slip. Board ferry and fasten bicycles to bicycle moorage points. At Winslow, leave ferry and head uphill on **State Route 305**.

0.2 Turn left at traffic light on **Winslow Way E.** through the Winslow shopping area.

0.8 Turn right and uphill on **Grow Avenue**.

1.1 Turn left on **Wyatt Way N.W.** and continue left around Eagle Harbor. Road changes name to **Eagle Harbor Drive**.

2.0 Turn left with Eagle Harbor Drive. Road changes name to **Rockaway Beach Drive, Halls Hill Road**, and finally **Blakely Avenue**.

6.8 Turn left on **N.E. Country Club Road**.

8.5 Entrance gate to Restoration Point Country Club. View surroundings and head back along route.

9.4 Turn left on **Toe Jam Hill Road** toward South Beach. Steep grades both up and down.

10.7 Bear right on **N.E. South Beach Road** along water's edge. Views of Rich Passage, populated in season with goldeneyes, surf scoters, baldpates, harlequin ducks, and aquaculture pens.

11.6 Continue on South Beach Road as Fort Ward Hill Road goes right. Go around gate and follow trail into Fort Ward State Park. Picnic tables and pit toilets by boat launch at mile 12.4. Exit Fort Ward State Park at mile 12.5 and continue on **Pleasant Beach Drive N.E.**

13.1 Keep left with Pleasant Beach Drive as Oddfellows Road goes right.

13.9 Turn left in Lynwood on **Point White Drive**. Road changes name to

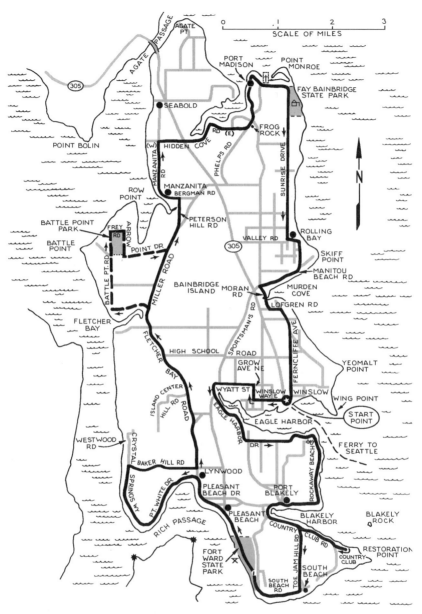

Crystal Springs Road.

16.5 Turn right on **N.E. Baker Hill Road** and climb over hill.

18.1 Turn left at stop sign on **Lynwood-Center Road**.

19.0 Turn left on **Fletcher Bay Road N.E.** Keep straight with main thoroughfare on **Miller Road** at mile 21.0 as Fletcher Bay Road swings left to a dead end. Grocery and restaurant at this intersection. *Note:*

Battle Point Road goes left at mile 21.4 to Battle Point Park; picnic tables. Optional side loop with return via Arrow Point Drive.

22.9 Bear left toward Manzanita on **Peterson Hill Road N.E.** If this turn is missed, go left on Bergman Road.

23.3 Turn left on **Bergman Road**, which is renamed **Manzanita Road** as it executes a dip and continues uphill.

24.6 Turn right on **Hidden Cove Road W.** Cross State Route 305 at mile 25.1 and continue on **Hidden Cove Road E.**

26.6 Turn left on **Phelps Road** toward Port Madison and Fay Bainbridge State Park. Continue past Frog Rock at mile 26.8.

26.9 Keep left at three forks by Port Madison historical monument and continue down to and along waterfront on **Euclid Avenue** in Port Madison. Follow Euclid uphill and left as it becomes a narrow, paved, tree-lined lane.

27.9 Turn left on **Fayette Avenue** toward Fay Bainbridge State Park. Kane Cemetery at mile 28.2. Road turns right in deep dip at mile 28.4 and is renamed **Sunrise Drive**.

28.6 Turn left into Fay Bainbridge State Park. This 17-acre state park has camping, clamming, swimming, picnicking, restrooms, and hot showers. Follow roadway through park.

29.0 Turn left on **Sunrise Drive** at park exit.

31.7 Turn left on **Valley Road** toward Manitou Beach as Sunrise Drive ends; grocery. Road bends right and becomes **N.E. Manitou Beach Road** at mile 31.9.

33.3 Turn left on **Moran Road** just before encountering State Route 305.

33.6 Turn left on **Lofgren Road**, which bends right at mile 34.0 and is renamed **Ferncliffe Avenue N.E.**

35.7 Turn right on **Winslow Way E.**

35.9 Turn left and downhill on **Olympic Avenue N.E. (State Route 305)**.

36.2 Winslow Ferry terminal; end of tour.

"Is this the day for the Chilly Hilly ride?"

43 KINGSTON–POINT NO POINT

STARTING POINT: Kingston in Kitsap County. From the north, take exit 181 (State Route 524, Lynnwood) from I-5 and follow signs to the Edmonds ferry terminal. From the south, take exit 177 (State Route 104) from I-5 to Edmonds ferry terminal. Turn right on Dayton Street past shopping center and park along Admiral Way.

DISTANCE: 28 miles.
TERRAIN: Hilly.
TOTAL CUMULATIVE ELEVATION GAIN: 1850 feet.
RECOMMENDED TIME OF YEAR: Any season.
RECOMMENDED STARTING TIME: Early morning ferry from Edmonds; consult current ferry schedule.
ALLOW: 5 hours.
POINTS OF INTEREST
Point No Point Lighthouse and Coast Guard Station
S'Klallam Indian Nation, Port Gamble Reservation

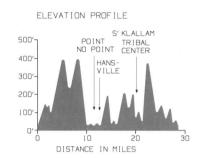

Our most vivid recollection of this ride is when a car roared past us, struck something in the road ahead, and careened on its way. We rode up and found the still-warm corpse of a male mink with gorgeous, chocolate-brown fur. We now have a tanned mink pelt.

Do not go on this ride to look for mink, however. Many other attractions await the bicyclist: seascapes, lighthouses, an Indian reservation, forest, and farmland. There are several opportunities for beachcombing near Point No Point and along Hood Canal. For a short, close-in ride, this has much to offer.

The rural aspects of this ride are apparent immediately upon leaving the Kingston ferry terminal. As soon as the inevitable ferry-landing hill is surmounted, the state highway is left behind, and woodland farms appear along little-used side roads. Great blue herons may rise ponderously out of any of the marshy areas along the road. The center road up to Hansville will have more traffic than the others on this ride, but not excessively so. Near the top of a hill at the eastern boundary of the Port Gamble Indian Reservation, the Klallam Indian Nation Store and Smoke Shop invites patrons. Several hills later, a long glide leads to the outskirts of Hansville and the turnoff to Point No Point.

At the point, parking space and access to the beach are severely limited by the Coast Guard station and adjoining private property. Bicycles may be parked along the fence by the road outside the station or wheeled out to the beach. Do not block the station's small parking lot. The beach is broad and sandy and is a good place to watch boaters searching for salmon. Foot traffic on the beach is unrestricted and beachcombing is permitted. The Coast Guard station and lighthouse are open to visitors in the afternoon. Along the way, a house has been built to resemble the bridge of a ship.

165

Bicyclists are always interested in knowing of local functions that offer food. At Buck Lake Park near Hansville, the Community Club prepares annual pancake breakfasts 8 A.M. to noon on the Saturday and Sunday closest to the Fourth of July. If Independence Day falls on a Wednesday, the breakfasts are prepared the following weekend. The menu consists of ham, eggs, and pancakes—all you can eat—at a reasonable price.

Leaving Hansville, the road climbs the hill overlooking Skunk Bay, but only occasional glimpses of the bay are possible. The road to Foulweather Bluff is also unrewarding for views. It is rough and full of chuckholes and can be ridden only with difficulty. The recommended route therefore turns south along Hood Canal Drive. Almost immediately, views open up across a new recreational development. The level riding here is deceptive, for soon the road turns a corner and heads steeply uphill. When it comes back down again and bottoms out on a sharp curve in a ravine, avoid the temptation to go shooting up the other side. A few steps down the ravine is an unusual view of Port Gamble and the Hood Canal Bridge. A foot trail leads to a wide, gravel beach. Trails also lead off into the forest along the bluff in either direction.

The tour through the Port Gamble Indian Reservation is most interesting and deserves a stop for examining the totem poles beside the Tribal Office Building and the Fire Hall-Health Center. A cemetery covers the grassy knoll above the water overlooking Port Gamble. Enjoy the rest stop, then tackle the long, steep hill out of the reservation to Hansville Road, followed by a downhill run to the state highway. The wide-shouldered highway provides for a rapid sprint to the Barber Cutoff Road, leading directly to Kingston and the ferry ride back to Edmonds.

MILEAGE LOG

0.0 Board ferry at Edmonds; secure bicycles to tie ropes, or position them where directed by ferry personnel. At Kingston, disembark and follow the exit route uphill through Kingston on **State Route 104**.

0.3 Turn left toward Indianola by community center, cross westbound lane of S.R. 104, and continue on **N.E. West Kingston Road**. Keep left at mile 0.7 as Barber Cutoff Road goes right.

0.9 Turn right and uphill with N.E. West Kingston Road.

2.6 Turn right on **Miller Bay Road N.E.** as West Kingston Road ends. Cross State Route 104 with traffic light at mile 3.6 and continue on **Hansville Road N.E.**; grocery. Klallam Tribal Store and Smoke Shop on the left at mile 5.6.

6.2 Turn right on **Old Hansville Road N.E.**, rejoining **Hansville Road N.E.** at mile 7.6.

10.5 Bear left on **Hansville Drive N.E.**

11.2 Rejoin **Hansville Road N.E.** and turn right toward Point No Point Lighthouse and Coast Guard Station. *Note: Buck Lake Park with restrooms and picnic tables is left on Buck Lake Road 0.7 mile.*

12.3 Point No Point U.S. Coast Guard Station. No beach fires or picnics. Return to Hansville Road N.E. and turn right through Hansville. Grocery in Hansville as the road bends left, changes name to **N.E.**

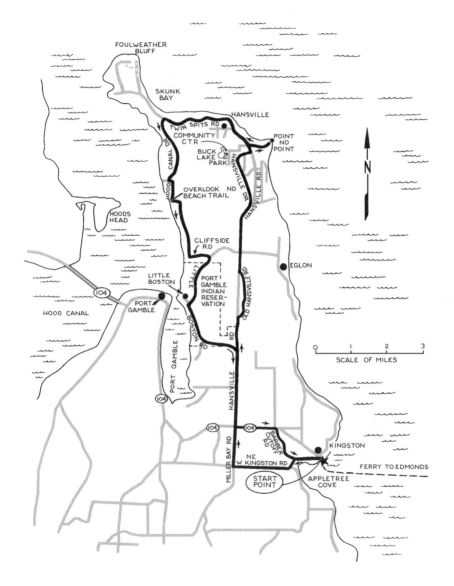

Twin Spits Road, and starts uphill.

15.5 Turn left on **Hood Canal Drive** and stay on it through several twists and turns of platted developments.

17.2 Turn left with Hood Canal Drive at T junction as Hood Canal Place goes right. At mile 18.2 at bottom of a dip where the road bends left, a trail leads right to a good viewpoint for Hood Canal and the bridge. Other trails lead down to the pebble-strewn beach. As road bends left at mile 19.1, it changes name to **N.E. Cliffside Road** and climbs an unusually steep hill.

19.7 Turn right and downhill on **N.E. Little Boston Road** as Cliffside ends. Enter Port Gamble S'Klallam Indian Reservation; Tribal Office Building, Fire Hall-Health Center, totem poles. Continue on Little Boston Road and proceed up a long hill.

23.2 Turn right on **Hansville Road N.E.**

25.2 Turn left at traffic light on **State Route 104 East**.

26.3 Turn right on **N.E. Barber Cutoff Road** as ferry holding lane begins. Parking area and trailhead for Nike Site County Park at mile 26.9.

27.3 Turn left on **N.E. West Kingston Road** as Barber Cutoff Road ends.

27.8 Turn right on **State Route 104** toward ferry terminal.

28.2 Ferry terminal. Board ferry and return to Edmonds.

Road Kill

44   SOUTHWORTH–PORT ORCHARD

STARTING POINT: Lincoln Park in West Seattle. From I-5 in Seattle, take exit 163 or 163A (Spokane Street and West Seattle). Cross Duwamish Waterway to West Seattle, climb hill, and at traffic signal continue through on Fauntleroy Avenue (follow Vashon ferry signs). Park in Lincoln Park (north parking lot), three blocks north of Fauntleroy ferry terminal.

DISTANCE: 29 miles.
TERRAIN: Moderately hilly.
**TOTAL CUMULATIVE ELEVATION
GAIN:** 1400 feet.
RECOMMENDED TIME OF YEAR:
Any season.
RECOMMENDED STARTING TIME:
9 A.M. ferry.
ALLOW: 5 hours plus lunch.
POINTS OF INTEREST
View of Bremerton Naval Yard
Manchester State Park

ELEVATION PROFILE

After a ferry ride from the Fauntleroy terminal in Seattle to Southworth in Kitsap County, the bicycle route follows the shoreline on secondary roads to Port Orchard. Views of Puget Sound, the Olympics, Blake Island, Seattle, Bainbridge Island, and the Bremerton Naval Yard open up along this route.

As the ride begins at Southworth, the western terminus of the ferry from West Seattle, the inevitable hill at the landing is a short one, and the route quickly leaves the main highway and threads through the narrow, curving streets of the residential section close to the shoreline. In the several shallow, sheltered coves between Southworth and Port Orchard, bird watchers will find flocks of wintering ducks paddling away in waves as bicycles approach. The pilings of the old ferry slip near Harper have been replaced by a fine new fishing pier.

Manchester has a good view of Seattle, being directly across from Alki Point. This little town passed its hundredth birthday in October 1971; it, too, hosted a ferry to Seattle at one time. A grocery store can provide food supplies. Gasoline storage tanks sprout out of the hillside on the naval reservation near Manchester. Visitors to Manchester State Park look across Rich Passage toward Fort Ward on the southern tip of Bainbridge Island. Old fortifications are fenced off for safety, but a former torpedo storage building now serves as a spacious picnic shelter. Interpretive trails and a well-appointed campground round out the park facilities.

Along the inland leg of this ride, pastures and forest line the road. Fragrant pink roses supply quantities of rose hips in the fall and winter. Wild honeysuckle drapes over trees and fences, with orange-colored blossoms in May and June, while clematis climbs high in the branches. White snow-berries hang on their bushes until late winter, reserved by the birds for emergency rations only because of their bitter taste.

The naval mothball fleet at the Bremerton Naval Yard comes into view as the rider turns south along Sinclair Inlet. Superferries rumble by on their way

169

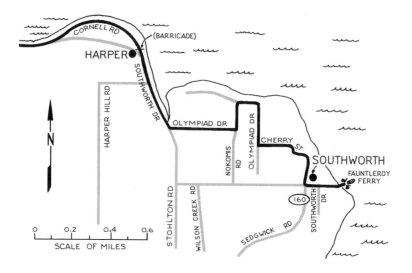

between Seattle and Bremerton. Perched high above the waterfront, the Veterans' Home at Retsil overlooks Port Orchard and busy Bremerton across the inlet. The Olympic Mountains provide an alpine background to this otherwise nautical scene. The turn-around point, Port Orchard, is the county seat of Kitsap County. After lunch head back along the same route. On many rides, returning along the same path can be monotonous, but here the changing of the tides varies the outlook. This is one of the few rides in which a different route could hardly heighten interest.

MILEAGE LOG

0.0   Lincoln Park, West Seattle. Leave parking lot, turn right, and head downhill toward the ferry landing.

0.5   Fauntleroy ferry terminal. Board ferry to Southworth. Leave the ferry at Southworth and head uphill.

0.8   Turn right on **Cherry Street** and follow it down, up, and around a few short, steep hills.

1.2   Turn right on **Olympiad Drive** and head down to the shoreline.

1.7   Turn right with Olympiad where Nokomis intersects. Landscaped pond on the left attracts ducks. Deer graze in the fields beyond.

2.0   Turn right on **S.E. Southworth Drive** as Olympiad ends. Pedal along the shoreline, where flocks of ducks gather in fall and winter.

2.5   In Harper, as the highway makes a sharp left turn, proceed straight ahead, push bicycles around a barrier, and continue along the shore-line on **Cornell Road**.

3.0   Turn right at stop sign on **S.E. Southworth Drive**.

4.0   Turn right on **Yukon Harbor Drive**.

4.9   Turn right on **Colchester Drive**. *Note: Miracle Mile Drive at mile 5.8 offers an optional short diversion from the thoroughfare.*

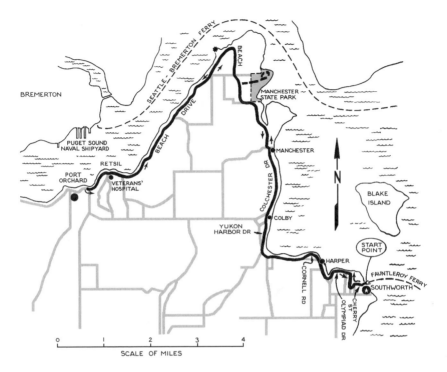

SCALE OF MILES

6.4 Turn left and uphill on **Main Street** in Manchester. Grocery store, small waterfront park, and pier to the right on Main Street.

6.5 Turn right on **Beach Drive** and stay on it all the way to Port Orchard. Naval gasoline storage tanks at mile 7.4. Side road to Manchester State Park at mile 8.5. Waterman Point horn at mile 9.4. Veterans home in Retsil at mile 13.0. Public fishing access at mile 13.1. Road is renamed **Bay Street** as it enters Port Orchard at mile 13.3.

14.1 Turn right at wye and continue on Bay Street.

14.3 Turn right with Right Turn Only lane toward Port Orchard Marina. There is a small park with restrooms and spacious shelters at the east end of this marina. Several restaurants available if a picnic lunch is not on the agenda. Retrace the route back to Southworth and enjoy the changing scenes.

29.0 Ferry terminal. Board ferry and return to West Seattle.

45 SHELTON–SKOKOMISH VALLEY–UNION

STARTING POINT: Kneeland Park, Shelton, Mason County. Take exit 104 (U.S. 101) from I-5 and proceed to first Shelton exit (State Route 3). One block after first traffic light at bottom of hill in Shelton, turn left on Turner Avenue to Kneeland Park. Park in public parking lot across Turner Avenue from park entrance.

DISTANCE: 49 miles.
TERRAIN: Half hilly, half flat.
TOTAL CUMULATIVE ELEVATION GAIN: 1450 feet.
RECOMMENDED TIME OF YEAR: Any season.
RECOMMENDED STARTING TIME: 9 A.M.
ALLOW: 6 hours.
POINTS OF INTEREST
Shay logging locomotive in Shelton
Christmas tree farms
Salmon and trout hatcheries in Skokomish Valley
Views of Skokomish River and Hood Canal

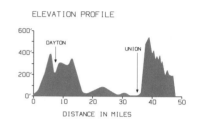

Cyclists touring the Olympic Peninsula loop or the Pacific Coast bicycle route pass many beckoning side roads but seldom have time to investigate. One of the more attractive areas for investigation is the Skokomish Valley area. A gray-green river with swirling rapids rushes past green, well-tended pastures down a quiet valley lined on either side with tall, forested hills. Within the space of a few miles, the river becomes estuarial and quietly empties into the heel of Hood Canal through a many-fingered delta. Two fish hatcheries capture the waters of tributary creeks to nurture young hatchlings destined for the sea and inland lakes. In the estuaries of the Skokomish River and the sheltered coves of Hood Canal, many varieties of waterfowl tempt the amateur bird watcher. In the lowlands, hundreds of acres of conical noble fir and sheared Douglas-fir Christmas trees indicate one of the principal industries of the region. Christmas tree plantations on the hill between Union and Shelton have been converted to timber growing.

MILEAGE LOG

0.0 Parking area by Kneeland Park along **Turner Avenue**. Proceed east to **First Street (State Route 3)** and turn left.

0.4 Turn left on **Railroad Avenue** at second traffic light as S.R. 3 goes right. Pass Shay locomotive on display. Beware of dangerous rail crossing at mile 1.0. U.S. 101 crosses overhead at mile 2.0.

7.6 Turn right on **Airport Road** toward waste disposal site. Washington Corrections Center on right at mile 9.9; Washington State Patrol Academy at 11.8.

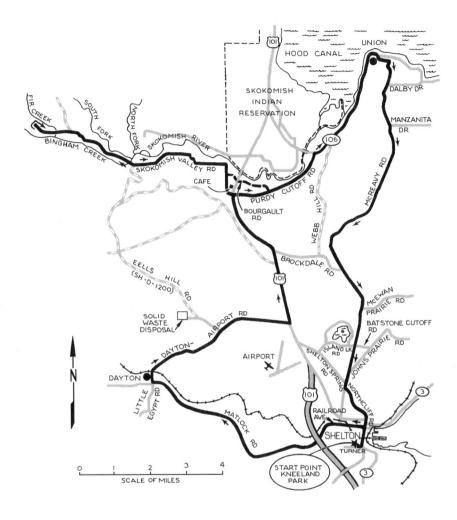

12.4   Turn left on **U.S. 101** from Dayton-Airport Road and continue on three-foot-wide shoulder.

16.4   Turn left on **Skokomish Valley Road** toward trout hatchery. Keep left on dead-end road at mile 22.1 and continue to end of road.

23.2   At end of paved road, turn around and retrace route down valley. *Note: Bourgault Road at mile 29.4 offers an optional shortcut.* Cross U.S. 101 at mile 30.1 and continue on **Purdy Cutoff Road**. Drive-in cafe 0.1 mile left on U.S. 101 offers good food at reasonable prices.

32.9   Turn right on **State Route 106** as Purdy Cutoff Road ends.

37.4   Turn right on **McReavy Road** in community of Union. Grocery, cafe (closed in winter months), and highway information sign describing

173

discovery of Hood Canal. Continue up steep hill.

43.3 Continue on **E. Brockdale Road** as it enters from the right. Road changes name to **N. 13th Street** at mile 47.0.

47.1 Get into left-turn lane as hospital buildings appear ahead and turn left on **Northcliff Road**. As it enters Shelton at bottom of hill, road is renamed **First Street**. Proceed through Shelton on First Street.

48.8 Cross bridge and turn right on **Turner Avenue** to Kneeland Park; end of tour.

"Leave the fenders off—it's not gonna rain."

46 SHELTON–SCHAFER STATE PARK

STARTING POINT: Kneeland Park, Shelton, Mason County. Take exit 104 (U.S. 101) from I-5 and proceed to first Shelton exit (State Route 3). One block after first traffic light at bottom of hill in Shelton, turn left on Turner Avenue to Kneeland Park. Park in public parking lot across Turner Avenue from park entrance.

DISTANCE: Loop A—total, 71 miles: first day, 41 miles; second day, 30 miles. Loop B—total, 94 miles: first day, 51 miles; second day, 43 miles.
TERRAIN: Loop A—moderately hilly. Loop B—hilly.
TOTAL CUMULATIVE ELEVATION GAIN: Loop A—1700 feet: first day, 1000 feet; second day, 700 feet. Loop B—3100 feet: first day, 2000 feet; second day, 1100 feet.

RECOMMENDED TIME OF YEAR: May through September.
RECOMMENDED STARTING TIME: 9 to 10 A.M.
ALLOW: 10 hours; 1 or 2 days.
POINTS OF INTEREST
John W. Eddy Tree Farm
Schafer State Park

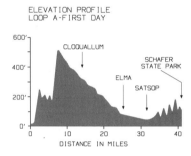

ELEVATION PROFILE
LOOP A-FIRST DAY

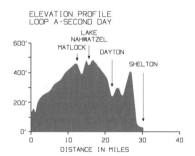

ELEVATION PROFILE
LOOP A-SECOND DAY

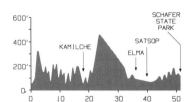

ELEVATION PROFILE
LOOP B-FIRST DAY

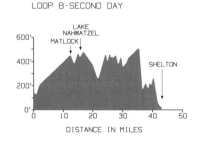

ELEVATION PROFILE
LOOP B-SECOND DAY

The area west of Shelton has many smooth-surfaced roads with low-density traffic. Forests, farms, camps, and resorts are the primary land uses outside the cities and towns. The John W. Eddy Tree Farm, purchased in 1870 and operated by the Blakely Mill, is a seemingly virgin stretch of forest, with informative signs describing its history. Schafer State Park, which is used for the overnight campground, has an attractive forest and river setting. In 1924 the 119 acres were presented to the state by the sons of John

D. and Anna Schafer in their memory. The relaxing atmosphere and low mileage of this overnight ride make it one of the best available.

There are two loop trips, of 71 miles and 94 miles. A major portion of each ride duplicates the other, but each also has separate features. The principal point in deciding between them is the number of miles the cyclist would like to ride. Although they are both described as overnight rides, a strong rider can do the shorter one as a one-day trip. The longer ride is not recommended for one day.

MILEAGE LOG

LOOP A—FIRST DAY

0.0   Entrance to Kneeland Park on **Turner Avenue**. Proceed east along Turner toward Shelton waterfront and turn right on **S. First Street** (**State Route 3**). Continue straight through traffic light on **Pioneer Way** at next block as S.R. 3 swings left on S. Olympic Highway.

0.6   Bear right on **Lake Boulevard** as Pioneer Way forks left. Road is renamed **W. Cloquallum Road** as it leaves Shelton at mile 1.4.

14.3   Bear left at wye toward Elma with Cloquallum Road. Enter Grays Harbor County at mile 19.1. Continue with Cloquallum Road at mile 23.3 as Hicklin Road goes left.

24.4   Bear right on **Elma-McCleary Road** as Cloquallum Road ends. Cafes and grocery in Elma at mile 26.0 and in Satsop at mile 30.0. The road is renamed **Monte Elma Road**.

31.6   Turn right toward Schafer State Park on **Middle Satsop Road**. West Satsop Road goes left to Swinging Bridge Park at mile 35.0. Cross West Fork Satsop River.

39.5   Turn right on **East Satsop Road** toward Schafer State Park as main road continues to Matlock. Cross Decker Creek and the East Fork Satsop River.

40.8   Entrance to Schafer State Park; picnic area to left along the East Fork Satsop with picnic shelter. Camping area on the right with coin-operated hot showers and over 50 campsites.

SECOND DAY

0.0   Turn left from campground entrance on **East Satsop Road**. Cross East Fork Satsop and Decker Creek.

1.3   Turn right toward Matlock as East Satsop Road ends.

12.3   Turn right toward Shelton in community of Matlock. Matlock Store at this intersection; groceries. Restaurant by Nahwatzel Lake at mile 16.8. Dayton grocery at mile 22.0. U.S. 101 goes overhead at mile 28.1. Enter Shelton on **Railroad Avenue** at mile 29.2.

29.6   Turn right at traffic light on **First Street** (**State Route 3**).

30.0   Turn right on **Turner Avenue** to start point at Kneeland Park.

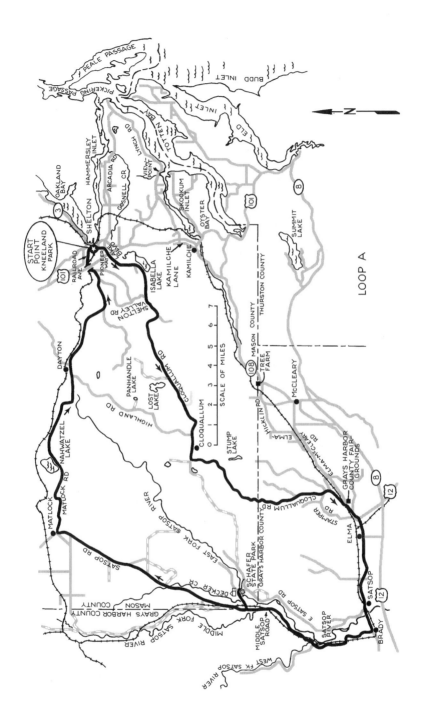

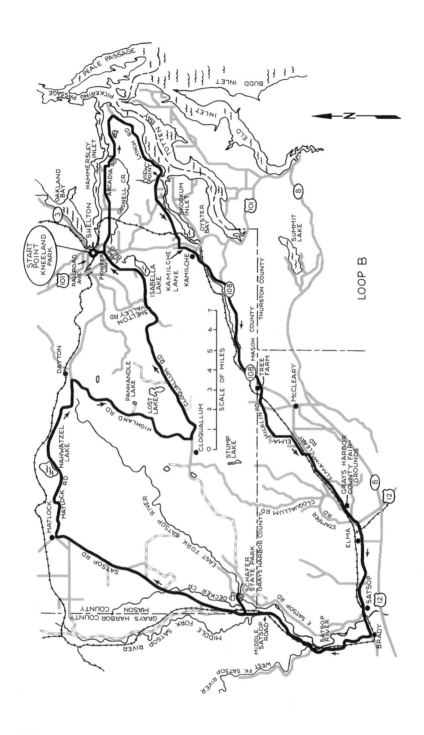

LOOP B—FIRST DAY

0.0   Entrance to Kneeland Park on **Turner Avenue**. Proceed east along Turner toward Shelton waterfront and turn right on **First Street** (**State Route 3**). Continue straight through traffic light on **Pioneer Way** at next block as S.R. 3 swings left on S. Olympic Highway.

0.6   Bear left with Pioneer Way as Lake Boulevard continues.

0.7   Turn left on **Arcadia Avenue**, which is renamed **S.E. Arcadia Road** as it crosses State Route 3 at mile 1.1.

8.1   Turn right on **Lynch Road** as Arcadia Road ends. View of Totten and Skookum inlets at mile 12.5.

17.0   Go past grocery and restaurant, cross U.S. 101, and turn left on **S. Kamilche Lane** as Lynch Road ends.

17.7   Turn right on **State Route 108** by U.S. 101 interchange and continue through small valley with farms. Enter the John W. Eddy Tree Farm at mile 26.0.

26.8   Turn right on **Elma-Hicklin Road**.

31.5   Turn right on **Elma-McCleary Road** as Elma-Hicklin Road ends. Cafes and grocery in Elma at mile 40.3.

42.0   Turn right toward Schafer State Park on **Middle Satsop Road** by Brady Store. Road winds up valley past crops of oats, wheat, peas, and potatoes. W. Satsop Road goes left to Swinging Bridge Park. Cross West Fork Satsop River.

49.9   Turn right on **East Satsop Road** toward Schafer State Park. Cross Decker Creek and East Fork Satsop River.

51.2   Entrance to Schafer State Park. Picnic area to the left with tables along the river and a rustic shelter. A plaque dedicates the park to John D. and Anna Schafer. Campground on right has coin-operated hot showers and over 50 campsites.

SECOND DAY

0.0   Leave campground entrance and turn left (north) on **East Satsop Road**. Cross East Fork Satsop and Decker Creek.

1.2   Turn right toward Matlock on **Middle Satsop Road** as East Satsop Road ends.

12.3   Turn right toward Shelton by Matlock Store. Cafe in resort by Nahwatzel Lake at mile 16.8.

21.8   Turn right on **Highland Road**.

29.7   Turn left on **Cloquallum Road** as Highland Road ends. As it enters Shelton, road changes name to **Lake Boulevard, Pioneer Way**, and then **First Street**.

43.0   Turn left on **Turner Avenue** to Kneeland Park; end of tour.

47 MILLERSYLVANIA–OLYMPIA

STARTING POINT: Millersylvania State Park, Thurston County. Take exit 95 (Maytown, State Route 121, state park) from I-5 and follow signs to state park, 3.5 miles east of the freeway. Park in the Kitchen Area #1 picnic area parking lot.

DISTANCE: 36 miles.
TERRAIN: Mostly flat, two hills.
TOTAL CUMULATIVE ELEVATION GAIN: 400 feet.
RECOMMENDED TIME OF YEAR: Any season.
RECOMMENDED STARTING TIME: 10 A.M.
ALLOW: 4 to 5 hours plus lunch and sightseeing.
POINTS OF INTEREST
Millersylvania State Park
Capitol Lake
Capitol grounds
Olympia Brewery
Tumwater Falls Park

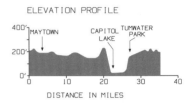

ELEVATION PROFILE

DISTANCE IN MILES

This combination rural and metropolitan ride features tours of Washington State's capitol and a major brewery. Rural roads or parkway sidewalks offer pleasurable riding most of the way, but a few miles of busy roads must be negotiated.

Although this tour may be taken at any season, there are special attractions throughout the year. Fall paints the Oregon ash trees a beautiful pale yellow, and the vine maples with pinks and reds. Fragrant wild rose blossoms in spring make for bright red rose hips in the fall. Horses and cattle graze the many green pastures.

The State Capitol grounds are famous for cherry blossoms in spring and for beautiful landscaping and fine architecture. Tours are conducted seven days a week in the Legislature Building from Memorial Day to Labor Day.

An interesting tour of the Olympia Brewery is available, and the nearby Tumwater Falls Park should be visited. In the falls and rapids of the stream so close to the city, water ouzels dart and splash in search of food. They are resident birds and nest along the moist, fern-covered banks of the falls. Autumn brings the chinook salmon run up the Deschutes River. This artificially induced run, maintained by the installation of the fish ladder at Tumwater Falls, is one of the most successful anywhere. Big fish, fighting their way upstream to their spawning grounds, can be seen at the dam that forms Capitol Lake and again at Tumwater Falls Park.

The route back to Millersylvania Park follows busy Capitol Boulevard, but as the airport is neared, an escape route around the west side presents itself, and the traffic is left behind. Scenes on the return ride include an extensive log dump, farms, and forest.

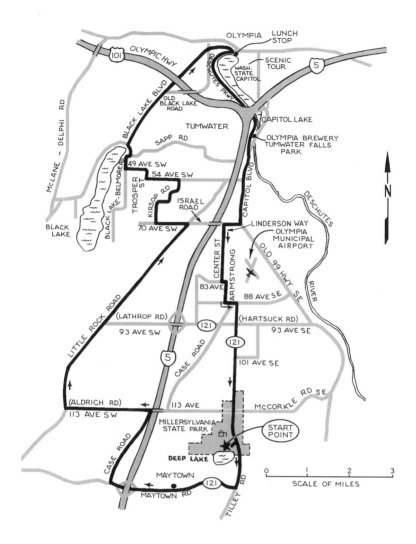

MILEAGE LOG

0.0 Picnic area parking lot, Millersylvania State Park. Leave park and turn right (south) on **Tilley Road S. (State Route 121)**.

0.9 Turn right with bike route sign on **Maytown Road S.W.** I-5 goes overhead at mile 3.4.

3.5 Turn right with Maytown Road toward Little Rock. Small cafe at this corner.

3.7 Turn right on **Case Road S.W.**

5.7 Turn left on **113 Avenue S.W.** as Case Road ends.

7.9   Turn right on **Little Rock Road S.W.** as 113 Avenue ends. Enter Tumwater at mile 10.5.

13.2   Turn left on **70th Avenue S.W.** as Israel Road goes right by corner grocery. Road bends right at mile 14.0 and is renamed **Kirsop Road S.W.**

15.5   Turn left on **54th Avenue S.W.** as Kirsop ends. Road bends right by power substation and becomes **Trosper Street S.W.**, bends left again, and is renamed **49th Avenue S.W.**

17.0   Turn right on **Black Lake-Belmore Road S.W.** by grocery store and then turn left with it at mile 17.3 as Sapp Road goes on.

17.5   Turn right on **Black Lake Boulevard S.W.** as Black Lake-Belmore Road ends. Bikeway begins at mile 19.2, followed by sidewalk. Proceed under U.S. 101 at interchange and head uphill. Road name changes to **Division Street**.

20.6   Turn right on **4 Avenue W.** Road is flat for a few blocks and then plunges down a steep hill.

21.3   Cross Olympic Way and turn right on sidewalk by Right Turn Only sign to avoid heavy traffic.

21.5   Cross **Deschutes Parkway** and continue left along sidewalk across dam at foot of Capitol Lake; viewing platform for chinook salmon run.

21.8   Picnic lunch site in Capitol Lake Park; restaurants nearby in downtown Olympia. *Note: Optional side trip proceeds up the hill to the State Capitol grounds.* Return along sidewalk and continue around the lake alongside **Deschutes Parkway**. I-5 goes overhead at mile 26.4. Olympia Brewery turnoff at mile 26.5; Tumwater Falls Park at 26.6. Road bends left at mile 26.8 as a freeway exit joins.

27.1   Turn right on busy **Capitol Boulevard**; four-lane, divided roadway with no shoulder.

29.0   Turn right by Point Tavern on **W. Israel Road**. Go past Tumwater High School.

29.5   Turn left on **Linderson Way**. Road name changes to **Center Street S.W.** as it goes through industrial area.

30.8   Turn left on **83rd Avenue S.W.** as Center Street ends. Road turns right at mile 31.0 and is renamed **Armstrong Road S.W.**

31.6   Turn left on **88th Avenue S.W.** as Armstrong is marked Dead End.

31.8   Turn right on **Tilley Road S.** toward Millersylvania State Park as Case Road goes sharply right.

35.4   Turn right into Millersylvania State Park. End of tour at mile 35.5.

48   MILLERSYLVANIA–RAINIER

STARTING POINT: Millersylvania State Park, Thurston County. Take exit 95 (Maytown, State Route 121, state park) from I-5 and follow signs to state park, 3.5 miles east of the freeway. Park in the Kitchen Area #1 picnic area parking lot.

DISTANCE: 32 miles.
TERRAIN: Moderate to flat.
TOTAL CUMULATIVE ELEVATION GAIN: 800 feet.
RECOMMENDED TIME OF YEAR: Any season.
RECOMMENDED STARTING TIME: 10 A.M.
ALLOW: 4 hours plus lunch.
POINTS OF INTEREST
Weir Prairie of Fort Lewis Military
   Reservation
Mima Mounds
Wolf Haven

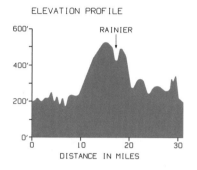

ELEVATION PROFILE

This is an enjoyable ride no matter what time of year. Weir Prairie, on the southwestern corner of the Fort Lewis training area, provides an interesting contrast with other parts of western Washington. Oregon ash trees are evident along this ride, particularly in fall, when they turn a pure, pale yellow. Oregon white oaks also are prevalent. In fall, the blue-berried elder is showy, and its fruit, black with blue bloom, is in sharp contrast to the yellows, reds, and pinks dotting the countryside. This ride passes fields of the small, round Mima Mounds.

After crossing the Deschutes River, the road winds past small farms and country homes. Then the farmlands end and the forest begins as the road enters the southwest corner of the Fort Lewis Military Reservation. Large fir and cedar trees form a forest here with little underbrush, interrupted by occasional dirt roads posted with no-trespassing signs. Close examination of roadside mounds reveals that ants have taken over many stumps and are devouring them. The ant hills appear as tall brown knolls covered with fir needles.

After several miles of forest, the road suddenly opens up to the sky and emerges onto Weir Prairie. Wide expanses of grassland, dotted here and there with perfectly shaped evergreen trees, spread out in a broad valley. Occasional barbed wire entanglements lie among the tall grasses. Meadow-larks sing their mellow, flutelike song from the tops of the singular fir trees. Visions of Old West cavalry maneuvers are easily conjured up as the rider passes through this prairie.

At the Fort Lewis boundary, the route heads downhill into the town of Rainier, where lunch may be purchased at a drive-in or grocery store. Little traffic is encountered as the route heads up the Deschutes Valley past several cattle ranches. The sights and sounds of avian residents, many apparently all year at the crossing of the Deschutes River, are greatly multiplied in summer months. Only glimpses of Offutt Lake will be had in

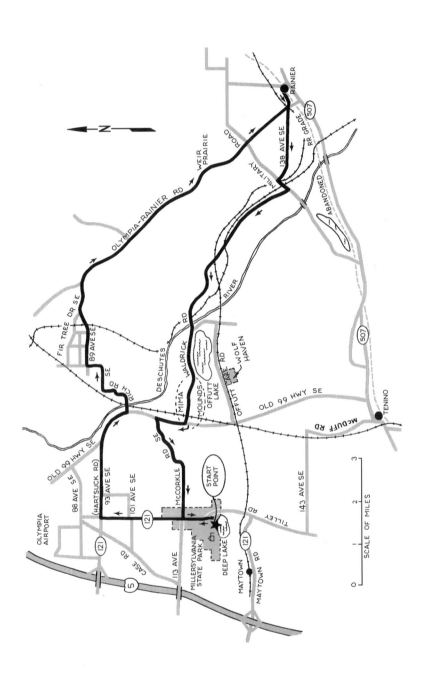

passing. More of the round Mima Mounds will be discernible behind a rustic, zigzag cedar fence just before the route crosses over the main-line tracks on a high bridge and joins the highway leading back toward Millersylvania Park.

MILEAGE LOG

0.0 Picnic parking area, Millersylvania State Park. Leave park and turn left (north) on **Tilley Road S. (State Route 121)**.

3.1 Turn right on **93 Avenue S.E.**

5.2 Turn right on **Old 99 Highway S.E.**

5.9 Turn left on **Rich Road** and immediately cross over the main-line Burlington Northern Railroad tracks. Cross the Deschutes River.

7.6 Turn right on **89 Avenue S.E.**

9.0 Turn right on **Fir Tree Drive S.E.**

9.7 Turn right on **Olympia-Rainier Road** (**Rainier Road S.E.**) and continue through a portion of the Fort Lewis Military Reservation. Cross Military Road at mile 15.2 and descend the hill. As it enters Rainier, the road is renamed **Minnesota Avenue**.

17.5 Junction with State Route 507 in Rainier; cafe, grocery. After lunch, return up the hill on **Minnesota Avenue** toward East Olympia. Road changes name to **Rainier Road S.E.**

18.4 Go straight on **138 Avenue S.E.** as Rainier Road swings right.

19.9 Turn left on **Military Road S.E.** as 138 Avenue ends.

20.3 Turn right on **Waldrick Road** and head down the Deschutes Valley past cattle ranches. Road plays leapfrog with railroad tracks. Cross the Deschutes River at mile 24.6; proceed past Offutt Lake and through a section of the Mima Mounds. *Note: Optional five-mile round trip to Wolf Haven at mile 24.7 on Offutt Lake Road; wolf exhibits.*

27.1 Turn right on **Old 99 Highway S.E.** as Waldrick ends.

27.7 Turn left on **McCorkle Road S.E.**; wind through a valley and up over a steep hill. Road name changes to **113 Avenue S.E.**

30.4 Turn left on **Tilley Road S.**

31.5 Turn right into entrance of Millersylvania State Park. End of tour at picnic parking area at mile 31.6.

49 SKOOKUMCHUCK

STARTING POINT: Millersylvania State Park, Thurston County. Take exit 95 (Maytown, State Route 121, state park) from I-5 and follow signs to state park, 3.5 miles east of the freeway. Park in the Kitchen Area #1 picnic area parking lot

.DISTANCE: 40 miles.
TERRAIN: Moderate.
TOTAL CUMULATIVE ELEVATION GAIN: 1100 feet.
RECOMMENDED TIME OF YEAR: Anytime
RECOMMENDED STARTING TIME: 9 to 10 A.M.
ALLOW: 6 hours.
POINTS OF INTEREST
Skookumchuck Dam
Mima Mounds

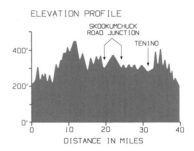

As the tour leaves the park entrance road and heads north along Tilley Road, it has more than a mile of state park to traverse. Few people realize just how large this park is. Waldrick Road is one of our favorites because of its intriguing Mima Mounds, oak trees, and natural prairies. Two sets of railroad tracks, including those of a private logging railway, wind along the hillside overlooking the Deschutes Valley. After skirting McIntosh Lake along the forested hillside south of the valley, the route is forced out onto State Route 507 (occasionally, we run out of backroads). Shoulder riding is soon over as Johnson Creek Road dives into a newly reforested woodland. Lavender-colored wild irises line the roadside in spring. Clearings, farm buildings, and animals eventually begin to appear. Then, quite unexpectedly, a roadside sign announces an evening restaurant just as the roadway emerges into the broad Skookumchuck Valley.

Skookumchuck Dam is unusual in that its primary purpose is not flood control, irrigation, or hydroelectric power. It was built to ensure a continuous supply of water to a coal-burning, thermal-electric power plant in the Hanaford Valley over the ridge to the south. The concrete spillway down the face of the dam is its most prominent feature. Formerly accessible for close viewing, the dam is now enclosed by a chain link fence and locked gate.

The ride out through the Skookumchuck Valley is a reminder of yesteryear. The road meanders from farm to farm and seems better adapted to the horse and buggy than to the very occasional automobile. Meadowlarks and savannah sparrows are constant companions on the ride and buteos soar high over the ridge. Even when the valley opens out into Frost Prairie and the road leads through to Tenino, the rural atmosphere is not dispelled. Another rural road continues almost to Millersylvania Park. This is neither a short ride nor an easy one, but the scenic rewards are commensurate with the effort.

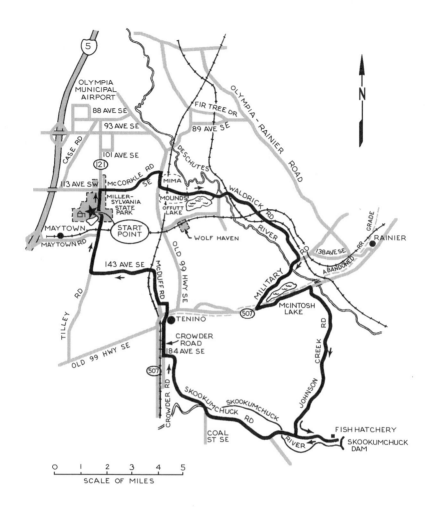

MILEAGE LOG

0.0 Picnic area parking lot, Millersylvania State Park. Leave park and turn left (north) on **Tilley Road** (**State Route 121**).

1.0 Turn right on **113 Avenue S.W.** and crank over steep hill. As it descends the other side, the road is renamed **McCorkle Road S.E.**

3.6 Turn right on **Old 99 Highway S.E.**, then take the next left on **Waldrick Road** at mile 4.1. Cross the Burlington Northern Railroad tracks on a high bridge and pedal through rolling Mima Mounds, past Offutt Lake, and across the Deschutes River. Fishing access on Offutt Lake at mile 5.5. *Note: Offutt Lake Road goes right at mile 6.5 to Wolf Haven wolf exhibit.*

10.9 Turn right on **Military Road** as Waldrick ends. Cross the Deschutes River and start up long hill. Fishing access on McIntosh Lake down a long hill on the left at mile 12.7.

13.5 Cross abandoned railroad grade and turn left on **State Route 507**.

15.6 Turn right on **Johnson Creek Road S.E.** by milepost 20.

22.0 Turn left on **Skookumchuck Road** as Johnson Creek Road ends. Continue to end of road by fish hatchery. Mowed green lawns edged by large rocks offer an impromptu picnic site. Turn around and return along **Skookumchuck Road**, passing Johnson Creek Road at mile 25.0. After two crossings of the river, the road changes name to **184 Avenue S.E.**

31.1 Turn right on **Crowder Road S.E.** just before 184 Avenue crosses the railroad tracks.

33.4 Cross abandoned railroad grade and bear right on **Park Avenue W.**, then take the next left on **McArthur** in Tenino. Cross Sussex Street (State Route 507) at mile 33.8 and continue on McArthur. *Note: Cafes and grocery to the right along S.R. 507 in Tenino.*

33.9 Turn left on **2nd Avenue** by Tenino High School as McArthur ends.

34.0 Turn right on **Wichman Street** as 2nd Street ends. As it leaves town, the road is renamed **McDuff Road**. Road bends left at mile 35.6 and is renamed **143rd Avenue S.E.**

38.0 Turn right on **Tilley Road S.**

40.1 Turn left into Millersylvania State Park. End of tour at mile 40.3.

THURSTON AND LEWIS COUNTIES

50 MORTON–MILLERSYLVANIA

STARTING POINT: Morton in Lewis County. Take exit 68 (U.S. 12, White Pass, Yakima) from I-5 and head east 32 miles to Morton. Park in public parking lot at Third and Main streets in Morton.
ALTERNATIVE STARTING POIINT: Millersylvania State Park, Thurston County. Take exit 95 (Maytown, State 121, state park) from I-5 and follow signs to the state park, 3.5 miles east of the freeway. Make arrangement with park ranger for overnight parking.

DISTANCE: Total, 129 miles: first day, 69 miles; second day, 60 miles.
TERRAIN: Lots of hills, partly flat.
TOTAL CUMULATIVE ELEVATION GAIN: 5250 feet: first day, 2550 feet; second day, 2700 feet.

RECOMMENDED TIME OF YEAR: May through September.
RECOMMENDED STARTING TIME: 9 A.M.
ALLOW: 2 or more days.
POINTS OF INTEREST
Mima Mounds near Offutt Lake
Millersylvania State Park

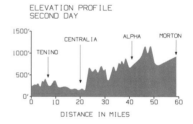

This is a long, strenuous ride covering parts of three counties: Lewis, Pierce, and Thurston. It can be completed in two days by strong capable riders, but the occasional rider should plan for three days. When camping for one night, Millersylvania State Park may be used. For a three-day trip, the cyclist will find camping facilities at a Department of Natural Resources (DNR) recreation area, Ike Kinswa State Park, and a KOA campground, or bed-and-breakfast accommodations in Morton and Eatonville (see B&B Index). If a two-day camping trip is planned, it is suggested that camping gear be left at Millersylvania State Park before transporting bicycles to the starting point at Morton.

As it leaves Morton, the route heads uphill at an even two-percent grade past lumber mills. An annual event in Morton is the Loggers Jubilee in August. Through green Douglas-fir forests, the smell of freshly cut lumber fills the air. Logging trucks rumble along the highway, occasionally blasting out with their compression braking. Tourists visiting Mt. Rainier National Park use this route, and traffic can be relatively heavy on summer weekends. Rusty railroad rails, climbing a parallel grade in the valley on the right, invite visions of worry-free rail-bike cycling. At mile 6.9, a bubbling spring-fed water fountain allows thirsty cyclists to fill their water bottles. From here

189

on, the grade becomes steeper, and the road reaches an elevation of 1800 feet before crossing Summit Creek. After several miles of relatively level riding, a tremendous downhill run begins. Forest and small open areas flash by before the glacial, silt-filled Nisqually River is crossed and the town of Elbe appears. Here the route turns left and follows State Route 7 for several miles along Tacoma City Light's Alder Lake, behind Alder Dam. Shoulder riding along the busy highway ends at the Alder Cutoff Road, which heads uphill past small country farms and much forest, and through a shallow valley where Mt. Rainier may be visible on the right. After climbing a moderate grade to a summit, the route heads downhill into Eatonville.

Between Eatonville and McKenna, the route traverses miles of rolling terrain past cattle and tree farms. To the east of the Nisqually River, the land flattens out and many irrigated pastures support dairy and beef cattle. Out of Yelm, the route stays fairly level until it leaves the highway and climbs the hill toward the Fort Lewis Military Reservation. Wild hazelnut trees along the road attract the Steller's jay at nut harvest time.

Weir Prairie is very different from most places west of the Cascade Mountains. Large groves of Oregon white oak are interspersed with Douglas fir trees, and there is little of the thick ground cover usually found in western Washington forests. Waldrick Road runs along the edge of a big ranch with black Angus cattle grazing in a lovely valley to the southwest.

Birds chittering along the way may include flickers, robins, jays, and chickadees. As the route crosses the Deschutes River, cedar waxwings swoop like flycatchers around the bridge and kingfishers watch from the trees. The road ascends a short grade, and Offutt Lake is glimpsed occasionally through the trees. This is Mima Mound country, and acres of these strange, round mounds stretch beyond a rustic rail fence.

Summertime overnighting

Residential buildings begin to appear as Millersylvania State Park is approached at the edge of Olympia's suburbia. This is a popular park, and its sylvan setting along the shores of Deep Lake makes it a very pleasant place. Swimming, fishing, picnicking, group camping by special reservation, hiking trails, and hot showers are offered. A food concession and small grocery are available at a resort immediately south of the park, but these are open only from Memorial Day to Labor Day. A small cafe at the Maytown Road interchange with I-5 is more reliable in its service.

From Millersylvania State Park, the route turns south along backroads to Tenino and from there wanders beside the Skookumchuck River to Centralia. Picturesque farms nestle in this narrow valley. The Oregon ash tree, with its decorative seed bunches and colorful leaves in fall, is quite prevalent. Swallows fill the air during the summer months.

As the road enters Centralia, a neighborhood grocery-delicatessen offers its wares; a larger chain store supplies the center of the city, but a detour is necessary to find it.

The route leaves Centralia along the broad, flat Salzer Valley. Soon it climbs a long hill to a plateau. This does not end the hill, however, as three forks of the Newaukum River must be crossed, each fork producing a long descent and a steep climb. On this backroad, very little traffic is encountered, and the surface is adequate. A few homes provide occasional breaks in the forest, but views are scarce, except when the road dips into a river valley. Just after the route passes Alpha, a secondary state highway is joined and the terrain assumes a less wild aspect.

Proceeding to Cinebar, the cyclist rolls through acres of Christmas tree plantations. The road then enters the Tilton River Valley and follows it to Morton. Ah! you say, all downhill from here. Not so. The road climbs the canyon wall to the north but dips again almost to the river level to negotiate the side streams. Finally, as the valley broadens, the road descends and behaves as it should. A short, flat ride is all that remains before the return to Morton and the end of the ride.

MILEAGE LOG

FIRST DAY

0.0   Morton in Lewis County. Turn left from **Main Avenue** on **State Route 7 (Second Street)** and head north and uphill. Fountain by the roadside at mile 6.9. Cross Summit Creek (elevation 1740) at mile 9.0. Begin a long downhill at mile 12.0. *Note: Pleasant Valley Road goes left 3.5 miles to the DNR Alder Lake Recreation Area at mile 14.3; secluded campsites, well with hand pump, picnic shelter.*

16.5   Cross Nisqually River, enter Elbe, and turn left with S.R. 7; cafe, grocery, steam-train rides, lodging. Proceed along Alder Lake.

21.4   Turn right and uphill on **Alder Cutoff Road E.** Road tops a summit at mile 26.0.

28.3   Enter Eatonville on **Center Street E.** Turn right on **Mashell Avenue N.** by bank and continue out of town. Cafes, grocery store, and bed-and-breakfast accommodations in Eatonville.

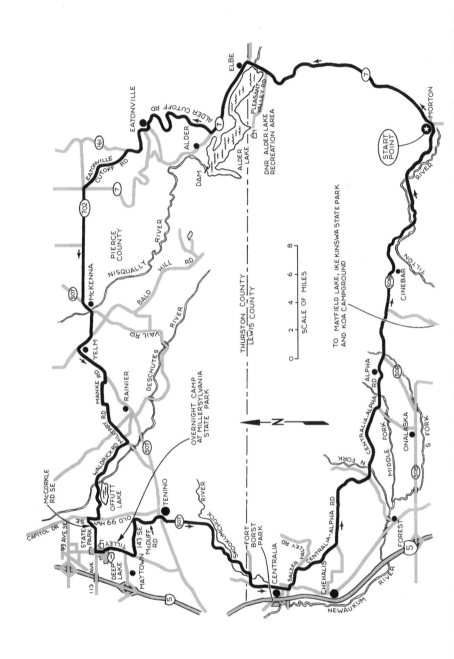

28.6   Turn left and downhill on **Washington Avenue N. (State Route 161)** as Mashell ends. Mt. Rainier viewpoint on the right at mile 31.7.

31.9   Turn left on **Eatonville Cutoff Road**.

36.6   Continue west on **State Route 702** as Eatonville Cutoff Road ends at an intersection with State Route 7.

46.0   Turn left on **State Route 507** as S.R. 702 ends. Enter McKenna, cross the Nisqually River, and enter Thurston County.

48.8   At a stop light in the center of Yelm, turn left (southwest) with S.R. 507 as Yelm Avenue (S.R. 510) continues across the railroad tracks.

51.8   Turn right on **Manke Road (118 Avenue S.E.)** and climb uphill past a poultry farm. Road bends left at mile 53.8 and is renamed **Fillman Road**; it bends right at mile 54.3 and is called **123 Avenue S.E.** Cross Rainier Road at mile 56.1 and go through a corner of the Fort Lewis Military Reservation on **Military Road**.

57.8   Turn right on **Waldrick Road** after bumping over two railroad grade crossings. Cross the Deschutes River at mile 62.1. Pass Mima Mounds at mile 63.8. Cross Burlington Northern main-line track on a high bridge at mile 64.5.

64.6   Turn right on **Old 99 Highway S.E.**

65.1   Turn left on **McCorkle Road S.E.** and crank over a hill. As it descends the hill, the road is renamed **113 Avenue S.E.**

67.7   Turn left on **Tilley Road S.**

68.7   Turn right into Millersylvania State Park.

SECOND DAY

0.0   Leave Millersylvania State Park and turn right on **Tilley Road S.**

2.4   Turn left on **143 Avenue S.E.** As road crosses railroad tracks and bends right, it is renamed **McDuff Road** at mile 4.7.

6.5   Enter Tenino on **Wichman**, which shortly ends at S.R. 507. Turn right on **State Route 507** and continue south on this highway toward Centralia.

16.8   Enter Centralia and follow **State Route 507 (Pearl Street)** through the center of town.

19.8   Continue on **S. Pearl Street** as S.R. 507 turns right toward I-5 and motels at a blinking red light.

20.2   Turn left (east) on **E. Summa Street**, cross railroad tracks and both one-way sections of old highway, and leave Centralia. Road name changes to **Salzer Valley Road**.

21.6   Turn right on **Centralia-Alpha Road**. Cross the valley and begin climb to a plateau. Start downhill at mile 30.3. Cross the north fork Newaukum River at mile 31.7 and climb over another summit.

40.0   Turn left on **State Route 508**. *Note: Ike Kinswa State Park and a KOA Campground at Silver Creek are approximately 8.0 miles right on Cinebar-Silver Creek Road at mile 44.7.* Summit of Bear Canyon at mile 48.8. Cross the Tilton River at mile 51.8 and continue alongside the river. End of tour in Morton at mile 60.0.

51 MILLERSYLVANIA–CENTRALIA

STARTING POINT: Millersylvania State Park, Thurston County. Take exit 95 (Maytown, State Route 121, state park) from I-5 and follow signs to state park, 3.5 miles east of the freeway. Park in the Kitchen Area #1 picnic area parking lot.

DISTANCE: 55 miles.
TERRAIN: Flat to moderate.
TOTAL CUMULATIVE ELEVATION GAIN: 700 feet.
RECOMMENDED TIME OF YEAR: Any season, but especially good in summer and fall.
RECOMMENDED STARTING TIME: 9 to 10 A.M.
ALLOW: 7 to 8 hours.
POINTS OF INTEREST
Scatter Creek Game Range
Fort Henness historical monument
Grand Mound-Rochester Cemetery
Lewis County Game Farm
Weyerhaeuser Forest Tree Nursery
Mima Mounds

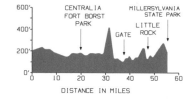

ELEVATION PROFILE

This is a long but surprisingly easy ride, for it has only one steep hill to climb. The open prairie country of Lewis and Thurston counties provides miles of good roads for the touring cyclist, with clear views of Mt. Rainier, Mt. St. Helens, and Mt. Adams. Interesting natural and cultural features are spaced along the ride, at convenient stopping points. Large hawks circle effortlessly in the thermal updrafts over the prairies on sunny days. Centralia's Fort Borst Park, with its picnic facilities and food concession, is the logical lunch stop.

Leaving Millersylvania State Park and starting south on Tilley Road, the route winds through dense forest. Douglas fir, cedar, hemlock, dogwood, cascara, and Oregon ash trees compete for space with thick ground cover of salal, Oregon grape, and huckleberry. As the rider turns west, the prairie begins, with occasional clumps of Oregon white oak and open, grassy fields becoming overgrown with Scotch broom. During the early summer months, lupine, daisies, campanula, and other wildflowers add spots of color. Flashy yellow goldfinches appear and meadowlarks sing at any season.

Scatter Creek Game Range covers many acres to the west of I-5. This is a public hunting range maintained by the State Department of Wildlife. *Note: Conservation license required for entry.* Hikers find this range especially interesting in April and May when there is no hunting. At the southwest corner of the game range is the Fort Henness historical monument to the 1855 Indian war. The Maple Lane State School is glimpsed near Grand Mound just before the route joins the busy concrete highway that heads south into Centralia. Traffic will be annoying here, but it can be left behind when Horsley Avenue is reached. A short detour through a residential section and past a cemetery leads quickly to Fort Borst Park. Several restaurants are near the park for those who do not wish to picnic.

Just after leaving the park, the cyclist sees the Lewis County Game Farm of the State Department of Wildlife, where colorful, exotic game birds are on exhibit. After crossing the Chehalis River, the route executes a sharp bend in the town of Galvin. Dairies line the lovely green valley along Lincoln Creek.

The air is clear and the sky bright blue as the prevailing winds sweep down over the Willapa Hills and bring clean ocean breezes. Breathe deeply, then tackle the mile of climbing through forest on the Michigan Hill Road. The whistling, freewheeling ride down the other side makes the uphill grind worth the effort. Another crossing of the Chehalis River takes the cyclist back into fertile prairie farmland, where blueberries thrive in the rich loam along the Black River near Gate.

The Weyerhaeuser Forest Tree Nursery is most interesting, with its expansive acres of infant trees. Little Douglas-firs, varying in height from a fraction of an inch to a couple of feet, march along the black soil, row after row as far as the eye can see. A gigantic sprinkling system satisfies their need for water. As the rider continues north on the Gate-Little Rock Road, the mysterious Mima Mounds appear. The mounds along Bordeaux Road have become a registered natural landmark, to be preserved in the interest of science and as a geologic mystery. Mt. Rainier, Mt. St. Helens, and Mt. Adams appear on the eastern horizon before the cyclist again enters forest, freewheels down into Little Rock, and continues past farms producing pork, beef, and dairy products. One last, steep hill must be negotiated before leaving the open prairie and returning to the "primeval forest" at Millersylvania State Park.

MILEAGE LOG

0.0 Millersylvania State Park. Leave the park entrance and turn south (right) on **Tilley Road S.**

4.8 Turn right on **Goddard Road (166 Avenue S.W.)**.

6.0 Turn left on **Gibson Road** and follow it as it zigs and zags across the prairie.

8.0 Turn right on **Old 99 Highway S.W.** for 0.1 mile, then bear right on **183 Avenue S.W. (Township Road)**. Olympia-Tenino Speedway at this corner. Pass Scatter Creek Game Range at mile 10.2.

10.9 Turn left on **Apricot Street S.W.** by Fort Henness historical monument to the 1855 Indian war.

11.6 Turn right on **191 Avenue S.W.** Cross diagonal Sargent Road.

12.2 Turn left on **Pecan Street S.W.**

12.9 Cross busy U.S. 12 and continue as the road swings left and southeast along railroad tracks and is renamed **Grand Mound Way**. The entrance to Maple Lane State School with its attractively landscaped grounds appears across the tracks on James Road at mile 13.8.

14.5 Turn right as Grand Mound Way ends, and cross the railroad tracks.

14.8 Bear left on **Old 99 Highway S.W.** at Y intersection. Stay on this busy old concrete highway for 3 miles.

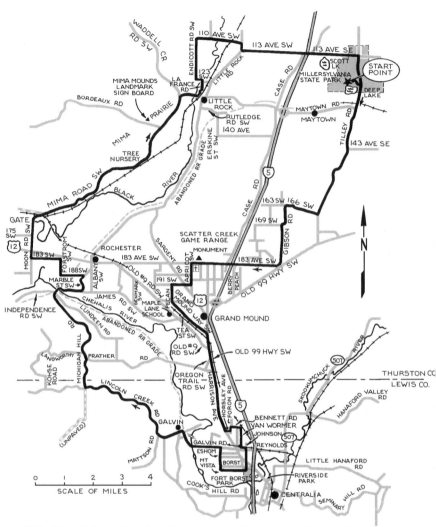

17.8 Turn left on **Horsley Avenue** by antique shop, then left again on **Foron Road**, followed by a right on **Bennet Road** and another right on **Van Wormer Road**. At mile 19.0, turn left through a cemetery for an interesting diversion.

19.3 Turn right at cemetery exit, cross Reynolds Road and continue south on **Johnson Road**. Enter west entrance of Fort Borst Park at mile 20.1. Log allocates 1.0 mile for touring the park. Route leaves the park from the west entrance, goes through the junior high school parking lot, past the tennis court, around the end of schoolyard fence, through gateway in second fence, and heads west on **Mt. Vista Road**. Pass Lewis County Game Farm at mile 21.9.

22.3   Turn right on **Eshom Road** past Centralia High School.

23.1   Turn left on **Galvin Road**. Cross the Chehalis River, proceed through Galvin, and enjoy the Lincoln Creek Valley.

29.1   Turn right on **Michigan Hill Road** and start uphill. Turn left with Michigan Hill Road at top of hill at mile 30.1 and start downhill as Prather Road goes right.

33.1   Turn right on **Independence Road S.W.** at stop sign and cross the Chehalis River.

34.1   Turn left on **Marble Street S.W.** at Y intersection.

34.7   Turn left on **188 Avenue S.W.**

35.4   Turn right on **Forstrom Street S.W.**

36.0   Turn left on **183 Avenue S.W.**

36.9   Turn right on **Moon Road**. Cross U.S. 12 at mile 37.2. Proceed north to Gate, bear right, and hug the hillside above the swampy Black River channel. Pass Weyerhaeuser Forest Tree Nursery at mile 42.5. As Bordeaux Road goes left at mile 44.4, a large marker proclaiming the Mima Mounds as a registered natural landmark is visible among the enigmatic mounds.

46.3   Enter Little Rock, cross railroad tracks, and turn left on **La France Road**.

46.8   Turn left on **123 Avenue S.W.** as La France Road ends. Cross the slow-moving Black River beside a dairy farm and turn right on **Endicott Road**.

48.9   Turn right on **110 Avenue S.W.** and cross the Black River again.

49.9   Turn right on **Little Rock Road**.

50.1   Turn left on **113 Avenue S.W.** Cross I-5 on an overpass at mile 52.1.

54.0   Turn right on **Tilley Road**.

55.0   Turn right into Millersylvania State Park; end of tour.

52 ORTING–KAPOWSIN–EATONVILLE

STARTING POINT: Parking area by Lions Club Park in Orting. Take the Valley Avenue exit from State Route 410 in Sumner and turn south to Orting on Valley Avenue, which becomes State Route 162.

DISTANCE: 20 to 40 miles.
TERRAIN: Moderate to hilly.
TOTAL CUMULATIVE ELEVATION GAIN: 700 feet or 1250 feet.
RECOMMENDED TIME OF YEAR: Any season.
RECOMMENDED STARTING TIME: 9:30 to 10 A.M.
ALLOW: 3 to 5 hours plus lunch.
POINTS OF INTEREST
Puget Sound Power and Light Company's Electron Park
Washington State Soldiers Home

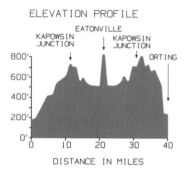

ELEVATION PROFILE

This ride, entirely within Pierce County, covers a pretty, rural area in the sparsely populated Ohop Valley and foothills near Orting. The broad, valley farmlands fall behind shortly after the cyclist leaves Orting, as the route heads south up the Puyallup River.

A high bridge crosses the river two miles before the turnoff to a park overlooking the hydroelectric plant at Electron. The one-mile side trip is worthwhile here. Built in 1903, this plant was the first in the power complex assembled by Stone and Webster to serve the cities of Tacoma, Seattle, and Everett. This generating station was also the start of the present-day Puget Sound Power and Light Company. An observation platform has been constructed on the bluff overlooking the facilities. A spectacular spray of water from the high-pressure turbines almost obscures the plant itself. Picnic tables, water fountain, and chemical toilet make this a fine rest stop. It can be used as the lunch stop for the short 20-mile loop ride between Orting and Kapowsin.

Back at the main road, an uphill grade takes the cyclist past Lake Kapowsin, which can be quite crowded on opening day for fishing season. The traffic from the Kapowsin junction through the Ohop Valley past Ohop Lake to Eatonville will be minimal. Most of the homes around Ohop Lake are for summer residence only, but this is also a popular lake for fishing. Ducks inhabit the lakes, of course, and the swampy lowland between the two lakes is the habitat of kingfishers and great blue herons.

The foothills region between Kapowsin and Orting has magnificent views of Mt. Rainier to the southeast. Here, the mountain towers over everything, as it is only 27 miles away. The separation of its summit into Liberty Cap on the left and Columbia Crest on the right is an unusual sight for the big-city dweller.

Picnic spots are available on this ride. The boat-launching ramp at Ohop

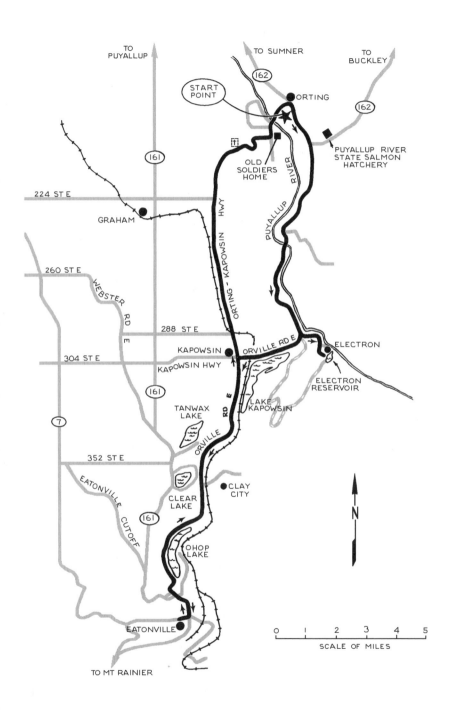

Lake provides toilet facilities. A small Lions Club park at the entrance to Eatonville provides green lawns for picnicking, but no water or other amenities. A grocery store is available in Kapowsin. There are also cafes and a grocery in Eatonville.

The downgrade just before reaching the Washington State Soldiers Home is quite steep and winding and may be a bit too thrilling for those who have neglected to keep brakes in good condition. A prominent *Visitors Welcome* sign invites the bicyclist to tour the Old Soldiers Home. New and old red-brick buildings are scattered about in a charming setting, and several pieces of vintage military equipment dot the landscape.

The Puyallup River is again crossed just before this ride is completed at Orting Park.

MILEAGE LOG

0.0 Lions Club Park in Orting. Head south on **State Route 162**, which runs through the center of Orting. Follow S.R. 162 as it turns west and then south again.

1.4 Turn right toward Electron on **Orville Road E.** Cross the Puyallup River on a high bridge at mile 4.8. Views of Mt. Rainier as the road bends at mile 7.0. A side road at mile 9.5 leads left and uphill to Electron Park. Lake Kapowsin Recreation Area (St. Regis Paper Company) on the left down a steep gravel drive at mile 9.9.

10.7 Turn left at blinking red light with Orville Road E. *Note: The shorter, 20-mile tour turns right on Orting-Kapowsin Highway E.* Grocery at this corner. Side road goes left across the valley at mile 15.0 to Mutual Materials' Clay City brick factory (closed). Public fishing area on Ohop Lake at mile 19.0; chemical toilets.

19.6 Turn left on rudimentary trail and go around traffic barrier and across old automotive bridge over Ohop Creek. Continue around barrier on other side on paved road.

19.9 Cross **State Route 161** (**Eatonville Highway**) at stop sign and continue left and uphill on shoulder of highway.

20.6 Turn right at *Welcome to Eatonville* sign and continue into Eatonville on **Business Route**. Cafes, grocery stores in Eatonville. After lunch, return on Business Route to **State Route 161** and continue left and downhill.

21.7 Go past Ski Park Road and bear right on next dead-end road, marked **116th Avenue E.** Go around traffic barrier, cross bridge, and turn right on **Orville Road E.**

30.8 Go straight through blinking red light at Kapowsin Junction and continue on **Orting-Kapowsin Highway E.** Large cemetery on left at mile 38.0 as road dives down steep hill. Washington State Soldiers Home at mile 39.2 as road bends sharp left. Road name changes to **Calistoga Street** as it enters Orting.

40.4 Lions Club Park in Orting; end of tour.

53   SOUTH PRAIRIE CREEK

STARTING POINT: White River Junior High School Annex in Buckley. From the south, take exit 127 (State Route 512) from I-5 to the State Route 410 interchange and take S.R. 410 east to Buckley. From the north, take exit 2A from I-405 and follow State Route 167 and State Route 410 to Buckley. Turn east on Park Avenue at the northeast edge of town and park along A Street by junior high school annex.

DISTANCE: 28 miles.

TERRAIN: Hilly with some flat; 4 miles of unpaved road; nontrivial creek ford.

TOTAL CUMULATIVE ELEVATION GAIN: 1200 feet.

RECOMMENDED TIME OF YEAR: Summer dry season for low water and minimum mud at creek ford.

RECOMMENDED STARTING TIME: 9 A.M.

ALLOW: 4 to 5 hours.

POINTS OF INTEREST
Lake Tapps Power Flume
Connell's Prairie Battle Monument
Wilkeson Cemetery
Trinity Orthodox Church in Wilkeson
Wilkeson Sandstone Quarry
Rainier State School

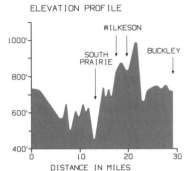

ELEVATION PROFILE

    This rather unusual ride requires the cyclist to ford South Prairie Creek. During late summer, the water will be low and bicycles can be pushed across safely, but in other seasons, the riders may have to carry their bicycles. After heavy rainstorms or during spring runoff, the crossing may be risky, so schedule this ride carefully. The historical and cultural background of this area make for interesting touring. Monuments, historic trails, an unusual cemetery, a sandstone quarry, and quaint towns vie for the cyclist's attention along roads carrying low volumes of traffic.

    History buffs will enjoy this ride. In the early 1850s, many white settlers moved into Washington Territory and took up land claims, receiving deeds from the U.S. Government. No one, however, had gotten around to negotiating for the land with the local Indians, the rightful owners. To rectify this situation, Governor Stevens in 1855 set out to obtain treaties with the tribes for all the land under his jurisdiction. He drove hard bargains and some claimed the Indians did not understand what they were signing. Leschi, a sub-chief of the Puyallup tribe, refused to sign the treaty at Medicine Creek and declared himself to be anti-establishment. With allies from the Klickitat and Yakima tribes, Leschi and his people set out to create disturbances. They massacred civilians at a settlement on the White River, ambushed a number of people along the Naches Trail, and attacked a group of soldiers dispatched to alleviate the problem. A monument near Connell's Prairie commemorates some of these events.

Another historical item is the aqueduct that carries water from the White River near Buckley to Lake Tapps. In 1910 the Pacific Coast Power Company of Stone and Webster built a flume to carry water between the White River and Lake Tapps, providing the energy source for the White River Power Plant at Dieringer below Lake Tapps. The power was used for the street railway systems of Tacoma and Seattle and for the electric interurban from Bellingham to Tacoma. This plant is now owned and operated by the Puget Sound Power and Light Company. A major portion of the open flume was converted to a buried aqueduct in 1990.

A Catholic cemetery in Wilkeson contains graves dating back to before the turn of the century. Wilkeson's early history was dominated by the booming industries of coal mining and logging. As the memorials in the cemetery indicate, the majority of Wilkeson's population were Croatian immigrants brought in to work the mines. The mines are no longer in operation, nor is the famous Wilkeson sandstone quarry that provided the building industry with its finest local stone. Washington State's Capitol was made of this beautiful stone. Wilkeson's Trinity Orthodox Church, with its bright blue Byzantine dome is a photographer's delight. In mid-July, Wilkeson holds a celebration with parades, food concessions, old machinery, and craft displays and sales.

For the nature lover, this ride has rural countryside, dairy farms, and miles of forest. In late summer and early fall, swallows flock in preparation for their flight south, robins and cedar waxwings feast on the wild berries, and in exposed locations vine maple is tinged with color. Foxglove and wild vetch add color to the roadsides in early summer.

The bicyclist looking for challenges will find the hill out of South Prairie to be one of the best. The long, unpaved hill down to South Prairie Creek requires brakes in good order.

MILEAGE LOG

0.0   White River Junior High School Annex in Buckley. Head south on **River Avenue**, turn right on **Main Street**, and cross State Route 410 with traffic light.

0.5   Turn left at stop sign on **Naches Street** as Main Street ends.

0.7   Turn right at stop sign on **Mason Avenue**. As it leaves Buckley, the road is renamed **Sumner Buckley Highway E.** Turn right at stop sign with Sumner Buckley Highway and cross power canal at mile 2.1 as Mundy Loss Road joins from the left.

5.3   Turn right on **Connell's Prairie Road E.**

5.9   Turn right on **Barkubein Road E.** by Connell's Prairie Battle Monument for a final look at the power canal. Return to the battle monument.

6.2   Turn right on **Connell's Prairie Road E.**

7.0   Turn left on **214 Avenue E.** for 0.3 mile and take the next right turn on **Kelly Lake Road E.**

7.7   Turn left and downhill with Kelly Lake Road as Church Lake Road continues on and uphill.

8.0   Turn right on **Sumner-Buckley Highway** as Kelly Lake Road ends.

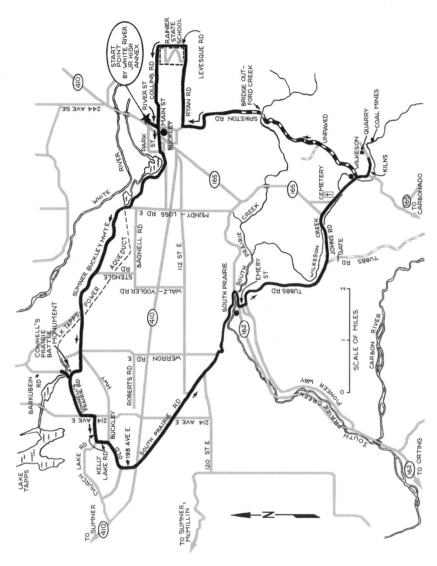

8.6 Turn left on **198 Avenue E.** at a wye, cross State Route 410, and continue south on **South Prairie Road E.** toward South Prairie.

13.1 Turn right at wye on **State Route 162** toward South Prairie.

13.3 Turn left on **Emery Street** in center of South Prairie; grocery store. Turn left on **E. Third Street** as Emery ends. Road bends right, is renamed **AP Tubbs Road**, and climbs a steep hill to a view of Mt. Rainier. Continue on paved **Johns Road E.** at mile 15.8 as gravel-surfaced Tubbs Road goes right.

17.2   Turn right on **State Route 165** and continue into Wilkeson. Catholic cemetery. *Note: A side trip into the Trinity Orthodox Church at 17.7 is worthwhile.* Continue through Wilkeson city center; cafe, grocery.

17.9   Just past the business district, bear left on **Railroad Avenue** past a row of old kilns. Bear left on gravel road at mile 18.7. If road is barred by chain, inquire at house for permission to enter quarry. Observe cut stone, old quarry face, stone-cutting machinery, and return to Wilkeson.

20.4   Immediately north of a group of stores in Wilkeson turn right on narrow, alleylike **Davis Street** just before State Route 165 crosses a small ravine. *Note: If recent rains have creeks running high, advise returning along S.R. 165 to Ryan Road near Buckley.* As the route leaves town, the pavement ends and the road is renamed **Spiketon Road**. Keep to the right as roads branch left near high-tension lines. Road surface may be muddy near bottom of hill.

23.1   Ford South Prairie Creek through rapids where road continuation can be seen on other side. Bicycles may need to be carried across, high on shoulder to avoid fast-moving water. Wring out socks and continue on Spiketon Road.

25.1   Turn right on **Ryan Road** at stop sign.

26.4   If desired, turn left into entrance of Rainier State School and tour slowly and carefully through grounds. Otherwise continue on thoroughfare around school as the road is renamed **Levesque Road** and **Collins Road**. Road bends left and right at mile 27.8 and is renamed **Spruce Street** and **Main Street**.

28.2   Turn right on **A Street** in Buckley or alternatively on **River Street**. End of tour at mile 28.4.

54 CARBON RIVER

STARTING POINT: Town of South Prairie on State Route 162 in Pierce County. Take State Route 410 south from Enumclaw through Buckley and the S.R. 162 turnoff to South Prairie, or take S.R. 410 to Sumner, then Valley Road and S.R. 162 to South Prairie. Park in graveled parking area opposite restaurant and church.

DISTANCE: 45 miles.
TERRAIN: Moderate.
TOTAL CUMULATIVE ELEVATION GAIN: 2500 feet.
RECOMMENDED TIME OF YEAR: May through October.
RECOMMENDED STARTING TIME: 9 A.M.
ALLOW: 6 hours.
POINTS OF INTEREST
Fairfax Bridge over Carbon River
Ipsut Creek Campground
Chenius Falls

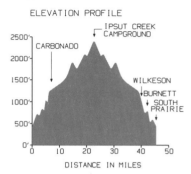

For those who want to ride to Mt. Rainier without fighting traffic on a major highway, this is the ride. Because of its dead-end nature, the Carbon River entrance road to Mt. Rainier National Park is less frequented than roads on the other sides of the mountain. Its scenery is superb, with displays of bounding, gray glacial rapids and immense trees of the rain forest. The Carbon River, named for the coal deposits in its drainage basin, accompanies the road through most of the ride. The high Fairfax Bridge over the Carbon River canyon presents a fine view, but be careful not to block traffic when stopped. The historic coal-mining towns of Carbonado and Wilkeson are quiet and pleasant. A word of advice: If good views of Mt. Rainier are desired, look early in the ride. When the hill is crested just out of South Prairie, a view is obtained, but it soon disappears behind the foothills and is seldom seen again. The scenery along the Carbon River also requires looking on the way in, because the temptation to whiz back down the river on the return is very strong.

As good as this ride is, a possible improvement could be made. An old, abandoned logging railroad grade parallels the highway up the canyon from Carbonado through the former settlement of Fairfax to within two miles of the park entrance. The observant cyclist will detect its presence at several points along this ride. Currently, the grade belongs to a timber company. With minor improvements, this could be a fine bicycle and pedestrian trail.

MILEAGE LOG

0.0   Parking area in center of South Prairie. Turn right on **State Route 162**, right on **Emery Avenue S.**, and then left on **E. Third Street** as Emery ends. The road bends right, is renamed **AP Tubbs Road**, and climbs a steep hill to a view of Mt. Rainier.

2.3   Turn right with Tubbs Road (marked Dead End) on gravel surface as paved Johns Road continues. Go under gate at mile 2.5 and under

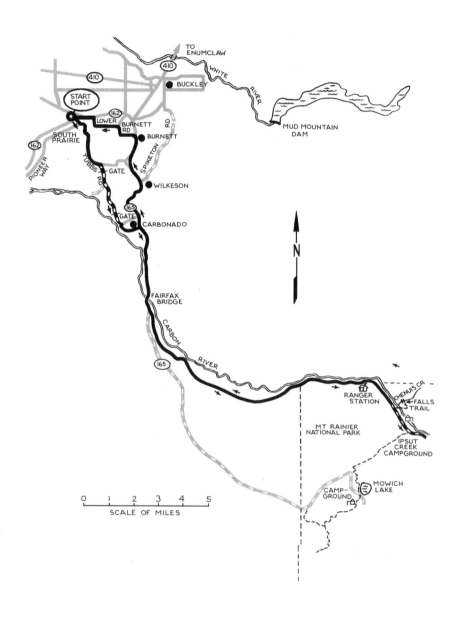

power lines at mile 3.5. Keep left and climb steep hill. Pavement resumes at mile 5.2. Keep right into Carbonado. Continue through Carbonado on **Pershing Street** past a row of diminutive company houses.

6.0 Turn right on **State Route 165**. Cross Fairfax Bridge at mile 8.9. Keep left with paved road as S.R. 165 goes right up steep, gravel road to Mowich Lake. Entrance gate to Mt. Rainier National Park at mile 17.3. *Note: Be prepared to pay entrance fee.* Pavement ends at mile 17.4. Trail goes left across Carbon River 0.2 mile to Chenius Falls at mile 20.9.

22.1 Ipsut Creek Picnic Area and Campground; trailhead for Carbon Glacier, Spray Park, and Mowich Lake. Enjoy it at leisure and return to and along **State Route 165**. Continue on S.R. 165 past Carbonado junction at mile 38.3 and through Wilkeson at mile 39.7; cafe, grocery.

42.6 Pedal through diminutive Burnett with its row of company houses and turn left on **Lower Burnett Road** just before S.R. 165 crosses Prairie Creek on a high bridge. Descend hill to creek, cross, turn left, and wind down valley.

44.3 Turn left on **State Route 162** and return to South Prairie. End of tour at mile 45.5.

"What kind of animal is that?

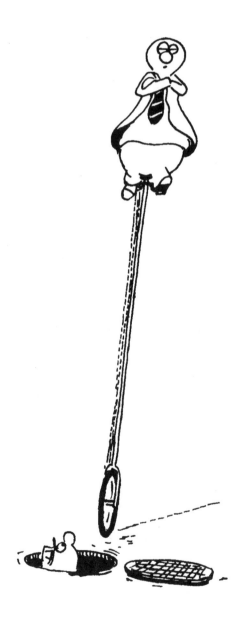

Appendix A

Excerpts applicable to bicycles from 1994 Revised Code of Washington (RCW).

Chapter 46.04

DEFINITIONS

46.04.071 Bicycle. "Bicycle" means every device propelled by human power upon which any person may ride, having two tandem wheels either of which is more than twenty inches in diameter, or three wheels, any one of which is more than twenty inches in diameter. [1982 ch 55 § 4; 1965 ex.s. ch 155 § 86.]

46.04.080 Business district. "Business district" means the territory contiguous to and including a highway when within any six hundred feet along such highway there are buildings in use for business or industrial purposes, including but not limited to hotels, banks, or office buildings, railroad stations, and public buildings which occupy at least three hundred feet of frontage on one side or three hundred feet collectively on both sides of the highway. [1975 ch 62 § 2; 1961 ch 12 § 46.04.080. Prior: 1959 ch 49 § 9; prior: 1937 ch 189 § 1, part; RRS § 6360-1, part; 1929 ch 180 § 1, part; 1927 ch 309 § 2, part; RRS § 6362-2, part.]

46.04.200 Hours of darkness. "Hours of darkness" means the hours from one-half hour after sunset to one-half hour before sunrise, and any other time when persons or objects may not be clearly discernible at a distance of five hundred feet. [1961 ch 12 § 46.04.200. Prior: 1959 ch 49 § 21; prior: 1937 ch 189 § 1, part; RRS § 6360-1, part.]

46.04.431 Highway. "Highway" means the entire width between the boundary lines of every way publicly maintained when any part thereof is open to the use of the public for purposes of vehicular travel. [1965 ex.s. ch 155 § 87.]

46.04.500 Roadway. "Roadway" means that portion of a highway improved, designed, or ordinarily used for vehicular travel, exclusive of the sidewalk or shoulder even though such sidewalk or shoulder is used by persons riding bicycles. In the event a highway includes two or more separate roadways, the term "roadway" shall refer to any such roadway separately but shall not refer to all such roadways collectively. [1977 ch 24 § 1; 1961 ch 12 §. 46.04.500. Prior: 1959 ch 49 § 54; prior: (i) 1943 ch 153 § 1, part; 1937 ch 188 § 1, part; Rem. Supp. 1943 6312-1, part. (ii) 1937 ch 189 § 1, part; RRS § 6360-1, part.]

46.04.670 Vehicle. "Vehicle" includes every device capable of being moved upon a public highway and in, upon, or by which any persons or property is or may be transported or drawn upon a public highway, including bicycles. The term does not include devices other than bicycles moved by human or animal power or used exclusively upon stationary rails or tracks. Mopeds shall not be considered vehicles or motor vehicles for the purposes of chapter 46.70 RCW. Bicycles shall not be considered vehicles for the purposes of chapter 46.12, 46.16, or 46.70 RCW. [1994 ch 262 § 2; 1991 ch 214 § 2; 1979 1st ex.s. ch 213 § 4; 1961 ch 12 § 46.04.670. Prior: 1959 ch 49 § 72; prior: (i) 1943 ch 153 § 1, part; 1937 ch 188 § 1, part; Rem. Supp. 1943 § 6312-1, part. (ii) 1937 ch 189 § 1, part; RRS § 6360-1, part; 1929 ch 180 § 1, part; 1927 ch 309 § 2, part; RRS § 6362-2, part.]

Chapter 46.37

VEHICLE LIGHTING AND OTHER EQUIPMENT

46.37.020 When lighted lamps and signaling devices are required. Every vehicle upon a highway within this state at any time from a half hour after sunset to a half hour before sunrise and at any other time when, due to insufficient light or unfavorable atmospheric conditions, persons and vehicles on the highway are not clearly discernible at a distance of one thousand feet ahead shall display lighted headlights, other lights, and illuminating devices as hereinafter respectively required for different classes of vehicles, subject to exceptions with respect to parked vehicles, and such stop lights, turn signals, and other signaling devices shall be lighted as prescribed for the use of such devices. [1977 ex.s. ch 355 § 2; 1974 ex.s. ch 124 § 2; 1963 ch 154 § 2; 1961 ch 12 § 46.37.020. Prior: 1955 ch 269 § 2; prior: 1937 ch 189 § 14, part; RRS § 6360-14, part; RCW 46.40.010, part; 1929 ch 178 § 2; 1927 ch 309 § 19; 1921 ch 96 § 22, part; 1919 ch 59 § 10, part; 1917 ch 155 § 15, part; 1915 ch 142 § 21, part; RRS § 6362-19.]

Chapter 46.61

RULES OF THE ROAD

46.61.160 Restrictions on use of limited-access highway—Use by bicyclists. The department of transportation may by order, and local authorities may by ordinance or resolution, with respect to any limited access highway under their jurisdictions prohibit the use of any such highway by funeral processions, or by parades, pedestrians, bicycles, or other nonmotorized traffic, or by any person operating a motor-driven cycle. Bicyclists may use the right shoulder of limited-access highways except where prohibited. The department of transportation may by order, and local authorities may by ordinance or resolution, with respect to any limited-access highway under their respective jurisdictions prohibit the use of the shoulders of any such highway by bicycles within urban areas or upon other sections of the highway where such use is deemed to be unsafe.

The department of transportation or the local authority adopting any such prohibitory regulation shall erect and maintain official traffic control devices on the limited access roadway on which such regulations are applicable, and when so erected no person may disobey the restrictions stated on such devices. [1982 ch 55 § 5; 1975 ch 62 § 25; 1965 ex.s ch 155 § 27.]

46.61.700 Parent or guardian shall not authorize or permit violation by a child or ward. The parent of any child and the guardian of any ward shall not authorize or knowingly permit any such child or ward to violate any of the provisions of this chapter. [1965 ex.s. ch 155 § 78.]

46.61.710 Mopeds—General requirements and operation. (1) No person shall operate a moped upon the highways of this state unless the moped has been assigned a moped registration number and displays a moped permit in accordance with the provisions of RCW 46.16.630.

(2) Notwithstanding any other provision of law, a moped may not be operated on a bicycle path or trail, bikeway, equestrian trail, or hiking or recreational trail.

(3) Operation of a moped on a fully controlled limited access highway or on a sidewalk is unlawful.

(4) Removal of any muffling device or pollution control device from a moped is unlawful. [1979 1st ex.s. ch 213 § 8.]

46.61.750 Effect of regulations—Penalty. (1) It is a traffic infraction for any person to do any act forbidden or fail to perform any act required in RCW 46.61.750 through 46.61.780.

(2) These regulations applicable to bicycles shall apply whenever a bicycle is operated upon any highway or upon any bicycle path, subject to those exceptions stated herein. [1982 ch 55 § 6; 1979 1st ex.s. ch 136 § 92; 1965 ex.s. ch 155 § 79.]

46.61.755 Traffic laws apply to persons riding bicycles. Every person riding a bicycle upon a roadway shall be granted all of the rights and shall be subject to all of the duties applicable to the driver of a vehicle by this chapter, except as to special regulations in RCW 46.61.750 through 46.61.780 and except as to those provisions of this chapter which by their nature can have no application. [1965 ex.s. ch 155 § 80.]

46.61.758 Hand signals. All hand signals required of persons operating bicycles shall be given in the following manner:

(1) Left turn. Left hand and arm extended horizontally beyond the side of the bicycle;

(2) Right turn. Left hand and arm extended upward beyond the side of the bicycle, or right hand and arm extended horizontally to the right side of the bicycle;

(3) Stop or decrease speed. Left hand and arm extended downward beyond the side of the bicycle.

The hand signals required by this section shall be given before initiation of a turn. [1982 ch 55 § 8.]

46.61.760 Riding on bicycles. (1) A person propelling a bicycle shall not ride other than upon or astride a permanent and regular seat attached thereto.

(2) No bicycle shall be used to carry more persons at one time than the number for which it is designed and equipped. [1965 ex.s. ch 155 sec 81.]

46.61.765 Clinging to vehicles. No person riding upon any bicycle, coaster, roller skates, sled or toy vehicle shall attach the same or himself to any vehicle upon a roadway. [1965 ex.s. ch 155 § 82.]

46.61.770 Riding on roadways and bicycle paths. (1) Every person operating a bicycle upon a roadway at a rate of speed less than the normal flow of traffic at the particular time and place shall ride as near to the right side of the right through lane as is safe except as may be appropriate while preparing to make or while making turning movements, or while overtaking and passing another bicycle or vehicle proceeding in the same direction. A person operating a bicycle upon a roadway or highway other than a limited-access highway, which roadway or highway carries traffic in one direction only and has two or more marked traffic lanes, may ride as near to the left side of the left lane as is safe. A person operating a bicycle upon a roadway may use the shoulder of the roadway or any specially designed bicycle lane if such exists.

(2) Persons riding bicycles upon a roadway shall not ride more than two abreast except on paths or parts of roadways set aside for the exclusive use of bicycles. [1982 ch 55 § 7; 1974 ex.s. ch 141 § 14; 1965 ex.s. ch 155 § 83.]

46.61.775 Carrying articles. No person operating a bicycle shall carry any package, bundle or article which prevents the driver from keeping at least one hand upon the handlebars. [1965 ex.s. ch 155 § 84.]

46.61.780 Lamps and other equipment on bicycles. (1) Every bicycle when in use during the hours of darkness as defined in RCW 46.37.020 shall be equipped with a lamp on the front which shall emit a white light visible from a distance of at least five hundred feet to the front and with a red reflector on the rear of a type approved by the State Patrol which shall be visible from all distances from one hundred feet to six hundred feet to the rear when directly in front of lawful lower beams of headlamps on a motor vehicle. A lamp emitting a red light visible from a distance of five hundred feet to the rear may be used in addition to the red reflector.

(2) Every bicycle shall be equipped with a brake which will enable the operator to make the braked wheels skid on dry, level, clean pavement. [1987 ch 330 § 746; 1975 ch 62 § 39; 1965 ex.s. ch 155 § 85.]

Chapter 63.32

UNCLAIMED PROPERTY IN THE HANDS OF CITY POLICE

63.32.010 Methods of disposition—Sale, retention, destruction, or trade. Whenever any personal property shall come into the possession of the police authorities of any city in connection with the official performance of their duties and said personal property shall remain unclaimed or not taken away for a period of sixty days from date of written notice to the owner thereof, if known, which notice shall inform the owner of the disposition which may be made of the property under this section and the time that the owner has to claim the property and in all other cases for a period of sixty days from the time said property came into the possession of the police department, unless said property has been held as evidence in any court, then in that event, after sixty days from date when said case has been finally disposed of and said property released as evidence by order of the court, said city may:

(1) At any time thereafter sell said personal property at public auction to the highest and best bidder for cash in the manner hereinafter provided;

(2) Retain the property for the use of the police department subject to giving notice in the manner prescribed in RCW 63.32.020 and the right of the owner, or the owner's legal representative, to reclaim the property within one year after receipt of notice, without compensation for ordinary wear and tear if, in the opinion of the chief of police, the property consists of firearms or other items specifically usable in law enforcement work; PROVIDED, That at the end of each calendar year during which there has been such a retention, the police department shall provide the city's mayor or council and retain for public inspection a list of such retained items and an estimation of each item's replacement value. At the end of the one-year period any unclaimed firearm shall be disposed of pursuant to RCW9.41.098(2).

(3) Destroy an item of personal property at the discretion of the chief of police if the following circumstances have occurred:

(a) The item has no substantial commercial value, or the probable cost of sale exceeds the value of the property;

(b) The item has been unclaimed by any person after notice procedures have been met, as prescribed in this section; and

(c) The chief of police has determined that the item is unsafe and unable to be made safe for use by any member of the general public;

(4) If the item is not unsafe or illegal to possess or sell, such item, after satisfying the notice requirements as prescribed in RCW 63.32.020, may be offered by the chief of police to bona fide dealers, in trade for law enforcement equipment, which equipment shall be treated as retained property for purpose of annual listing requirements of subsection (2) of this section; or

(5) If the item is unsafe or illegal to possess or sell, but has been or may be used, in the judgement of the chief of police, in a manner that is illegal, such item may be destroyed. [1988 ch 223 § 3; 1988 ch 132 § 1; 1981 ch 154 § 2; 1973 1st ex.s. ch 44 § 1; 1939 ch 148 § 1; 1925 ex.s. ch 100 § 1; RRS § 8999-1.]

Chapter 63.35

UNCLAIMED PROPERTY IN HANDS OF STATE PATROL

63.65.010 Definitions. Unless the context clearly requires otherwise, the definitions in this section apply throughout this chapter.

(1) "Agency" means the Washington State patrol.

(2) "Chief" means the chief of the Washington State Patrol or designee.

(3) "Personal property" or "property" includes both corporeal and incorporeal personal property and includes, among other property, contraband and money.

(4) "Contraband" means any property which is unlawful to produce or possess.

(5) "Money" means all currency, script, personal checks, money orders, or other negotiable instruments.

(6) "Owner" means the person in whom is vested the ownership, dominion, or title of the property.

(7) "Unclaimed" means that no owner of the property has been identified or has requested, in writing, the release of the property to themselves, nor has the owner of the property designated an individual to receive the property or paid the required postage to effect delivery of the property.

(8) "Illegal items" means those items unlawful to be possessed. [1989 ch 222 § 1.]

63.35.020 Methods of disposition—Sale, retention, destruction, or trade. Whenever any personal property shall come into the possession of the officers of the state patrol in connection with the official performance of their duties and said personal property shall remain unclaimed or not taken away for a period of sixty days from the date of written notice to the owner thereof, if known, which notice shall inform the owner of the disposition which may be made of the property under this section and the time that the owner has to claim the property and in all other cases for a period of sixty days from the time said property came into the possession of the state agency, unless said property has been held as evidence in any court, then in that event, after sixty days from date when said case has been finally disposed of and said property released as evidence by order of the court, said agency may:

(1) At any time thereafter sell said personal property at public auction to the highest and best bidder for cash in the manner hereinafter provided;

(2) Retain the property for the use of the state patrol subject to giving notice in the manner prescribed in RCW 63.35.030 and the right of the owner, or the owner's legal representative, to reclaim the property within one year after receipt of notice, without compensation for ordinary wear and tear, if, in the opinion of the chief, the property consists of firearms or other items specifically usable in law enforcement work: PROVIDED, that at the end of each calendar year during which there has been such a retention, the state patrol shall provide the office of financial management and retain for public inspection a list of such retained items and an estimation of each item's replacement value;

(3) Destroy an item of personal property at the discretion of the chief if the chief determines that the following circumstances have occurred:

(a) The property has no substantial commercial value, or the probable cost of sale exceeds the value of the property;

(b) The item has been unclaimed by any person after notice procedures have been met, as prescribed in this section; and

(c) The chief has determined that the item is illegal to possess or sell or unsafe and unable to be made safe for use by any member of the general public;

(4) If the item is not unsafe or illegal to possess or sell, such item, after satisfying the notice requirements as prescribed in this section may be offered by the chief to bona fide dealers, in trade for law enforcement equipment, which equipment shall be treated as retained property for purpose of annual listing requirements of subsection (2) of this section; or

(5) At the end of one year, any unclaimed firearm shall be disposed of pursuant to RCW 9.41.098(2). Any other item which is not unsafe or illegal to possess or sell, but has been, or may be used, in the judgement of the chief, in a manner that is illegal, may be destroyed. [1989 ch 222 § 2.]

63.35.030 Notice of sale. Before said personal property shall be sold, a notice of such sale fixing the time and place thereof which shall be at a suitable place, which will be noted in the advertisement for sale, and containing a description of the property to be sold shall be published at least once in a newspaper of general circulation in the county in which the property is to be sold at least ten days prior to the date fixed for the auction. The notice shall be signed by the chief. If the owner fails to reclaim said property prior to the time fixed for the sale in such notice, the chief shall conduct said sale and sell the property described in the notice at public auction to the highest and best bidder for cash, and upon payment of the amount of such bid shall deliver the said property to such bidder. [1989 ch 222 § 3.]

63.35.040 Disposition of proceeds. The moneys arising from sales under the provisions of this chapter shall be first applied to the payment of the costs and expenses of the sale and then to the payment of lawful charges and expenses for the keep of said personal property and the balance, if any, shall be forwarded to the state treasurer to be deposited into the state patrol highway account. [1989 ch 222 § 4.]

63.35.050 Reimbursement to owner. If the owner of said personal property so sold, or the owner's legal representative, shall at any time within three years after such money shall have been deposited in the state patrol highway account, furnish satisfactory evidence to the state treasurer of the ownership of said personal property, the owner or the owner's legal representative shall be entitled to receive from said state patrol highway account the amount so deposited therein with interest. [1989 ch 222 § 5.]

Chapter 63.40

UNCLAIMED PROPERTY IN HANDS OF SHERIFF

63.32.010 Methods of disposition—Sale, retention, destruction, or trade. Whenever any personal property, other than vehicles governed by chapter 46.52 RCW, shall come into the possession of the sheriff of any county in connection with the official performance of his duties and said personal property shall remain unclaimed or not taken away for a period of sixty days from date of written notice to the owner thereof, if known, which notice shall inform the owner of the disposition which may be made of the property under this section and the time that the owner has to claim the property and in all other cases for a period of sixty days from the time said property came into the possession of the sheriff's office, unless said property has been held as evidence in any court, then in that event, after sixty days from date when said case has been finally disposed of and said property released as evidence by order of the court, said county sheriff may:

(1) At any time thereafter sell said personal property at public auction to the highest and best bidder for cash in the manner hereinafter provided;

(2) Retain the property for use of the sheriff's office subject to giving notice in the manner prescribed in RCW 63.40.020 and the right of the owner, or his or her legal representative, to reclaim the property within one year after receipt of notice, without compensation for ordinary wear and tear if, in the opinion of the county sheriff, the property consists of firearms or other items specifically usable in law enforcement work; PROVIDED, That at the end of each calendar year during which there has been such a retention, the sheriff shall provide the county's executive or legislative authority and retain for public inspection a list of such retained items and an estimation of each item's replacement value. At the end of the one-year period any unclaimed firearm shall be disposed of pursuant to RCW 9.41.098(2);

(3) Destroy an item of personal property at the discretion of the county sheriff if the following circumstances have occurred:

(a) The property has no substantial commercial value, or the probable cost of sale exceeds the value of the property;

(b) The item has been unclaimed by any person after notice procedures have been met, as prescribed in this section; and

(c) The county sheriff has determined that the item is unsafe and unable to be made safe for use by any member of the general public;

(4) If the item is not unsafe or illegal to possess or sell, such item, after satisfying the notice requirements as prescribed in RCW 63.40.020, may be offered by the county sheriff to bona fide dealers, in trade for law enforcement equipment, which equipment shall be treated as retained property for purpose of annual listing requirements of subsection (2) of this section; or

(5) If the item is not unsafe or illegal to possess or sell, but has been or may be used, in the discretion of the county sheriff, in a manner that is illegal, such an item may be destroyed. [1988 ch 223 § 4; 1988 ch 132 § 3; 1981 ch 154 § 3; 1973 1st ex.s. ch 44 § 4; 1961 ch 104 § 1.]

Appendix B

MORE ABOUT DOGS

This section is written, not as a personal vendetta, but out of concern over the alarming rate of serious dog-involved bicycle accidents. In metropolitan areas, other bicycles and automobiles are by far the most serious hazards. In backroad rural touring, dogs are involved in most bicycle accidents.

Dogs are found wherever human residences occur, yet only in certain areas are they a serious problem. In densely settled metropolitan areas, dogs are usually accustomed to cyclists and pay them little attention. Farm dogs may bark, but they seldom dispute the road right of way. In fringe areas, however, between the city or suburb and the truly rural countryside, the dogs are poorly trained and see only occasional groups of bicyclists. They regard the road in front of their house as part of their guarded territory, and guard it they will. Beware of the dog who runs off the road ahead of you into his driveway. He may be waiting to attack you from within his territory.

In tour descriptions, we have indicated the more serious dog-problem areas. Conditions may change rapidly in certain areas as outstanding troublemakers are "trained" by bicyclists using chemical deterrents. Other areas, with higher dog densities, will take longer to pacify. We hope our warning will speed the process by alerting cyclists to have their control techniques ready.

To keep the canines from spoiling an otherwise enjoyable ride, it is helpful to understand dog attitudes and habits. Attitudes may be classed in order of increasing concern as follows:

1. Indifference—couldn't care less
2. Watch dog—warns of your approach and passage
3. Friendly—glad to see you
4. Chaser—finds it fun to run after anything that moves
5. Guard—tries to drive you from his territory
6. Vicious

Fortunately, the vicious dog is almost never allowed to run loose, and dog bite is one of the least common of bicyclist injuries. Categories 3, 4, and 5 are the most common problem, either distracting the rider or getting in the way. A dog will often concentrate on the bicycle ahead of him, running into the path of a following cyclist and causing upset. A second dog, chasing after the first, may crash into a moving bicycle, throwing it out of control. The first rider of a group, although usually stronger and more prepared for trouble, may have fewer encounters than the cyclists behind him. The dog spots the leader from his yard and heads for the road, but by the time he gets there, the first target has gone on by and others have appeared. This can be a particularly bad problem in family touring groups.

Dog-control techniques take various forms, depending upon the situation and the skills of the rider. Rule number one is to be aware of the complete situation and not to panic. A sudden swerve may lead to a collision with a tree, a ditch, another bicycle, or an automobile. A sudden stop may cause loss of control or a crash from behind by another cyclist. Neglecting to brake on a hill because of dog distraction may cause a crash or spin-out at the bottom of the hill. Look and think before you react! With this in mind, let us go on to the various techniques.

A. Ignore. This is all right for the short-legged yappers and friendlies. Just be sure to keep out of their way.

B. Vocal. A sharp command or rough growl will often deter categories 2 and 3. Screaming usually produces the opposite effect.

C. Speed up. On a flat or downhill run, most dogs can be outdistanced. On an uphill slope, however, this seldom works.

D. Chemicals. Pressurized cans of cayenne pepper solution sold under trade names *Halt* and *Dog Shield* will project a stream of liquid "fire" up to ten feet. This is quite effective when contact is made with eyes or nostrils.

E. Mechanical. Whips, chains, cables, bicycle pumps, and assorted other clubs have been used with varying success, but these may lead to trouble with dog owners. A well-aimed, sudden kick sometimes works, if the dog is close and can be surprised.

F. Confrontation. A leader of a tour group, spotting a chaser or guard-type dog, may stop to confront the animal until the remainder of the group passes. As soon as the leader gets ready to leave, however, the dog is usually after him again.

G. Firearms. The use of firearms is seldom effective unless the intent is to kill the dog. Blanks have little effect. Either way, the dog owner will be seriously irritated. Firearms are **not** recommended.

H. Acoustic "Dazer." This is a battery-operated, sonic generator, and is practically useless: the dog will be startled the first time it is used, but not deterred. Subsequent applications have little or no effect.

The legal aspects of a bicycle-dog accident are not clear-cut, unless the dog unquestionably attacks without provocation. In any case, if an accident or incident occurs, be certain to obtain identification of witnesses and the dog owner if possible. But let us hope this situation never arises and that we all enjoy many years of HAPPY CYCLING!

ALPHABETICAL INDEX

MILEAGE INDEX–DAY TOURS

MILEAGE INDEX–OVERNIGHT TOURS

TOURS WITH BED-AND-BREAKFAST ACCOMMODATIONS

TOUR NO.	TOUR NAME	B&B LOCATION	TELEPHONE NO.
1	Mercer Island	Mercer Island	(206) 232-2345
5	Renton–Maple Valley	Maple Valley	(206) 432-1409
10	Upper Snoqualmie	North Bend	(206) 888-0799
		North Bend	(206) 888-3572
		Snoqualmie	(206) 888-1637
11	Fall City–Snoqualmie Falls	Snoqualmie	(206) 888-1637
15	Issaquah–Snoqualmie Falls–Fall City	Issaquah	(206) 392-1196
20	Vashon Island	West Vashon Is.	(206) 567-4832
		East Maury Is.	(206) 463-2646
23	Snohomish Valley	Snohomish	(360) 568-9622
		Snohomish	(360) 568-1078
27	Skykomish–Index–Jack's Pass	Index	(360) 793-2312
		Index	(360) 793-0100
		Skykomish	(360) 677-2345
35	Arlington-Rockport	Concrete	(360) 826-4333
37	Skagit Flats	Mt. Vernon	(360) 428-1990
		La Conner	(360) 466-3366
		La Conner	(360) 466-4675
		La Conner	(360) 466-3207
		La Conner	(360) 466-4578
		La Conner	(360) 445-6805
		La Conner	(360) 466-4626
39	Lopez Island	MacKaye Harbor	(360) 468-2253
		Aleck Bay Road	(360) 468-2506
		Aleck Bay Road	(360) 468-2028
40	Orcas Island	Orcas	(360) 376-4300
		Crow Valley Rd	(360) 376-4914
		Westsound	(360) 376-2340
41	San Juan Island	Friday Harbor	(360) 378-2783
		Friday Harbor	(360) 378-5907
		Friday Harbor	(360) 378-2070
		Friday Harbor (boat)	(360) 378-5661
		Beaverton Vly Rd	(360) 378-4138
		Pear Point Road	(360) 378-5604
		Cattle Point Rd	(360) 378-3186
42	Bainbridge Island	Lynwood	(206) 842-3926
44	Southworth–Port Orchard	Port Orchard	(360) 876-9170
		Beach Drive	(360) 871-5582
45	Shelton–Skokomish Valley–Union	Union	(360) 898-4862

TOUR NO.	TOUR NAME	B&B LOCATION	TELEPHONE NO.
47	Millersylvania–Olympia	Olympia	(360) 754-0389
		Olympia	(360) 754-9613
		Olympia	(360) 786-8440
50	Morton–Millersylvania	Eatonville	(360) 832-6506
		Morton	(360) 498-5243
52	Orting–Kapowsin–Eatonville	Eatonville	(360) 832-6506

TOUR JUNCTIONS

Note: Tours 55 through 93 are found in *Bicycling the Backroads of Northwest Washington*, and tours 94 through 139 are found in *Bicycling the Backroads of Southwest Washington* (The Mountaineers, Seattle, Washington).

Tour Junction	Tour Numbers	Tour Junction	Tour Numbers
Morton	50	Skykomish	27
Mt. Vernon	37,70,71,73	Snohomish	21,22,23,24,89
Mukilteo	22,59,85,86	Snoqualmie	10,11
North Bend	10,93	Snoqualmie Falls	10,11,15
Olympia	47,118,119	South Prairie	53,54
Orcas Island	40	Southworth	44,94,95
Orting	52,101	Stanwood	30,38
Oso	35,36	Sultan	17,25
Port Orchard	44,95	Tacoma	20
Rainier	48,121,122,123	Tenino	49,50
Redmond	18,19	Tukwila	2,3
Renton	4,5,6	Tumwater	47,119
Rochester	51,120,124	Union	45,106
Rockport	35	Vashon Island	20
San Juan Island	42	Wilkeson	53,54
Satsop	46,114,116	Winslow	42,82
Seattle	20,42,44,82,94,95	Woodinville	18,89
Sedro Woolley	35,70,74	Yelm	50,121
Shelton	45,46,106		

Authors Erin and Bill Woods have put more than 50,000 miles on their bicycles researching and updating the three books in their cycle tour guide series that also includes *Bicycling the Backroads of Northwest Washington* and *Bicycling the Backroads of Southwest Washington*. Residents of King County near Redmond, WA, they are active members of the Boeing Employees Bicycle Club.

THE MOUNTAINEERS, founded in 1906, is a nonprofit outdoor activity and conservation club, whose mission is "to explore, study, preserve, and enjoy the natural beauty of the outdoors. . . ." Based in Seattle, Washington, the club is now the third-largest such organization in the United States, with 15,000 members and four branches throughout Washington State.

The Mountaineers sponsors both classes and year-round outdoor activities in the Pacific Northwest, which include hiking, mountain climbing, ski-touring, snowshoeing, bicycling, camping, kayaking and canoeing, nature study, sailing, and adventure travel. The club's conservation division supports environmental causes through educational activities, sponsoring legislation, and presenting informational programs. All club activities are led by skilled, experienced volunteers, who are dedicated to promoting safe and responsible enjoyment and preservation of the outdoors.

The Mountaineers Books, an active, nonprofit publishing program of the club, produces guidebooks, instructional texts, historical works, natural history guides, and works on environmental conservation. All books produced by The Mountaineers are aimed at fulfilling the club's mission.

If you would like to participate in these organized outdoor activities or the club's programs, consider a membership in The Mountaineers. For information and an application, write or call The Mountaineers, Club Headquarters, 300 Third Avenue West, Seattle, Washington 98119; (206) 284-6310.

Send or call for our catalog of more than 300 outdoor titles:

 The Mountaineers Books
1001 SW Klickitat Way, Suite 201
Seattle, WA 98134
1-800-553-4453